"This wonderfully presented volume is an inviting guide to reading the Bible. I think this volume would be an ideal companion for any Christian following a plan to read through the Bible. This work would not only enhance one's reading and understanding of Scripture, but would help the reader anticipate what would be encountered along the journey."

—**Clinton E. Arnold**, research professor of New Testament,
Talbot School of Theology

"Commitment to the exposition of the entire Bible has been Dallas Seminary's core identity since its founding. This volume continues that ongoing legacy by putting an accessible handbook to the Scriptures into readers' hands. Coupled with useful introductions and sidebars, the surveys of each biblical book present an outline, key themes, and practical discussion points. This is a helpful manual for anyone desiring a handle on the breadth of the Scripture's content and a sense of its relevance for life today."

—**M. Daniel Carroll**, Scripture Press Ministries Professor
of Biblical Studies and Pedagogy,
Wheaton College and Graduate School

"For a century, the faculty members at Dallas Theological Seminary have continued to demonstrate an unflinching commitment to the full truthfulness and authority of the Bible. Those familiar with Dallas Seminary will know that the teaching of all 66 Bible books has been characteristic of the seminary's curriculum through the years. Building on these commitments, the DTS faculty, both past and present, have provided a wonderful introduction to the Bible's overarching story, its historical meaning, and its contemporary message. By offering background information regarding context and setting, each Bible book is explored in light of its historical and canonical setting. Helpful guidance and applicable questions for reflection are included with each book. In addition, illuminating articles regarding the nature and interpretation of Scripture from all former presidents and others who have shaped the seminary's history are included. I heartily recommend *Exploring Christian Scripture* as a remarkable resource for Christ followers who want to strengthen their understanding of God's written Word."

—**David S. Dockery**, president, International Alliance
for Christian Education and president,
Southwestern Baptist Theological Seminary

"Kudos to the Dallas Theological Seminary faculty and alumni for producing this outstanding book! *Exploring Christian Scripture* is a most helpful and beneficial resource that will assist Christians around the world to study and to understand the Bible more fully. I recommend it highly."

—**J. Daniel Hays**, professor of Biblical Studies Emeritus,
Ouachita Baptist University and senior professor of Old
Testament, Southwestern Baptist Theological Seminary

"Accessible and insightful. *Exploring Christian Scripture* helps orient today's Bible readers to the beauty and depth of God's Word."

—**Jason K. Lee**, professor of theological studies,
Cedarville University

"Exploring Christian Scripture is an extremely user-friendly guide to exploring how each book of the canon fits into the total story of redemption. Drawing from the past and present DTS tradition, the collaborators of this coast-to-coast flyover of the Bible show the beauty of the full collective breadth of Scripture while making the contribution of each individual book shine with its own aura. This is a great work for new believers and seasoned saints to have nearby to grasp the significance of both the parts and whole of the biblical story for enjoying God more."

—**Eric C. Redmond**, professor of Bible,
Moody Bible Institute

EXPLORING CHRISTIAN SCRIPTURE

EXPLORING CHRISTIAN SCRIPTURE

A Guide to the World of the Bible in Celebration of
Dallas Theological Seminary's 100th Anniversary

General Editors

GLENN R. KREIDER, MICHAEL J. SVIGEL,

and MARK M. YARBROUGH

ACADEMIC
BRENTWOOD, TENNESSEE

Exploring Christian Scripture: A Guide to the World of the Bible in Celebration of Dallas Theological Seminary's 100th Anniversary

Copyright © 2024 by Dallas Theological Seminary

Published by B&H Academic
Brentwood, Tennessee

ISBN: 978-1-4300-9699-3

Dewey Decimal Classification: 220.6
Subject Heading: BIBLE--CRITICISM \ BIBLE--STUDY
AND TEACHING \ BIBLE--READING

Cover design by Darren Welch. Cover image sourced from cjp/iStock.

Printed in China

29 28 27 26 25 24 RRD 1 2 3 4 5 6 7 8 9 10

CONTRIBUTORS

John Adair

Joe Allen

Jim Allman

Mark Bailey

Brian Bain

Michael Balbier

Scott Barfoot

Darrell Bock

Stephen Bramer

Michael Burer

Lanier Burns

Donald Campbell

Lewis Sperry Chafer

Robert Chisholm

Gary Cook

John Dyer

Sue Edwards

Buist Fanning

Joe Fantin

Kevin Gandy

Kenneth Gangel

Brian Gault

Alex Gonzalez

John Hannah

Hall Harris

Dipa Hart

Howard Hendricks

George Hillman

Harold W. Hoehner

Richard Hon

Gordon Johnston

Will Johnston

Glenn R. Kreider

Jenny McGill

Nate McKanna

Rodney Orr

J. Dwight Pentecost

Ramesh Richard

Jay Sedwick

Ben Simpson

Daniel Steffen

Wayne Stiles

Michael J. Svigel

Charles R. Swindoll

Jim Thames

Stanley D. Toussaint

John F. Walvoord

Paul Weaver

Mark M. Yarbrough

Timothy Yoder

Roy B. Zuck

Special thanks for additional editorial assistance from John Adair, Juliene Anderson, Michael Banks, Marci Monro, Christopher Reynolds, Jack Riniker, Autumn Wilson, and Josh Winn.

CONTENTS

Part III: Explorer's Guide to the New Testament

Part IV: Where Do You Go from Here?

INTRODUCTION:
HOW TO USE THIS GUIDE

Oh no. You're lost.

Again.

Not long ago you turned your back on the familiar surroundings of home and boarded a plane. You realized you were in trouble when you stumbled off the plane and everybody around you spoke a language you'd never heard before. After following a herd of travelers through a maze of tunnels, you find yourself thrust out a one-way door and standing in the middle of a bustling city.

This isn't the fun-filled sightseeing tour you had in mind.

Disoriented and overwhelmed, you don't even know which way is north. You're not sure if the street you're on leads downtown, uptown, or to the city dump. The street signs label roads you can't pronounce. And you wouldn't know an important landmark if you were sitting on it.

You need a map and a guidebook. Something to let you know where you are and where you need to go. Landmarks. Boundaries. Anything to point you in the right direction. If you're going to get anything from this tour besides a migraine, you need two things: an *orientation* and an *overview*.

Ever been there before? Lost? Confused? Wishing you could retrace your steps and be back in the comfort of your own home? You're not alone. An entire travel-guide industry thrives by addressing this almost universal problem. People just like you and me trying to travel on their own in a foreign land need guidance.

The same holds true when people crack open the Bible.

When stepping out of our high-speed modern world into the strange world of the Bible, most of us feel like lost travelers—disoriented and overwhelmed. Not sure where to start our exploration, we quickly find ourselves wandering aimlessly through a desert of detailed genealogies . . . or hacking through a jungle of unpronounceable names . . . or tripping through the ruins of an irrelevant culture. We just don't know where or how to get a grasp on the strange world of Scripture. Should we start in the Old Testament or the New? Skim or take notes? What do we need to know to help us understand what we're looking at? Why do some people seem to get so much out of the Bible while we barely find our way around?

Like a lost tourist in a strange city, we need a guide for orientation and overview.

The book you're holding in your hands is like your travel guide through Scripture, perfect for both first-time visitors and repeat explorers. Not only will it lead you along well-worn paths to the most frequented landmarks of the Bible, but it will also point out overlooked sights that lie off the beaten path. It will let you know where you are, how various parts of the Bible fit together, and the most important facts to make the most of your visits.

Exploring Christian Scripture differs from other introductions to the Bible in some significant ways. For starters, instead of just dropping these books on a "timeline," we connect them to a "plotline," so you'll have a clear idea of how each episode fits into God's grand story of creation, fall, redemption, and restoration. You'll never be lost in the rapidly changing highways of history. This will help you better understand their central focus—the person and work of Christ in his first and second coming.

Second, after you've read through this introduction and familiarized yourself with the big picture, you're free to begin your exploration *anywhere*. Pick a place and start exploring. Like a handy travel guide, we include general comments for a quick overview as well as detailed information about each "location." We cut through all the distractions and let you know why each book is important, how it functions in its part of the biblical world, and how it's related to other points in the biblical story. With straightforward descriptions and helpful hints and tips, we make exploring these books both informative and rewarding.

Third, to keep things simple, we provide a handful of standard features for each book of the Bible. The "Snapshot" at the beginning sums up the content of each book in a few lines. The "Orientation" chart summarizes key information, like date, authorship, audience, and outline. The "You Are Here" feature reminds you where you are in the context of the Bible's big picture. Then it's time to dive in with the "Exploring" section, which explains the book's contribution to faith and life. The "Start Your Journey" feature provides some pointers on how to work through the book in ways that will inspire and equip you for Christian living.

Fourth, *Exploring Christian Scripture* contains additional unique features to help you economize the time you spend in each book. Besides some sidebars to provide additional information, the "Going Deeper" and "Q&A" features will point out intriguing people and events, key passages to ponder, and practical principles to apply, as well as expert information on various topics. Like an experienced tour guide pointing out landmarks, photo ops, and the best places to shop or dine, we ease you into the Bible with valuable insights to really explore Scripture, not just rush through its pages or wade through its passages.

Finally, this book can only scratch the surface of exploring Christian Scripture. So, we are giving you access to a whole library of additional materials at a website specifically designed to supplement this book. You can access that website with the link below or by scanning the QR code to continue your exploration of Scripture with trusted guides.

https://www.dts.edu/exploringchristianscripture

In short, we've designed *Exploring Christian Scripture* to be a reliable tool for everyone—from the beginner to the experienced adventurer. Use it for personal Bible reading, in-depth Scripture study, or as a handbook for leading others through the Bible's bustling streets and quaint avenues.

No need to feel lost or confused.

Take a deep breath, relax, and turn the page.

PART I

HIGH-ALTITUDE SURVEY

If you've ever visited a museum dedicated to a particular person, event, or period of history, you likely spent the first fifteen to twenty minutes of the tour in a small theater watching a video overview (after, of course, standing in line for ten minutes waiting for the previous group to clear out!). If the museum focuses on a particular location, it may have even included a flyover of the area, giving you a literal "high-altitude survey" of the land. In fact, some take the whole thing to another level with 3D glasses or a multimedia presentation. We've even had fake wind blown in our faces and water sprayed at us to make us feel like we're really "there."

The purpose of those presentations (besides controlling the flow of people in the museum) is to provide the visitors with context. On the other side of the theater exit, you'll be walking among countless exhibits, artifacts, names, places, events, dates—a barrage of individual facts that somehow add up to a story. So, knowing the big picture in advance helps you put the pieces together. Why is this that important? Where does this chair fit into the story? Who published that propaganda article and for what reason? What's the point of this rifle hanging behind thick glass? Knowing the story

5

behind the displays will prevent confusion and frustration . . . and make for a much more rewarding experience.

The same is true when cracking open the pages of the Bible. Without a high-altitude survey of Scripture that tells its basic story and orients you to its world, you might feel like a clueless visitor meandering from relic to relic trying to figure out what it's all about. So, in the following sections, we overview the biblical narrative, including a chart that places each book of the Bible in one of the story's "episodes." Then we orient you to "The World of Scripture," including an introduction to its languages, literature, lives, and lands.

So sit tight, get comfortable, and be our guest in this brief overview. Before you know it, the lights will come on, the door will open, and you'll begin your self-guided exploration of Scripture.

The Biblical Story of Redemption

Every good story has a beginning, in which the author sets the context for what will happen. Then some tension or conflict enters the author's imagined world. The story ultimately ends with some resolution. In some way, we witness restoration or redemption. Remember those classic children's stories you heard growing up? They started with "once upon a time," conflict ensued, and with the resolution everyone lived "happily ever after."

How should we understand the Bible's story? Is it just a collection of stand-alone vignettes? Or is it an epic with a unified story arc, like a multiseason drama? Does it have its own equivalent to the "once upon a time" and "happily ever after" of classic narratives? The Bible *is* a kind of anthology of writings in a variety of genres, written over a long period of time in several languages and in a variety of cultural contexts. But it tells one grand story, the story of redemption—the story of the relationship between the Creator and the world he created.[1] Let's preview that story in eight "episodes."

---

[1] Christians agree on the basic plotline of the Bible although different traditions view the details differently.

Episode 1: The Beginning	Episode 2: Sin (and Grace)	Episode 3: Promise and Hope	Episode 4: The Kingdom Rises	Episode 5: Division and Judgment	Episode 6: Return from Exile	Episode 7: Dawn of a New Era	Episode 8: The End and New Beginning
Gen 1 ↑ Gen 3	Gen 3 ↑ Gen 10	Gen 11 ↑ 1 Sam 16	1 Sam 16 ↑ 1 Kgs 12	1 Kgs 12 ↑ 2 Chron 36	2 Chron 36 ↑ Neh 13	Matt 1 ↑ Acts 28	Acts 28 ↑ Rev 22
Genesis 1 Chronicles	Genesis 1 Chronicles	Genesis Exodus Leviticus Numbers Deuteronomy Joshua Judges Ruth 1 Samuel 1 Chronicles Job	1 Samuel 2 Samuel 1 Kings 1 Chronicles 2 Chronicles Psalms Proverbs Ecclesiastes Song of Solomon	1 Kings 2 Kings 2 Chronicles Psalms Proverbs Isaiah Jeremiah Lamentations Ezekiel Daniel Hosea Amos Obadiah Jonah Micah Nahum Habakkuk Zephaniah	2 Chronicles Ezra Nehemiah Esther Joel Haggai Zechariah Malachi Psalms	Matthew Mark Luke John Acts Romans 1 Corinthians 2 Corinthians Galatians Ephesians Philippians Colossians 1 Thessalonians 2 Thessalonians Philemon James	1 Timothy 2 Timothy Titus Hebrews 1 Peter 2 Peter 1 John 2 John 3 John Jude Revelation

Episode 1: The Beginning

The biblical story begins with God's glorious act of creation (Gen 1–2). Once there was nothing except God; then, through divine speech, God brought the universe into existence. Into darkness, he spoke light and separated light from darkness. Into the chaos of a water-covered earth, he spoke and separated water from land. To a sparse earth, God spoke, and vegetation of various kinds sprang up from the ground. Again, God spoke, and birds filled the skies, fish swam in the seas, and land animals populated the earth. To the creatures who inhabited the skies and the water, God spoke blessing—blessing demonstrated through fruitfulness. Then God created humans—male and female—in his image and likeness. To them and to all their descendants, he gave the blessing of fruitfulness and the privilege of caring for the created world. The Creator was pleased with his work; he pronounced it very good.

But this glorious "once upon a time" didn't last long.

Into the garden in which the humans dwelled, the adversary appeared in the form of a serpent. He contradicted the command of God, challenged the goodness of God, and presented an alternative narrative. Instead of blessing through obedience to God's instructions and a lifetime of serving as the ambassadors of the Creator in the world he had made, the serpent offered them wisdom, self-sufficiency, and independence. The tension is short-lived; they quickly and enthusiastically chose the wrong path—the path away from God.

From that ground zero of rebellion, devastation erupted.

Tragically, what was good is now not good; everything has been negatively impacted by sin. What was a place of blessing is now a place of cursing. What was intended to be joyful fulfillment in relationship with one another and with God is now pain and suffering. And what was intended to be life that never ends now results in death.

The "fall" (Gen 3), which usually describes the moment sin entered the grand narrative, brings an end to the first act of the story, and it introduces the bulk of the Bible's plotline.

Episode 2: Sin (and Grace)

But God.

Throughout Scripture, those words continue to remind us that in the darkest, most hopeless circumstances, God shows up. In the place where humans turned their backs on him, God promises that this story won't end in cursing, but in blessing. It won't end in darkness, but in light. It won't end in death, but in life. It won't end in isolation and loneliness, but in eternal fellowship with all creation and with the Creator.

One day, the serpent will no longer have access to the creation. One day, the dead will be raised and live forever. One day, the curse on creation will be lifted. One day, God will make his eternal home on the earth.

And this *one day* will never end.

As God consistently and persistently engages with his creatures in the world he created, he is faithful to his promises, gracious and merciful toward rebellious people, and always at work to make all things new. He is patient, long-suffering, committed to the reclamation project for the long haul—as long as it takes.

This is the good news! The God who had the first word will also have the last. Thus, his people have hope—not hope as in wishful thinking, but hope founded in the character of a kind and gracious God, a God who is always good and always acting in a way which is good for those he loves.

We don't need to go much further in the biblical story before we see God respond in a gracious way. When the first humans rebelled against God and ate the fruit of the tree of the knowledge of good and evil (Gen 3), God came to them in the garden and gave them the opportunity to confess. They hid from him and refused to take responsibility. God did judge them, cursed the ground because of them, and drove them from the garden; but he also graciously extended their lives. God's plan for his creation cannot be thwarted by human rebellion.

These two humans who rebelled against God experienced the conse-quences of sin every day of their lives as they groaned in anticipation of all things being made new (Rom 8:22). They wrestled with creation to provide food and shelter, they succumbed to sickness and disease, they experienced the stages of aging and pain in childbearing, and they struggled with the challenges of child-rearing. In short, they experienced what every human after them has experienced. They spent their lives in a fallen world. And as the Creator said, death entered. Murder occurred (Gen 4). Purity of life was now tainted by sin. And eventually, like every living thing, people died (Gen 5).

Their lives are the archetype of what every human since them has experienced.

This would be an ongoing tragedy were it the end of the story. But in his judgment against their rebellion, the Lord introduced a glimmer of hope when he said to the serpent, "I will put hostility between you and the woman, and between your offspring and her offspring. He will strike your head, and you will strike his heel" (Gen 3:15). Many Christians see in this the first declaration of the gospel, the *protoevangelium*—the "first proclamation of the gospel." As the biblical story unfolds, it becomes clearer that the offspring of the woman, the Messiah (or "Christ," which means "anointed one"), would in fact crush the serpent and bring an end to evil's access to the world God had created.

This hope grows in intensity as the story continues.

Yet sin, particularly violence, intensifies too.

Eventually things get so bad that God's grief and pain result in his decision to destroy all life on earth with a flood (Gen 6:6–7). However, the gracious and compassionate God preserves animal life and the lives of Noah's family in an ark. When the flood ends, God makes a covenant with Noah and his descendants along with the animals and the earth. He promises "that never again will every creature be wiped out by floodwaters; there will never again be a flood to destroy the earth" (Gen 9:11).

Far from abandoning his damaged creation to complete destruction, God is committed to the earth and its inhabitants for the long run.

Episode 3: Promise and Hope

In the early chapters of Genesis, God reveals himself to individuals and walks with them (Adam, Enoch, and Noah, for example). Then, in Genesis 11–12, he chooses one man through whom he promises to bless all peoples on earth (see Gen 12:1–3). He makes a covenant with Abraham (see Gen 15, 17), promising that Abraham would be the father of many nations and that he would mediate blessings to all peoples. This covenant looks forward in hope to the ultimate offspring of Abraham—Jesus, the Messiah (Gal 3).

Abraham's son, Isaac, inherits these promises, as does Isaac's son Jacob, whose name God changes to "Israel." As a nation descended from Abraham, Israel is significant in the biblical story because through that chosen nation the Messiah would come. That Messiah, the offspring of Abraham, will also be the offspring of the woman hinted at way back in Gen 3:15. With each promise, we see God's plan of redemption and restoration unfolding before our eyes.

The descendants of Jacob are enslaved in Egypt for four hundred years until, through Moses, God redeems them from bondage. Through ten plagues and the miraculous deliverance at the Red Sea, God fulfills his promises to bring them to the land he had promised to Abraham, Isaac, and Jacob. But again, his people refuse to enter the land, so God judges them by allowing them to wander in the wilderness.

And yet, God's people didn't wander alone; God went with them (Deut 2:7; 8:2). He provided food and water for them, as well as protecting them from enemies, including disease (Deut 8:2–5). Moses summarizes God's relationship with them during the forty years: "For the Lord your God has blessed you in all the work of your hands. He has watched over your journey through this immense wilderness. The Lord your God has been with you these past forty years, and you have lacked nothing" (Deut 2:7).

God's law, the Ten Commandments (and the subsequent laws presented in the Torah), was given to protect them and also direct them toward God. This covenant made with the nation (Exod 20–24) was different than the covenants before. It was conditional. Simply put, they would be blessed if they faithfully followed God; curses awaited if they rebelled. Unfortunately, a familiar theme appears once again in the story: disobedience. Due to his own rebellion against God, Moses doesn't enter the promised land. And the nation? Some rebelled as well—leading one generation to die in the wilderness! The question remained regarding future generations. Would they receive blessings for following God or suffer consequences for rejecting him? In regard to Moses, his sin was costly. He did not enter the land of promise. Instead, Joshua leads the Israelites into the land to conquer and settle the land of Israel. Through judges and prophets, God mediates his rule over his people until . . . the people demand a king.

Episode 4: The Kingdom Rises

God's plan for his chosen nation—and for the world—always assumed a king. Thus, God gave parameters for choosing one. The law of Moses includes detailed regulations for this king and establishing a kingdom (Deut 17:14–20), among them, "Appoint a king from your brothers. You are not to set a foreigner over you, or one who is not of your people" (Deut 17:15). The problem with Israel's request for a king was not the idea of a king but the timing and their motivation: "We must have a king over us. Then we'll be like all the other nations" (1 Sam 8:19–20).

The prophet Samuel "considered their demand wrong" (1 Sam 8:6), so he took it to the Lord. God's response was chilling: "Listen to the people and everything they say to you. They have not rejected you; they have rejected me as their king. They are doing the same thing to you that they have done to me, since the day I brought them out of Egypt until this day, abandoning me and worshiping other gods. Listen to them, but solemnly warn them and tell them about the customary rights of the king who will reign over them" (1 Sam 8:7–9). Samuel warns the people of what will happen: The king will take your children, your freedom, and your money through taxes (1 Sam 8:10–18). The people insisted, so God gave them Saul (2 Sam 9). Saul was the people's choice.

As often happens when people stubbornly push their own agenda against God's, Saul's monarchy ended in failure. He disobeyed God and offered a sacrifice, rashly assuming the role of a priest (1 Sam 13). The final straw was his disobedience in the battle against the Amalekites (1 Sam 15). Samuel declared to him: "Because you have rejected the word of the LORD, he has rejected you as king" (1 Sam 15:23).

God himself then chose David as Saul's replacement. David was the opposite of Saul in stature and heart. David was well-known to Saul, having killed the giant Goliath (1 Sam 17) and served as a musician in Saul's court (1 Sam 16). But Saul became jealous of David, partly because the people loved David (1 Sam 18:8). So Saul plotted to kill him. God delivered David from the threat of Saul numerous times. Eventually Saul was killed in battle, and David became king (1 Sam 31; 2 Sam 2).

David was a poet; many of the Psalms are attributed to him. Unlike Saul, he was a good and faithful king. He was not perfect, as witnessed by his violence (1 Chron 22:6–8) and his abuse of power in the case of Bathsheba and Uriah (2 Sam 11–12). But God was gracious to him; he made a covenant with him (2 Sam 7). In this shocking covenant, God promised to bless David's family, to establish a kingdom that would never end. This promise led the nation to anticipate a Messiah, one who would be greater than David. This covenant would eventually be fulfilled in the Son of David, who will reign on the throne of his father David forever (Luke 1:32–33).

Episode 5: Division and Judgment

David's son Solomon succeeded him as king, and God blessed him with renowned wisdom (1 Kgs 3). Wise living is the focus of biblical books associated with Solomon himself—Proverbs and Ecclesiastes. Solomon's wisdom, although greater than most, foreshadowed the ultimate heir of the kingdom, the incarnate wisdom of Jesus (1 Cor 1:30). Solomon built the first temple in Jerusalem, which looked forward to the temple his descendant Jesus will build (1 Kgs 6–8; 1 Cor 3:16–17).

Yet not all wisdom is created equal. For political reasons, Solomon added many wives and concubines, and his heart was led astray. Worst of all, he led the Israelites to worship other gods (1 Kgs 11). In terms of spiritual leadership, he failed. He directly did what God said his king should never do (Deut 17). Thus, God was angry with Solomon and promised him that his kingdom would be divided. Yet God would not reject Solomon's ultimate offspring and heir of the kingdom because of the promise God had made to David.

As predicted, the kingdom split in two. Solomon's son Rehoboam and Jeroboam, a servant of king Solomon, led military campaigns to demonstrate power. Ultimately, the kingdom's division occurred through a civil war. The precipitating cause was Rehoboam's plan to tax Israel even more heavily than his father had (1 Kgs 12). The tribes of Judah and Benjamin remained loyal to Rehoboam (known as Judah [the southern kingdom]). The remaining ten tribes submitted to Jeroboam (known as Israel [the northern kingdom]).

Generation after generation of Davidic kings failed to keep the law (the Mosaic covenant), failed to live up to the high standard set by God, and failed to lead the people in righteousness. At the same time, generation after generation of Israelites lived in anticipation of a coming king who would establish an eternal kingdom of righteousness and justice. They waited for the Messiah, the offspring of Abraham, of Israel, of David. They waited for the ultimate "image of God," who would fulfill the promise of the offspring of the woman (Gen 3:15).

God exhibited great patience with his people, calling them to repent through his prophets like Isaiah, Jeremiah, and Ezekiel, pleading with them to soften their hearts toward God and to exercise mercy and justice toward others, urging them to keep the covenant with God as they had promised centuries earlier in the desert with Moses.

Eventually, though, God executed judgement against the divided nations. The northern kingdom of "Israel" was the first to face judgment; in 722 BC, they fell to the Assyrians (2 Kgs 17). Then, in 586 BC, the southern kingdom, "Judah," fell to the Babylonians (2 Kgs 25). The marauding Babylonians destroyed Solomon's temple. Many Israelites were killed, and others were taken into captivity. Among those hauled away to captivity were Daniel and his companions. While Daniel was in Babylon, God revealed to him in a series of dreams his plans for the nations—plans to return his people to the promised land, to restore them under a coming king, and to bless them as he had promised long ago.

Episode 6: Return from Exile

God is gracious and merciful; his judgment is not forever. His promises to Abraham and his descendants were that they would live in the land of promise forever as recipients of great blessing that would be for all nations (see Gen 13:15; 17:4–8). In 538 BC, the Persian king Cyrus gave permission for the exiles to return to the land of Israel. They did so in three primary groups under the leadership of Zerubbabel, Ezra, and Nehemiah. Those who returned from exile rebuilt the city of Jerusalem and restored the temple, even in the midst of stout opposition from a variety of sources. When the temple was completed, the exiles mourned as they observed the second temple; it was not as glorious as the one Solomon had built (Hag 2:3).

Just as the earlier prophets had done prior to the exile, the later prophets called the people back to the Mosaic covenant—to repent and live under the blessing of God. At the same time, they looked forward to that same coming messianic offspring of Abraham, Isaac, Jacob, Judah, and David, a perfect king who would establish his kingdom forever. Jeremiah promised a new covenant (Jer 31:31–34) that would replace the old covenant made through Moses at Sinai.

In that future messianic era, the provision of the Spirit would enhance the relationship between God and his people by internalizing the law of God and providing the power to do his will. That coming age would also result in universal knowledge of God and would experience the complete removal of sin and its consequences: suffering, death, disease, injustice, and pain. These themes are found throughout the prophets, as in Ezekiel 36–37, Joel 2, and Malachi 3–4. Other prophets predicted a coming judgment, the day of the

BC—AD? BCE—CE?

Dating Events of the Old and New Testaments

The Old and New Testaments straddle two dating systems—before the advent of Christ and after his advent. The abbreviation *BC* stands for the English phrase "Before Christ" and always follows the date (that is, "100 BC," not "BC 100"). Because BC dates count backwards from the time of Christ, the larger the number, the earlier the event. So, the Assyrian invasion of Israel in 722 BC took place 136 years before the destruction of Jerusalem in 586 BC. In the modern era, as the cultural force of Christianity has waned in the West, many historians have opted for the more theologically neutral *BCE*, meaning "Before the Common Era," though the dates still count backward from the time of Christ. Thus, many scholarly writings today would refer to the destruction of the temple in 586 BCE rather than 586 BC.

For events since the time of Christ, the traditional designation, *AD*, always comes before the date (that is, "AD 100," not "100 AD"). It stands for the Latin phrase *Anno Domini*, which means "in the year of our Lord." The modern designation drops the theologically weighty phrase and opts for *CE*, meaning "Common Era," and follows the date. That is, the destruction of the temple by the Romans in the first century occurred according to the traditional system in AD 70; according to the modern system, it occurred in 70 CE. Events after the advent of Christ count in the right direction—an event in AD 50 is earlier than an event in AD 1950.

One final note on dating. Even though the dating system BC/AD originally intended to count backward and forward from the birth of Christ, long after the system was established, historians rightly discovered that the birth of Christ had been misplaced relative to other events! Instead of completely redating everything (for example, changing the date for the Declaration of Independence from AD 1776 to 1780), the history books just adjusted the birth of Christ to 4 BC!

Lord, before the establishment of the messianic kingdom. Malachi 4 ends the Old Testament Scriptures with the promise that before that time of judgment, Elijah would come, preaching a message of repentance.

Episode 7: Dawn of a New Era

After approximately 400 years without prophets, the long-awaited time had finally come.

The silence was broken when an angel from heaven announced to a priest named Zechariah that his son John would be a prophet "in the spirit and power of Elijah" (Luke 1:17). Matthew identified John as the one who would fulfill the promise of Isa 40:3, the one who would prepare for the coming of the Lord (Matt 3:3). John's message was simple: "Repent, because the kingdom of heaven has come near" (Matt 3:2), language which echoes the words of Mal 4:5–6.

An angel also announced the birth of Jesus to Mary (Luke 1:26–38) and to Joseph (Matt 1:20–21). Matthew explains that this miraculous birth would fulfill Isa 7:14, which predicted the virgin birth of Immanuel, God with us (Matt 1:21–23). In taking on flesh, the Son of God added full humanity to his complete and perfect deity. He is, literally, *God with us*.

Jesus was born in Bethlehem, as the prophet had predicted (Mic 5:2; Matt 2:5–6). Angels announced his birth to shepherds (Luke 2:8–15). Magi—wise scholars—followed a star to find the newborn offspring of David (Matt 2). Seeing the birth of the King of Israel as a threat, the illegitimate king Herod—like the Egyptian Pharoah years earlier (Exod 1–2)—commanded the execution of male children. Joseph, the adoptive father of Jesus, took the young Messiah to Egypt as instructed by an angel (Matt 2:13–18).

In fulfillment of his calling, the prophet John baptized Jesus, whose earthly ministry was preceded by temptations from the same adversary who had at one time tempted Adam and Eve and plunged humanity into death. Yet instead of succumbing to the serpent's deceit, the long-awaited offspring resisted the temptations and sent the serpent slithering away in defeat (Matt 3:13–4:11). Jesus then began his public ministry with the same message as his predecessor, John: "Repent, because the kingdom of heaven has come near" (Matt 4:17).

The four gospels—Matthew, Mark, Luke, and John—record Jesus's public ministry of preaching, doing miracles, serving others, and calling people to repentance. In their own way, all the Gospel writers demonstrate that Jesus is the fulfillment of all of the Old Testament covenant promises. Many people believed in him and followed him. But many rejected him, especially among the political and religious elites whose power and prestige were threatened by the arrival of the Son of God. Opposition to Jesus and his message grew so strong that he was murdered by Pontius Pilate in a conspiracy that included some of Israel's leaders. Yet, it was more than a murder. Jesus willingly laid down his life. And the Father himself "did not even spare his own Son but gave him up for us all" (Rom 8:32). Jesus, the Son of God, was crucified; he died and was buried in a tomb. But on the third day, he was raised from the dead.

This was, after all, the plan of God for the salvation of the world.

Before he ascended to heaven, Jesus reminded his disciples to wait for the coming of the Spirit (Acts 1:4–5). On the day of the Jewish feast of Pentecost, the Spirit came upon the disciples and those gathered in Jerusalem; the church was born (Acts 2). The book of Acts of the Apostles narrates the spread of the gospel, from about 120 believers in a room in Jerusalem (Acts 1:15) to thousands of followers of Jesus throughout the world (Acts 1:8).

Episode 8: The End and New Beginning

As the events in the book of Acts unfold, several apostles wrote letters ("epistles") to churches and individuals, interpreting the person and work of the promised Messiah for the generations that would follow. These epistles address challenges in these early churches (e.g., the two letters to the church in Corinth), summarize the need for and impact of the gospel (Romans), encourage Christians during times of persecution (Prison Epistles), instruct pastors how to structure the church (Pastoral Epistles), help believers practice wisdom (James), elevate Christ over the old covenant (Hebrews), and encourage followers to have assurance of salvation and confidence in the gospel (epistles of Peter, John, and Jude). Collectively, they articulate what Christians believe and how they are to live in a fallen world under the power of the Holy Spirit.

The New Testament canon concludes with a series of otherworldly, prophetic visions given to the apostle John (Revelation). This book first presents specific messages to seven churches and then describes in graphic detail 1) a cataclysmic time on planet earth, 2) the physical return and reign of Christ, and 3) the promise of a new heaven and earth. During these events, God completes all of his covenant promises to Israel, judges sin once and for all, and brings in complete restoration as seen in a new Jerusalem and access to the tree of life (Rev 22). The curse of sin is once and for all removed, and all of the redeemed live in complete, unhindered fellowship with God.

In the end, night is no more, and the light of the Lamb is eternal.

The gospel message of the New Testament is clear. Jesus is descended from Abraham and is the offspring promised to Abraham. He fulfills all the provisions of the Abrahamic covenant (Gal 3:15–18). He kept the law of Moses perfectly, thus fulfilling its requirements (Gal 3:19–26). He is the Son of David and will fulfill the promise of the Davidic covenant of righteousness, peace, and prosperity (Acts 2:32–36). His kingdom will be physical and eternal. Jesus inaugurated the new covenant (Luke 22:20), sending the Holy Spirit (Acts 2:33), who is the down payment and guarantee of our inheritance (Eph 1:13).

Post resurrection, Jesus gave his followers their instructions, the Great Commission, which commands them to make disciples of all nations (Matt 28:18–20). While making disciples, believers are also called to serve him as they await his return. In this messy world, Christians demonstrate his love, by love (John 13:35). What about those that die while awaiting his return? Their bodies are planted in the ground. But their souls go to be with the Lord (2 Cor 5:8). Their bodies await the full day of redemption.

Prior to his ascension, Jesus promised to return to the earth. Through the message of the angels: "This same Jesus, who has been taken from you into heaven, will come in the same way that you have seen him going into heaven" (Acts 1:11). This return of Christ will move toward the final fulfillment of God's plan of redemption. In his vision of the end, John saw Christ return to the earth (Rev 19), establish a kingdom during which Jesus will reign over all creation (Rev 20), and then establish a new heaven and new earth in which the triune God makes his dwelling on the earth forever: "God's dwelling is with humanity, and he will live with them. They will be his peoples, and God himself will be with them and will be their God" (Rev 21:3).

The Bible ends with the promise of Jesus himself: "He who testifies about these things says, 'Yes, I am coming soon'" (Rev 22:20a). The apostle John responds with the longing of every generation of believers since: "Amen! Come, Lord Jesus!" (Rev 22:20b). Finally, the benediction promises, "The grace of the Lord Jesus be with everyone. Amen" (Rev 22:21).

The biblical story begins with the great act of creation, but it's quickly followed by the fall, as the first humans chose to listen to the serpent and eat from the tree God had forbidden. But, thanks be to God, the story doesn't end with rebellion, sin, and death. God has a plan of redemption, and he immediately put that plan into action through a sacrificial system for the forgiveness of sins, a system that looked forward to the ultimate sacrifice of "the Lamb of God, who takes away the sin of the world!" (John 1:29). But the sacrifice for sin is not the culmination of God's plan. He promises that unrighteous people will be righteous (Rom 3:21–26), by grace alone through faith alone in Christ alone (Eph 2:8–10). God's plan of redemption culminates in the resurrection of the dead and a new creation, where sin and death will never be found again.

The World of Scripture

Behind the amazing, true biblical narrative stands the world of Scripture, the times and places, individuals and communities, events and cultures that form the backstage of the story itself. God inspired the books of the Bible through real people facing real problems, experiencing real pain, and clinging to real promises. Among the raw realities of flesh-and-blood mortals like you and me, God's revelation appeared through the beauty and order of creation, by visions and dreams, from angels and prophets, in the written words of the Old and New Testaments, and in the person and work of the Son of God himself.

For people unfamiliar with the Bible or the Christian faith, their picture of the world of Scripture is usually informed by random images gathered from here and there, like a sloppy collage of photos cut and pasted from magazines. Here's Charlton Heston's "Moses" from *The Ten Commandments*. There's "Jesus" from Mel Gibson's *The Passion of the Christ*. In this corner we have some grumpy-looking Pharisees in long robes. Down there is a bright cartoon of a smiling Noah posing in front of a big boat, a parade of happy animals, and a rainbow. Here's an angel. There's a snake and an apple tree.

You'd think those of us raised learning about the Bible would have a much clearer picture. Yet often we've not really grown beyond the images in our children's Bibles. We may know more Bible stories, and we may be able to identify people and events of the Old and New Testaments and even put them in some kind of order. Yet often we talk about "Bible characters" and "Bible stories" as though the world of Scripture is more like a theme park than an actual city—a place people visit and experience, but not where people live normal lives.

Before we embark on brief guided tours of the books of the Bible, let's spend a little time exploring the world of the Scripture—its languages, its literature, its lives, and its lands.

The Languages of Scripture

Though it has been translated into countless languages, the Bible was originally written in three. Most of the Old Testament comes to us in the Hebrew language. A few chapters of Daniel are recorded in the Aramaic language, similar to Hebrew. And the New Testament was written in a form of Greek common in the first century.

Hebrew. Biblical Hebrew—the language in which most of the Old Testament was written—is part of the "Semitic" family of languages of the ancient Near East, from Babylonia and Assyria to Syria, Canaan, Arabia, and even parts of Africa. The language was mostly confined to the finger of land that is modern-day Israel. By the time of the New Testament, many Jews spoke Aramaic, a close relative of Hebrew. The language of the inspired Scriptures had to be explained and interpreted for people who did not understand the biblical language as in previous generations. Also, by the time of Christ, the Old Testament had been translated into Greek, known as the Septuagint.

Aramaic. Aramaic—the language of the region of Aram (modern Syria)—was spoken as the everyday language in much of the ancient Near East toward the close of the prophets and the period of exile and return. By the first century, Aramaic had replaced Hebrew as the everyday language in the land of Judea. As a Semitic language, much of its vocabulary and grammar are similar to ancient Hebrew and later Syriac. Whole chapters of the Old Testament were written in Aramaic: Dan 2:4–7:28; Ezra 4:8–6:18 and 7:12–26.

Greek. Through the influence of Alexander the Great, "koine" or "common" Greek became the international language (*lingua franca*) from India to Greece. After the consolidation of the Mediterranean world under Rome, Greek continued to operate as the common language, while Latin was increasingly used for official purposes. Because of the universal use of Greek, the Septuagint was the main version of the Old Testament used by the earliest Christians, and the apostles and prophets wrote the New Testament texts themselves in Greek. Greek continued as the main language in the eastern Byzantine Empire and Greek Orthodox Church, which uses the Greek Septuagint as its standard Old Testament version to this day.

Latin. None of the Old or New Testament books were written in Latin. However, because Latin became increasingly popular in the western Roman Empire after the first century, the Old and New Testaments were translated into Latin fairly early. And in the fourth century, Jerome provided a fresh translation originally from the Greek Septuagint and New Testament. He later updated his Old Testament translation based on his study of Hebrew texts. The Latin Vulgate (or "common") Bible became the standard translation used in the western Roman Catholic Church.

Ten Hebrew and Greek Words Helpful to Know

Hebrew		Greek	
Amen	אמן	ἀγάπη	Agape
Cherub(im)	(כרוב)ים	ἀδελφός	Adelphos
Hallelujah	הללויה	ἀπόστολος	Apostolos
Hosanna	הושענה	χάρις	Charis
Messiah	משיח	κύριος	Kurios
Sabbath	שבת	λόγος	Logos
Satan	שתן	ἐκκλησία	Ecclesia
Seraph(im)	(שרפ)ים	Θεός	Theos
Shalom	שלום	κοινωνία	Koinonia
Torah	תורה	Χρίστος	Christos

The Literature of Scripture

The Bible tells a single story, but it tells that story through a number of different types of writing. For instance, the five books of Moses—the Pentateuch—serve as a kind of foundational section. Though the books set forth a sweeping narrative from creation to the threshold of the Promised Land, they also contain in themselves elements of the kinds of literature characteristic of the rest of the Bible. Historical narrative with keen theological insight holds the books together. In these first five books, we find examples of origin accounts (Gen 1 and 2), genealogies (Gen 4, 10, 46; Num 26), poetry/song (Exod 15), prophecy (Gen 49; Num 23–24), and even apocalyptic visions and dreams (Gen 37, 40–41). Although Moses lived through the time of most of the Pentateuch, he was not born until after the events recorded in Genesis. He wrote that historical book in the context of the Exodus.

Following the Pentateuch, the twelve books of history continue the story employing the established conventions of interpretive history. That is to say, even the books described as "historical" are not primarily interested in presenting a "just-the-facts," bare-bones account of historical events. In fact, the Bible itself points outside itself to more comprehensive records of the facts and figures—see the repeated cross-reference to the "Historical Records" in 1 Kgs 14:19, 29, and so on. The historical narrative is meant to display the facts of history rightly interpreted in the light of God's bigger story of creation, fall, and redemption. Even when God is not explicitly mentioned by name (as in Esther), we see his fingerprints on every scene, hear his voice echo across every landscape, and feel his glorious presence illuminate every event.

After the books of history, the five books of wisdom and poetry provide light and life to God's people in the form of verse, song, and memorable maxims. From the highly stylized musical dramas of Job and Song of Solomon to the pointed and punchy Proverbs and introspective musings of Ecclesiastes to the profound musical ruminations of the Psalms, this collection reminds us that eternal truth can be conveyed through imaginative artistic expression.

Finally, the Old Testament concludes with the five Major Prophets—Isaiah through Daniel—and twelve Minor Prophets—Hosea through Malachi. Employing a combination of rich imagery and poetry, prophetic oracles and apocalyptic scenes, warnings and promises, the messages of the prophets point God's people upward to faith, outward in love, and forward in hope.

The New Testament kicks off with four Gospels, which tell the story of Jesus from four distinct perspectives, emphasizing who he is and what he taught and accomplished in his earthly ministry. Following the Gospels, the one historical book, the book of Acts, chronicles the story of the church of the first generation. Then, twenty-one Epistles (Romans to Jude) address specific issues faced by the newly established churches and their leaders. Finally, the New Testament ends with the book of Revelation, or Apocalypse, which predicts the future through revelatory visions given to the apostle John.

The Lives of Scripture

Adam, Eve, Noah, Job, Abraham, Sarah, Hagar, Isaac, Rebekah, Jacob, Leah, Rachel, Joseph, Moses, Aaron, Joshua, Rahab, Gideon, Deborah, Naomi, Ruth, Samuel, David, Solomon, Elijah, Elisha, Jonah, Ezra, Nehemiah, Mary, Joseph, Anna, Elizabeth, John the Baptist, Jesus, Peter, James, John, Lydia, Paul, Phoebe, Aquila, Priscilla. . . .

Most Christians raised in the faith have known these names—and many, many more—from their earliest days. They appear in Sunday school lessons. They fill the pages of Bible story books. We've sung songs about them from early on. Even non-Christians or new believers could probably identify half the names in that sampling and even provide some basic biographical info about them: you know, trivia-game kind of stuff like "Noah built the ark," "Moses parted the Red Sea," and "David killed Goliath."

Now, putting them in chronological or biblical order? That might be tough for a lot of people. Providing book and chapter for even some of the big names? Even tougher. Placing them in the right historical period or even century? That's just cruel. Yet one thing is certain—God revealed his plan for creation and redemption *through* people, *to* people, and *for* people. In fact, when he finally focused full attention on the revelation of the center of his plan of salvation, God shined the spotlight on a *person*—the Lord Jesus Christ—"born of a woman, born under the Law" (Gal 4:4), "who has been tested in every way as we are, yet without sin" (Heb 4:15).

One thing about the lives of Scripture that stands out: they're normal. Like you and me. Though some Christian traditions have hallowed and haloed, painted and pedestaled the people of the Bible, even a cursory examination of their lives reveals feeble, fickle, and faulty people. Think of Moses. He was so paralyzed with some kind of speech impediment that he had to have his brother Aaron speak for him before Pharaoh (Exod 4:10–16).[2] Consider David. When the prophet Samuel told Jesse to line up his sons so the Lord could instruct the prophet whom to anoint as the next King over Israel, Jesse didn't even bother to call little Davey from the field (1 Sam 16:10–13). And when you peruse the unlikely cast of characters in the uncanny drama of God's redemptive history, you find shockingly flawed men and women. Grumblers. Footdraggers. Runaways. Doubters. Deceivers. Adulterers. Murderers. Flip-floppers. Hardly a person worth emulating in the list.

Yet God used these men and women mightily. To accomplish his plan, God's Spirit worked in, through, with, and often *in spite of* those normal believers. The word of the Lord to Zerubbabel to encourage him to finish rebuilding the temple in Jerusalem in the midst of obstacles could be spoken to all God's servants, whatever their task: "'Not by strength or by might, but by my Spirit,' says the LORD of Armies" (Zech 4:6). When we read the accounts of average people called and equipped to accomplish miraculous things, we should always see the God who is working out his purposes according to his plans. It should encourage us to know that he can use us— *even us*—in the continual telling of his story of redemption.

At the same time, the lives recorded in Scripture provide us with bad examples to avoid as well as good models to follow. We can learn valuable lessons from the victories and defeats of those who have gone before us. This concept of looking back to the saints of old for inspiration goes all the way back to the first century. After Hebrews 11 reviewed the lives of the Old Testament men and women of faith, the author concluded, "Therefore, since we also have such a large cloud of witnesses surrounding us, let us lay aside every hindrance and the sin that so easily ensnares us. Let us run with endurance the race that lies before us" (12:1). And Paul warned the

---

[2] See Gerald R. McDermott, *Famous Stutterers: Twelve Inspiring People Who Achieved Great Things while Struggling with an Impediment* (Eugene, OR: Cascade, 2016), 1–14.

Corinthians to avoid the folly and wickedness of the people of Israel in their sojourn in the wilderness: "Nevertheless God was not pleased with most of them, since they were struck down in the wilderness. Now these things took place as examples for us, so that we will not desire evil things as they did. . . . These things happened to them as examples, and they were written for our instruction, on whom the ends of the ages have come" (1 Cor 10:5–6, 11). It would be wrong to reduce the Bible to merely a collection of anecdotes from which to draw moral principles. It is much more than that. Yet drawing principles and illustrating truths about God, about people, and about our relationship with him is an important purpose for the inspiration and preservation of his word. But, ultimately, all of these people in some way point forward to the perfect one, the God man, who alone is a trustworthy example we can always follow.

The Lands of Scripture

Though historical events fill its pages, the Bible isn't a textbook for global history. And though its teachings affect all people in all places in all times, it doesn't recount detailed histories of the Americas, the Orient, the tip of remote regions of Africa, the outback of Australia, or the frigid coasts of Antarctica. If you glance at the maps in the back of most Bibles, you'll notice the lands of Scripture are limited to a few central locations—mostly the lands around the Mediterranean Sea. Yet the bookends of the Bible— Genesis and Revelation—cast the scope of the Bible's story far beyond the boundaries of that slender segment of the globe. In fact, the story begins and ends with reference not only to the earth but to the heavens, which includes everything you could see with the most powerful telescope and even the unseen world of spiritual things.

But let's not get ahead of ourselves. It's easy enough to get lost in the handful of lands mentioned in Scripture without worrying about the unseen realm!

Most of the action in the Bible takes place in or around *THE land*—the "Promised Land." Originally called the "land of Canaan" (Gen 12:5), God later identified that finger of territory east of the Mediterranean by the various nations dwelling in it: "the land of the Canaanites, Hethites, Amorites, Perizzites, Hivites, and Jebusites" (Exod 3:17). Later, after the exodus and conquest of the land by the tribes of Israel, the same place is called "Israel's territory" (Judg 20:6). After the split between the northern and southern kingdoms, the land to the south around Jerusalem is called "the land of Judah" (2 Kgs 23:24), while the northern kingdom is called "Israel's land" (2 Kgs 6:23).

By the time of the New Testament, several kingdoms had conquered the region—the Assyrians, Babylonians, Persians, Greeks, and finally the Romans, who gave the province the name of "Judea," meaning "land of the Jews" (Matt 2:22). In the second century AD, after the Romans put down one of many Jewish revolts, they renamed the region "Palestine," meaning "land of the Philistines." It kept that name for centuries until the twentieth century, when the nation of Israel was established in 1948.

Why do the majority of recorded events center on this sliver of land roughly the size of New Jersey? A land that represents not even 0.00006 percent of the globe? *Because of God's covenant with Abraham.* In Genesis 15, God swore to Abraham: "I give this land to your offspring, from the Brook of Egypt to the great river, the Euphrates River: the land of the Kenites, Kenizzites, Kadmonites, Hethites, Perizzites, Rephaim, Amorites, Canaanites, Girgashites, and Jebusites" (Gen 15:18–21). Since that promise, the story of Abraham, Isaac, Jacob, and the people of Israel centered on that land. More specifically, their relationship to the land was like a thermometer for their relationship with God. As they grew spiritually cool toward Yahweh and his law, the land withered; as their hearts froze, they found themselves expelled from the land. As they warmed toward Yahweh in faith, repentance, and obedience, they enjoyed peace, safety, and prosperity in the land. Yet these repeated cycles of blessing, hardship, judgment, exile, and return kept their hopes of an ultimate restoration and fulfillment alive, as it does even to this day among the Jewish people.

Yet the Promised Land isn't the only land of the Bible. Surrounding nations played a role in the affairs of God's people. To the south, Egypt alternated as a place of refuge and a political and military opponent (Gen 12:10). From there Moses led the people of Israel from bondage (Exod 3:17). The Bible mentions other southern nations such as Edom, Cush, Put, Lud, Libya, and Ethiopia (Cush) (Num 33:37; Isa 11:11; Ezek 30:5; Acts 8:27). To the east, nations like Assyria, Babylon, Persia, Arabia, and even India are mentioned (1 Kgs 10:15; 2 Kgs 24:1; Esth 1:1; Isa 19:23; Ezek 38:5). To the north we encounter Lebanon, Syria, Armenia (Deut 1:7; 2 Kgs 19:37; Isa 7:8), and the mysterious "Gog/Magog" along with Tubal and Meshech (Ezek 27:13). There's even passing reference to remote lands like Tarshish (Jonah 1:3).

When the gospel of Jesus Christ moves beyond Jerusalem, Judea, and Samaria toward the "ends of the earth" (Acts 1:8), the map of the lands of the Bible expands. Paul's first missionary journey introduces us to "Asia Minor"—a name given collectively to the various regions in modern-day Turkey, such as Galatia, Pamphylia, and Phrygia (Acts 14:24; 16:6). Then, in ever-larger circles, the church reached new regions—Macedonia, Achaia (Greece), Italy, and even as far as Spain (Acts 19:21; 27:6; Rom 15:28). Yet these regions were only the beginning. Though not explicitly mentioned in the New Testament, God's vision for the gospel and the witness of the church was to reach every nation of the world (Matt 24:14; Acts 13:47). One day, regardless of political boundaries or ethnic backgrounds, "a vast multitude from every nation, tribe, people, and language" will stand before the throne of God (Rev 7:9).

GOING DEEPER

"The Word of God: Why I Trust the Bible"

— John F. Walvoord —

T he earliest memories from my childhood remind me that I recognized the Bible as a very special book. In Sunday school, as well as in our home, the Bible had a place given to no other book.

While I cannot recall my father ever reading a newspaper at the dinner table, it was our family custom to read a portion of Scripture and have family prayer each day. Even before I could read, I was taught to memorize short verses of the Bible. Later I joined with the rest of the family in reciting almost daily some portion of Scripture that we were learning together, such as Psalm 1, Psalm 23, or Psalm 103, which were favorite psalms. The Bible was presented to me as a holy book, the Word of God.

In more than fifty years of preaching and teaching scriptural truth, I was impressed with the comprehensive evidence supporting the conclusion that the Bible is indeed the Word of God, absolutely accurate in its statements—a book that can be trusted to teach us spiritual truths. Many large volumes have been written in support of the inspiration and inerrancy of the Bible, but certain facts stand out in my own experience.

The Bible clearly claims to be inspired of God. According to 2 Tim 3:16–17, "All Scripture is inspired by God and is profitable for teaching, for rebuking, for correcting, for training in righteousness, so that the man of God may be complete, equipped for every good work." Peter expressed the same concept in 2 Pet 1:21—"No prophecy ever came by the will of man; instead, men spoke from God as they were carried along by the Holy Spirit." These direct statements of the inspiration of the Bible are confirmed by dozens of references throughout the Old and New Testaments. The Bible is "the Word of God" and "your Word," an assertion made in various ways over 100 times in the Old Testament alone.

In the New Testament, whenever Christ and the apostles quoted the Old Testament, they cited it as absolute authority and often indicated that the writers of Scripture had been guided in what they wrote by the Spirit of God. We find illustrations of this in Matt 22:43–44 and in frequent quotations of the Old Testament in the New Testament. For instance, in Acts 1:16, Peter referred to Ps 109:8 when he said, "It was necessary that the Scripture be fulfilled that the Holy Spirit through the mouth of David foretold about Judas."

One of the most dramatic statements about the Bible's accuracy comes from the lips of Christ himself: "For truly I tell you, until heaven and earth pass away, not the smallest letter or one stroke of a letter will pass away from the law until all things are accomplished" (Matt 5:18). Here Christ referred to the smallest letter of the Hebrew alphabet—and to the smallest part of a letter that would change its meaning.

This points to an important conclusion: those who attack the written Word of God also attack the incarnate Word of God, Jesus Christ. If the Bible is in error, then Christ is in error too. The two stand or fall together. For this reason, evangelical Christians insist that the Bible is indeed the inspired Word of God and that the authors were guided by the Spirit so that they wrote the truth without any error.

Even a casual reader of the Bible becomes impressed by the uniqueness of the Bible. Where in all the world could sixty-six books be collected from more than forty authors, written over a period of more than

1,600 years, and yet form one united and continual presentation of divine truth? The unity of Scripture is one of the convincing evidences that the Bible is not a natural book, but a book that God himself directed and produced through human authors.

Most Christians, while unfamiliar with many of the technical arguments for the inspiration of the Bible, are convinced that the Bible is the Word of God because of what it has done in their own lives. The influence of the Bible on millions of those who have put their trust in it is an attested fact of history. Many who have been moral wrecks and victims of drink and drugs have been marvelously redeemed through the power of the Word of God. They have been made new into intelligent, useful citizens and members of the church. The power of Scripture is described in Heb 4:12—"For the word of God is living and effective and sharper than any double-edged sword, penetrating as far as the separation of soul and spirit, joints and marrow. It is able to judge the thoughts and intentions of the heart."

Wherever the Bible has been constantly applied, it has dramatically changed the civilization and culture of those who have accepted its teaching. It has raised women from debased slavery to a position of honor, love, and purity. It has led to the abolition of slavery. It has energized movements supporting human life and dignity. The Bible recognizes, on the one hand, humankind's innate sinfulness and depravity and, on the other hand, the value of human life and the dignity of humanity. In civilizations where only some of the people were consistent Christians, their presence had the effect of influencing the entire social and political structure. No other book has ever so dramatically changed individual lives and society in general.

Since the Bible is indeed the Word of God, those who read it are confronted with moral decisions. The truth of the Scriptures must first be believed and comprehended, and this requires careful Bible study, proper methods of interpretation, and understanding how one portion of Scripture casts light on another.

And as the Word of God, the Bible is as essential to our spiritual life as food is to our physical life. The Bible should be read daily, and its truths allowed to cast their light on our path.

The Bible, however, is more than a book to be admired and revered, more than a book to be placed in a special category as a holy book. Its moral commands and spiritual values demand commitment. People who really believe the Bible allow it to lead them to faith in Jesus Christ. The comprehensive sweep of the Bible, as it looks at history from God's point of view and then presents the glorious future that is awaiting the Christian, gives them lives of meaningful activity. It includes a system of values that transcends the materialism of our day and a glorious hope in a world where there is much hopelessness.

The Bible was written for people as they are, but it points the way to what we can be by the grace of God. As we meditate on it and profit by our study of it, our spiritual lives will grow, our lives will become more fruitful in the service of the Lord, and we will be preparing for our eternal destiny.

No other book can do more for those who put their trust in its truth. No other book is inspired of God, given by inspiration of the Holy Spirit, revealing God's truth without any mixture of error. The Bible is as trustworthy as God Himself.[1]

---

[1] Adapted from John F. Walvoord, "The Word of God: Why I Trust the Bible," *Kindred Spirit* 25, no. 3 (Fall 2001): 2–3. © 2001 Dallas Theological Seminary.

Q&A

"The Lands of the Bible"

With Dr. Wayne Stiles

Dr. Wayne Stiles (ThM, DMin, Dallas Theological Seminary) is author of *Going Places with God* and *Walking in the Footsteps of Jesus*, which show the practical application of the Bible lands to life. For decades, he has led countless pilgrims through the lands of the Bible, and he has made his expertise available through an immersive online Holy-Land journey at www.walking thebiblelands.com.

Q: When some people hear the word *geography*, they have flashbacks to map quizzes back in school. Why would knowing more about the lands of the Bible be important for exploring Scripture?

A: In short, the better we understand the lands of the Bible, the better we will understand and apply the Bible itself. Reading God's Word "in context" means more than the words on the page. That's because the land God chose for his people played an essential role in shaping their lives.

Q: Can you give a few examples? How did God use the land to shape his people?

A: When we look at Israel on a map, we see how it stands as a natural land bridge at the crossroads of three continents—Asia, Africa, and Europe. All who traveled to or from Egypt had to pass through Israel on this international highway. As a result, God's people were uniquely positioned to influence the world for God. (They also had to trust the Lord for protection from invading nations who constantly wanted to control Israel's land.) Jesus made use of this highway's potential when he relocated to Capernaum in order to have greater influence (Matt 4:13, 24).

Q: This sounds like it might even apply to believers today.

A: Exactly! Israel's geography illustrates a question we can also ask ourselves: *Who is influencing whom?* God has put us where we are to influence others for him. We either lead them toward God, or they draw us away from him. Like Christ, we need to think and act strategically about where God has placed us.

The Lord also put his people in a land where rain was its primary source of water—and rain comes from God. Unlike Egypt or Mesopotamia, which had abundant rivers, Israel had to walk faithfully with God in order for the land to get rain. Talk about motivation! The Lord said it this way: "But the land you are entering to possess is a land of mountains and valleys, watered by rain from the sky" (Deut 11:11). Our own lives feel this same tension too, don't they? God often puts us in a context of lack, and it keeps us dependent on the Lord to provide.

Q: OK, so God used the land of Israel to teach his people to trust him. But do you have an example of how using those maps in the back of our Bibles helps us better understand a specific passage?

A: Of course. Let's say we're reading in Numbers 21 about the Hebrews' victory against the King of Arad. When we find Arad on the map (just west of the Dead Sea) and follow the direction the Lord led his people, we see that God took them far south to the Red Sea—not north into the Promised Land. This shows us why "the people became impatient because of the journey" (Num 21:4). But as we keep reading, we also see how God led them to enter the Promised Land not from the south but from the center—at

Jericho—which strategically divided the land in two. In our own lives, this reminds us that God sees the map from above and knows the best way to proceed—even when the long way seems the wrong way to us.

Q: That's great. What about actually visiting the land? Any thoughts on that?

A: Absolutely! Try to wrap your mind around this amazing fact: *99 percent of those who journey to Israel say it has a profound effect on their spiritual lives.* I have experienced this personally, and I have seen the difference the journey makes in the lives of thousands of people I have led on tours. Why so significant? It's like taking a journey inside the Bible. You experience a context you can get no other way.

Q: That's a great line: *taking a journey inside the Bible.* **But many people won't be able to take that journey. What resources would you suggest for those who can't see the Holy Land for themselves?**

A: Many great atlases, photo libraries, commentaries, and websites offer insights from our desks at home. In fact, I developed my virtual tour videos to show the sites to those who can't travel to see them all. The lands of the Bible offer us so much insight into God's Word! Everyone can experience those life-changing lessons on some level. It just requires taking the first step.

PART II

EXPLORER'S GUIDE TO THE OLD TESTAMENT

In the city of Boston, Massachusetts, visitors year-round can follow the famous "Freedom Trail." This two-and-a-half-mile walk from Boston Commons to Bunker Hill will lead you through sixteen historic sites, like Paul Revere's house, the Old North Church, and the U.S.S. Constitution. Unfamiliar with those locations and their place in early American history? No problem. Signs at each stop will tell you where you are, orient you on the timeline in history, associate it with other places and events, and usually give you opportunities to step inside for a longer visit. And as soon as you're ready to move on, the Freedom Trail is still there—a literal red line of bricks built into the walkway to lead you on to the next location.

Like Boston's Freedom Trail, the following "Explorer's Guide" will help you journey through the books of the Bible. With the basic overview behind us in the high-altitude surveys, it's time to lace up our walking shoes and hit the path. You can start anywhere—Old Testament, New Testament, Historical Books, Wisdom literature . . . even the Book of Revelation. But maybe for your first time through—or first time in a long time—starting at the beginning might make good sense. Or find a book you want to explore, read the one- or two-page overview, then dig into the book itself.

Snapshot—briefly summarizes the content of the book

Orientation—features date, authorship, audience, and outline

You Are Here—informs readers where they are in the context of the Bible's storyline

Exploring—explains helpful details of the book's contribution to faith and life

Start Your Journey—advice for readers on how to get the most from the book

Exploring the Old Testament

Approximate Centuries in Which Recorded Events Likely Occurred, Poetry Written, or Prophets Prophesied

	Pre-15th	15th–13th*	14th–11th	11th–10th	10th–9th	9th–6th	6th–5th
PENTATEUCH	Genesis	Exodus, Leviticus, Numbers, Deuteronomy					
HISTORY		Joshua	Judges, Ruth	1 Samuel · 2 Samuel	1 Kings	2 Kings	Ezra, Nehemiah, Esther
			1 Chronicles		2 Chronicles		
WISDOM	Job			Psalms	Proverbs		
					Ecclesiastes, Song of Solomon		
MAJOR PROPHETS						Isaiah, Jeremiah, Lamentations	
						Ezekiel, Daniel	
MINOR PROPHETS						Hosea, Amos, Obadiah, Jonah, Micah, Nahum, Habakkuk, Zephaniah	Joel, Haggai, Zechariah, Malachi

(Job may be later, and Proverbs may include earlier sayings composed prior to its collection.)

KEY

- PENTATEUCH
- HISTORY
- WISDOM
- MAJOR PROPHETS
- MINOR PROPHETS

*The century of the exodus (and thus the conquest of the land of Canaan under Joshua and the period of the judges) is unsettled among biblical historians; the range of centuries indicates this.

GENESIS

SNAPSHOT

Why is there something rather than nothing? Why are we even here? Our exploration of Scripture begins with God, whose works of creation, preservation, and redemption anchor the story of the Bible. This book of beginnings explains where we came from, what went wrong with the world, and how God has begun his plan of restoration through promise.

ORIENTATION

Date:	Between 15th and 13th centuries BC
Author:	Moses
Audience:	Early Israel, beginning with the people of the exodus
Outline:	1. Pristine Creation (1–2)
	2. Primeval History: The Fall, The Flood, and the Tower (3–11)
	3. Patriarchal Narratives: Abraham, Isaac, Jacob, and Joseph (12–50)

YOU ARE HERE

Episode 1: The Beginning → Episode 3: Promise and Hope

As the first book of the Pentateuch, Genesis sets the course for God's relationship to the universe and humanity. It sets forth the account of creation, fall, and the hope of redemption.

EXPLORING GENESIS

Without Genesis, there is nothing else. Literally! This book is the *first* main point of an extended unit of Scripture (Genesis to Deuteronomy). Its subdivisions deal with the first ages and stages of global history, geography, and people. In the account of creation, God deems and declares all creation "good." Created in God's image as male and female, humanity's distinct purpose is to be fruitful and multiply, to fill and subdue the earth, to work and keep the garden, and to rule over the earth as God's stewards—to *image* God to and in creation (Gen 1–2).

Adam and Eve, the genealogical ancestors of all humanity, disobeyed God and flouted his clear commands (Gen 3). The consequences of their sin spelled death and destruction of cosmic, global, and personal proportions. The grim specter of death began immediately (Gen 5). Massive destruction multiplied exponentially at the levels of individuals and families, nature, and nations (6–11). What started with a forbidden bite resulted in a moral and spiritual meltdown.

However, the Creator's redemptive mission of mercy and grace accompanied his decisive justice. His salvation intent from Genesis is cross-referenced throughout Scripture.

- The tempter in the garden was cursed, but human sinners have provision of redemption through blood (Gen 3:21; Heb 9:22).
- God promised a fatal crushing of the archenemy, who will wound but will be vanquished by the final "seed" of the woman (Gen 3:15).

- The first Adam plunged humanity into ruin, but Jesus, the "second Adam," is the source and authority of human salvation (Rom 5; 1 Cor 15).
- Widespread, unprecedented rebellion provoked decisive judgment (Gen 6–8), but a covenant sealed with a rainbow promised divine mercy (Gen 9).
- Humans jointly aspired for a great name in disobedience to God by building a tower to heaven; God acted in dispersing humanity (Gen 10:1–11:9).

Several key figures anchor the foundational story of Genesis. God made an unconditional commitment to make Abram's name great and to bless *all* the families of the earth *in him* (12:3). God repeats the unconditional dimensions of his unbreakable covenant—land, lineage, and blessings forever—promised to Abraham, Isaac, and Jacob (Gen 21, 26, 28). Jacob, renamed "Israel," becomes the father of twelve sons, who are themselves the patriarchs of the twelve tribes. Then Genesis ends with one son, Joseph, exalted to a high position in Egypt—providentially placed by God to preserve the growing nation of Israel. Along the way, this lineage of Abraham, Isaac, and Jacob (Israel) made sinful choices, or they suffered under the shenanigans of others. But they continued to experience the grace, mercy, and sovereign goodness of God.

The story of Genesis concludes with hope. Though families of Israel are refugees in Egypt, displaced from their land of promise, Joseph leaves them with prophetic words of promise: "I am about to die, but God will certainly come to your aid and bring you up from this land to the land he swore to give to Abraham, Isaac, and Jacob" (50:24).

START YOUR JOURNEY

- The men and women of Genesis provide both positive and negative examples for believers today. For example, we avoid Lot's worldly compromises that led him into moral calamity (Gen 19). Or we can follow Joseph's examples of integrity in the crucible of temptation (Gen 39). As you read through Genesis, take note of decisions and actions and how they reflect faith, hope, and love.

- Over half of the famous "Hall of Faith" in Hebrews refers to men and women from the book of Genesis. We think of Genesis as the book of beginnings, and that's true. But it's also a book of *faith*. These women and men died without receiving the promises of God (Heb 11:39–40).

- Disclosing his dreams of ascendance arouses competitive jealousy among Joseph's brothers. Though sold as a slave, his vital spirituality continues. He trusts the God who organizes, accompanies, and utilizes evil circumstances for his good purposes (Gen 37–50). Raised from destitute circumstances, Joseph's declaration of God's mysterious, meticulous, and marvelous providence climaxes the book of Genesis. "You planned evil against me; God planned it for good to bring about the present result—the survival of many people" (Gen 50:20; cf. Rom 8:28). In this, Joseph is a type of Christ, the one who will come and make all things new.

EXODUS

SNAPSHOT

Ever feel abandoned by God? Trapped in an inescapable situation? Oppressed by your own sin or the wickedness of others? For millennia, the book of Exodus has reminded God's people that patience pays off, God keeps his promises, and he can be trusted to deliver his people from whatever is keeping them in a state of bondage.

ORIENTATION

Date: Between 15th and 13th centuries BC

Author: Moses

Audience: Early Israel, beginning with the people of the exodus

Outline:
1. Bondage in Egypt (1)
2. The Calling and Preparation of Moses (2–4)
3. Moses vs. Pharoah: Plagues and Passover (5–13)
4. Deliverance from Egypt: Red Sea and Wilderness (14–18)
5. Giving of the Law and Tabernacle (19–31)

YOU ARE HERE

Episode 3: Promise and Hope

As the second book of the Pentateuch, Exodus continues the history of the people of Israel, focusing on how God not only keeps his promises but also protects and provides for his people.

EXPLORING EXODUS

"Let my people go!" In the confrontation between Moses and Pharaoh, God repeats those words to that mighty earthly emperor at least seven times, illustrating the hardness of Pharoah's heart and the tenacity of God's redeeming love for his people. Throughout that confrontation between the powerful ruler of Egypt and the powerless people of Israel, God shows up with devasting plagues that demonstrate that even the mighty Pharoah must bow to the almighty God who created the heavens and the earth!

At the start of the story of Israel's redemption, it seems many of the people of Israel had lost hope of God keeping his promises to their forefathers. Yet behind the scenes, often in ways unnoticed by the people, God was working toward a dramatic rescue operation. He protected the infant Moses from Pharoah's order to slaughter the infant Israelite boys, and he providentially orchestrated events so Moses was adopted by Pharoah's daughter and nursed by his own mother (1:20–21; 2:1–10)! When the time was right, God revealed himself to Moses in a burning bush, sharing with him his name, "I AM," related to the Hebrew name *Yahweh* (3:1–15). Far from forgetting his people in their plight, the God of Abraham, Isaac, and Jacob saw to it that his people would be rescued . . . in God's timing.

When Moses returns to the new Pharoah's court, with his brother Aaron at his side and the power and authority of God Almighty going before him, a dramatic confrontation ensues. Through Moses and Aaron, God demands that Pharoah release the Israelites. As the Egyptian ruler refuses, God strikes the land of Egypt with a series of ten plagues that not only demonstrate his power over all creation but also serve up a slap in the face of Egyptian religion. Eugene Merrill notes, "Each plague was an assertion of the sovereignty of Yahweh over the deity (or deities) responsible for the area of nature particularly under attack."[1]

The final plague—the death of the firstborn—establishes the observance of the Hebrew feast of "Passover," when God's judgment passed over those who had applied the blood of a sacrificed lamb on the doorpost of their home, a foreshadowing of the blood of Christ who would be the ultimate Passover sacrifice (1 Cor 5:7). Humbled and humiliated, with his firstborn son dead because of his hard-heartedness, Pharoah finally lets the Israelites go . . . then changes his mind when they flee. The result was an astonishing deliverance when God split the Red Sea, allowing his people to pass on dry land and swallowing up the army of Egypt in judgment (Exod 14:1–31).

Having rescued Israel from their bondage in Egypt, God organizes the people under a covenant made at Mount Sinai, first in the form of the Ten Commandments, then in a detailed system of laws and rituals designed to provide order, justice, and righteousness, and the Tabernacle which provided a place of worship for the new nation about to return to the land promised to Abraham, Isaac, and Jacob (Exod 19–31). Yet even after witnessing such a miraculous deliverance, the people of Israel rebelled, groaned, and grumbled about their conditions (15:24; 16:2; 17:2; 32:1)—foreshadowing a shaky on-again, off-again relationship between God and his people, Israel, that would continue for generations. But God persisted in his faithfulness to them.

In spite of Israel's fickleness, God's character throughout the exodus from Egypt remains consistent, summarized beautifully in 34:6–7: "The LORD is a compassionate and gracious God, slow to anger and abounding in faithful love and truth, maintaining faithful love to a thousand generations, forgiving iniquity, rebellion, and sin. But he will not leave the guilty unpunished, bringing the consequences of the fathers' iniquity on the children and grandchildren to the third and fourth generation."

---

[1] Eugene H. Merrill, *Kingdom of Priests: A History of Old Testament Israel*, 2nd ed. (Grand Rapids: Baker Academic, 2008), 81.

START YOUR JOURNEY

- If you're stuck in a seemingly hopeless situation, don't lose hope! Just as the Israelites cried out to God from their bondage and oppression, you can lift your own voice to God, who hears your groanings and will come to your aid.

- Whether you're dealing with an oppressive bully, an unrelenting illness, or a besetting sin, reflect on the early chapters of Exodus for both comfort and motivation to persevere in faith even in the midst of deep struggles.

- God always protects and provides for his people . . . but not always in the ways we anticipate. When they were pinned against the shores of the Red Sea, instead of obliterating the Egyptian army in a burst of divine wrath, God split the sea to allow Israel through and to crush the army under the water. When they were hungry and thirsty in the wilderness, God gave miraculous manna, a swarm of quail, and water from a rock. In the same way, God protects and provides for us in his own timing and by his own means through Jesus, the true deliverer who is greater than Moses.

LEVITICUS

SNAPSHOT

Do you ever feel like something's missing in your worship experience? If you're like many Christians living in a secular culture, part of the problem may be that you've unwittingly neglected the importance of holiness as the basis for worship. Reading the book of Leviticus and considering what it says about holiness can reinvigorate your life and worship.

ORIENTATION

Date: Between 15th and 13th centuries BC
Author: Moses
Audience: Originally the first generation of Israelites out of Egypt
Outline: 1. Ritual Regulations: Cultic Traditions (1–16)
                  a. Rituals for Obtaining/Maintaining Cultic Holiness (1–5)
                  b. Ritual Consecration of Priests and Tabernacle (6–10)
                  c. Rituals for Obtaining/Maintaining Cultic Purity (11–15)
                  d. Ritual Day of Atonement: Yom Kippur (16)
              2. Ethical Regulations: Moral Laws (17–27)

    a. Ethical Holiness of the People and Priests (17–22)
    b. Annual Festivals and Sabbatical Years (23–25)
    c. Blessings for Obedience/Curses for Disobedience (26)
    d. Regulations about Vows (27)

YOU ARE HERE

Episode 3: Promise and Hope

As the middle book of the Pentateuch, Leviticus occupies the central place in the Torah, the first of the three portions of the Hebrew Scriptures: Law, Prophets, and Writings.

EXPLORING LEVITICUS

After delivering the Israelites from slavery in Egypt (Exod 1–15), Yahweh brought the people to Sinai (Exod 16–18), where he formally entered into covenant with Israel (Exod 19–24). Since Israel had already believed in Yahweh when they saw his redemptive actions in Egypt (Exod 4:31; 14:31), the covenant at Sinai did not establish her relationship with God. Rather, it transformed it. Through the covenant, the faithful individuals and clans became a unified people called to obey and serve him: "'if you will carefully listen to me and keep my covenant, you will be my own possession out of all the peoples, although the whole earth is mine, and you will be my kingdom of priests and my holy nation'" (Exod 19:5–6). Thus, obedience was not the basis of Israel's *salvation*, but the basis of Israel's *service*.

    Yahweh's commands and covenant stipulations at Sinai consisted of two types of instructions: (1) the moral regulations in Exodus 20–23, composed of the Decalogue ("Ten Commandments") in Exodus 20 and practical case laws in 21–23, and (2) the ritual regulations in Leviticus 1–27. Thus, God gave two types of laws at Sinai: the moral laws and the ritual laws (Jer 7:22–23). The order was significant: God gave the moral laws first and the ritual laws second. To be sure, God wanted Israel to obey both, but he would not accept obedience to the ritual laws in place of obedience to the moral (e.g., 1 Sam 15:22–23; Isa 1:10–20; Hos 6:6; Amos 5:21–24). Ritual worship was to be rendered out of an obedient heart that flowed from faith in and love for Yahweh.

A popular misconception is that Leviticus is only concerned about ritual and sacrifice. While Leviticus 1–16 focuses on ritual holiness, Leviticus 17–27 combines ritual holiness and ethical holiness. Moses rejected the separation of ancient Israel's life into secular and spiritual. He called the Israelites to live fully integrated lives of ritual purity and ethical integrity. For example, the detailed instructions for the ritual of Yom Kippur culminate in the reminder: "You must humble yourselves . . . this day atonement is to be made for you to cleanse you from all your sins; . . . you must humble yourselves" (Lev 16:29–31, NET; cf. Lev 23:27, 32; Num 29:7).

Those who live in Western secular societies often struggle to understand the legitimate role of ritual in the life of ancient Israel. They often have a superficial view about the nature of ritual and its role in human society in general and religious communities such as ancient Israel in particular. Levitical ritual had many facets:

- Sacred symbolism provided both a model *of* reality—showing Israel how to interpret the world in categories of the "holy" and "profane" (e.g., Lev 10:10; 27:33; Ezek 44:23)—as well as a model *for* reality—illustrating the quest for moral holiness through the quest for ritual holiness.
- Sacred routine performed in a set order at regular seasons created a cultural system to provide social order, which imposed meaning on an otherwise disordered and chaotic life in a fallen world.
- Sacred liturgical rites performed in compliance with detailed rules encouraged an acceptance of the moral authority of Yahweh and religious authority of the priests, promoting social order and stability.
- Sacred invariance of ritual in a timeless repetition created continuity between the past, present, and future, forming a sense of

connectedness with a community spanning the ages and helping individuals find their place in the world.

- Sacred scriptedness of regulated ritual effectively communicated that God had not called Israel merely to believe the right doctrine, but to live and act the right way.
- Sacred rites of passage from a ritually unclean to a clean state, as well as from a ritually profane to a holy state, marked the spiritual journey of individuals leaving their old way of life and entering a new way of life by following Yahweh's law.

START YOUR JOURNEY

- As you read Leviticus, try not to not get lost in the details but consider its basic theology. Consider what the rituals in chapters 1–16 teach about God's holiness and what the regulations in chapters 17–27 communicate about ethical purity in daily life.
- If you're a member of a nonliturgical church, the strict schedule and ritual of Leviticus might seem rigid and lifeless. Yet God has given us symbols, rites, and repeated reminders to continually point us back to him, like weekly Sunday worship, devotional time, and observance of the ordinances.
- Praise God for sending his Son as the perfect once-for-all sacrifice for our sins! Our great High Priest, Jesus Christ, has removed our sins through his death on the cross and intercedes for us before God the Father through his resurrection and ascension into heaven.

Why Does My Bible Sometimes Have *LORD* instead of *Lord*?

In most modern English translations, when you see the word *LORD* in all capital letters, it indicates the underlying Hebrew word *YHWH*, that is, the proper name of God, often pronounced "Yahweh." Among Hebrew readers, who didn't want to utter the name of God for fear of offending him or inadvertently breaking the third commandment (Exod 20:7), when they reached the name YHWH in Scripture, they would instead pronounce the general title, *Adonai*, which means "lord." In fact, later scribes who copied the Old Testament intentionally left the symbols for vowel sounds out of the name YHWH in the Hebrew text in order to make it difficult to pronounce the name even if somebody tried. Instead of translating the four-letter name for God, called the Tetragrammaton, or "four letters," as "Yahweh," "Jehovah," "YHWH," or some other unlikely pronunciation, English translators opted for a compromise between the Hebrew stand-in *Lord* and the original *YHWH*—the all-caps *LORD* you see in your English Bible. Just remember, whenever you see that word, it stands for the name of God—YHWH, which means "self-existing one" or "I AM."

NUMBERS

SNAPSHOT

How do sin and rebellion impact a people's relationship with God? Will God remain faithful even to rebellious people, or is his relationship with them conditional? Does God's judgment of his people result in rejection? As Moses faces multiple challenges to his leadership and God defends him and judges the rebels, God continues to graciously provide for his people.

ORIENTATION

Date: Between 15th and 13th centuries BC; forty years after the
              exodus (Num 36:13; cf. Josh 5:6)
Author: Moses
Audience: Early Israel, beginning with the people of the exodus as they
              prepare to cross the Jordan into the land of Canaan
Outline: 1. Preparations for Travel (1:1–10:10)
              2. The Journey to Kadesh Barnea (10:11–14:45)
              3. The Journey to the Plains of Moab (15:1–22:1)
              4. The Moabites and Balaam (22:2–25:18)
              5. Final Preparations for Entering Canaan (26–36)

YOU ARE HERE

Episode 3: Promise and Hope

Numbers is the fourth book of the Pentateuch. The name comes from the English translation of the name given to the book in the Septuagint, the Greek translation of the Hebrew Scriptures.

EXPLORING NUMBERS

The book begins with Moses taking a census of the people of Israel and a description of the organization of the tribes as they traveled and as they worshipped at the tabernacle. Explicit instructions for the worship of God indicate how seriously God takes the practice of worship. Included in this section is the set of instructions for the Nazirite vow, an act of consecration to the Lord. Men or women who choose this vow are to "abstain from wine and beer" (6:3), refrain from cutting their hair (v. 5), and avoid contact with dead bodies (v. 6). The instructions about the vow are followed by the familiar words Aaron and his sons are commanded to use in blessing the Israelites: "May the Lord bless you and protect you; may the Lord make his face shine on you and be gracious to you; may the Lord look with favor on you and give you peace" (vv. 24–26).

The Israelites celebrated their second Passover (Num 9) and then began to move toward the land of Canaan (Num 10). As they did, the people "began complaining openly before the Lord about hardship. When the Lord heard, his anger burned, and fire from the Lord blazed among them and consumed the outskirts of the camp" (11:1). Then the people complained about having to eat manna every day, and again, "The Lord was very angry; Moses was also provoked" (v. 10). When Moses complained to the Lord about how hard it was to lead the people, the Lord instructed Moses to choose seventy elders to help him. The Lord declared, "I will take some of the Spirit who is on you and put the Spirit on them. They will help you bear the burden of the people, so that you do not have to bear it by yourself" (v. 17).

Rebellion against the Lord and Moses's leadership also came from Moses's own family as his sister Miriam and brother Aaron criticized Moses's Cushite wife (Num 12:1–2). This criticism seems to be particularly offensive since "Moses was a very humble man, more so than anyone on the face of the earth" (v. 3).

In chapter 13, Moses sends a representative from each tribe to scout out the land. The majority return with a negative report; although the land is "flowing with milk and honey" (13:27), it is populated by powerful peoples. They conclude, "We can't attack the people because they are stronger than we are!" (v. 31). Joshua and Caleb disagree: "If the LORD is pleased with us, he will bring us into this land, a land flowing with milk and honey, and give it to us" (14:8). The people threaten to kill the two of them, and the Lord is angry. He declares to Moses his intention to "strike them with a plague and destroy them" (v. 12). Moses's response is to plead for the Lord to forgive the people. The Lord agrees but declares that none of this generation would enter the land (vv. 26–35).

Moses faces another challenge to his leadership as Korah leads a rebellion. This threat ended when "the earth opened its mouth and swallowed them and their households, all Korah's people, and all their possessions" (16:32).

When the people again complained about Moses and his leadership because they lacked water, the Lord instructed Moses to speak to the rock and there would be water (20:8). Instead, Moses angrily struck the rock, and the Lord pronounced judgment on him: "Because you did not trust me to demonstrate my holiness in the sight of the Israelites, you will not bring this assembly into the land I have given them" (v. 12).

In chapter 21, the people again murmur against Moses, and the Lord sends venomous snakes among them in judgment (21:6). When they repent, the Lord heals them when they look at a bronze serpent Moses mounts on a pole (vv. 8–9), which looks forward to the Messiah's crucifixion and the salvation he provides (John 3:14).

Balak, from Moab, hired Balaam to curse the Israelites, but the Lord forbade him to do so (Num 22:6). Balaam set out to do it anyway, and his life was saved when the Lord spoke to him through his donkey (vv. 22–35). In Balaam's fourth oracle, he predicted, "A star will come from Jacob, and a scepter will arise from Israel" (24:17), which seems to be the reason the magi traveled to Israel when Jesus was born (Matt 2).

The book ends with the Israelites poised to enter the land promised to Abraham, Isaac, and Jacob.

START YOUR JOURNEY

- The Nazirite Vow was a voluntary act of consecration to the Lord. How might new covenant believers similarly indicate their devotion to God?
- Numbers 14 emphasizes again that God is slow to anger and abounding in faithful love, forgiving iniquity and rebellion (cf. Exod 34:6–7) and that he will remain present with his people. Even in judgment, God's people have confidence that they will not be abandoned by God. Reflect on the significance of this promise, which is fulfilled in Jesus, for your relationship with God.
- Leadership is difficult, and no one can do it alone. Moses needed help. What does this indicate about the benefits of shared or team leadership today?
- The people of Israel seem to have a short memory. When things are going well, they trust God. When facing difficulty, they consistently murmur, complain, and rebel against their leader and the Lord. Consider how your own story parallels this one.

GOING DEEPER

"Four Reliable Truths from Caleb's Life"

— Roy B. Zuck —

Tension filled the air. Israel stood waiting to hear the report of twelve men appointed by Moses to go on a forty-day reconnaissance trip to explore the land of Canaan that God had promised them. And the twelve were divided. Ten said the inhabitants were powers, the cities fortified, and giants resided there (Num 13:27–28). But two men, Caleb and Joshua, gave a different report. In a response briefer than that of the ten, these two leaders said, "Let's go up now and take possession of the land because we can certainly conquer it!" (v. 30). But the ten retorted, "We can't" (v. 31). This story and its outcome reveal four truths.

The majority is sometimes wrong. In the case of the negative report, the majority was wrong. The pessimistic assessment of the ten caused an entire generation of Israelites to die in the desert—everyone twenty-one years of age and older. Imagine the countless funerals to bury the thousands who questioned what God had promised. Sometimes the majority may be right, but not in this case. As William Penn said, "Right is right, even if everyone is against it; and wrong is wrong, even if everyone is for it."

God is bigger than circumstances. Yes, we should consider our circumstances and our environment. But we should not let our circumstances take our eyes off the Lord. When a man asked his friend how

he was doing, the response was, "I'm okay under the circumstances."
Then he realized, "What am I doing under there?" Keeping our eyes on
the Lord can help us look beyond the circumstances to God's character
and promises.

God's rewards often require waiting. When Caleb spied the land, he
was forty years old (Josh 14:7). But he did not possess any of it until he
was eighty-five years old (v. 10). Imagine having to wait forty-five years
to see the fulfillment of God's promise.

Waiting is difficult, but the Bible tells us this is what we must do.
Twice in Ps 27:14 the writer tells God's people to wait on the Lord.
And waiting for him is mentioned numerous other times in the Psalms
(33:20; 37:7, 34; 38:15; 119:166; 130:5). God's timing, although it calls
for patience, is always best.

The Lord said, "But since my servant Caleb has a different spirit
and has remained loyal to me, I will bring him into the land where he
has gone, and his descendants will inherit it" (Num 14:24). Although
God did not fulfill his promise immediately, the Lord did keep this word
about Caleb.

God is our help. Caleb and Joshua had determination and commitment, but they also placed their confidence in the Lord. In fact,
Caleb said, "Perhaps the Lord will be with me and I will drive them
[Canaanites] out as the Lord promised" (Josh 14:12). And he did. Caleb
knew that without the Lord's help he would fail. And like Caleb, we can
carry out God's will only with the Lord's help and his strength.

Are circumstances weighing you down? Do you feel like you are facing giants? Do you feel small as a grasshopper? Keep your eyes on the
Lord. Remember that the majority is often wrong, that circumstances
need not dictate our actions, that God is present even in delays, and that
in all we do, God is our help.[1]

---

[1] Adapted from Roy B. Zuck, "Four Reliable Truths from Caleb's Life," *Kindred
Spirit* 38, no. 1 (Spring/Summer 2014): 17. © 2014 Dallas Theological Seminary.

DEUTERONOMY

SNAPSHOT

In Deuteronomy, Moses gives a series of "farewell sermons" to the nation of Israel, which reflect their past troubles and serve as a hopeful reminder to live faithfully to the law once they enter the Promised Land. On the brink of entering their homeland, Moses's poetic exposition is equally a recounting of God's faithfulness, as well as a charge to live holy lives and keep the covenant.

ORIENTATION

Date: Between 15th and 13th centuries BC
Author: Moses
Audience: Israelites before they entered the Promised Land
Outline: 1. The Introduction (1:1–5)
                2. First Speech: History of Their Journey (1:6–4:43)
                3. Second Speech, Part 1—Keeping the Law and Commandments (4:44–11:32)
                4. Second Speech, Part 2—Ceremonial, Civil, and Social Laws (12:1–26:19)
                5. Third Speech, Part 1—Next Steps: Entering Canaan (27:1–28:68)

6. Third Speech Part 2—Next Steps: Getting Settled in Canaan (29:1–30:20)
7. Leadership Succession Plans (31:1–32:52)
8. Final Blessing and Death of Moses (33:1–34:12)

YOU ARE HERE

Episode 3: Promise and Hope

The fifth book of the Pentateuch, Deuteronomy, was written after the Israelites' forty years of wandering in the desert while located on the plains of Moab, ready to enter the Promised Land.

EXPLORING DEUTERONOMY

As soon as we step into this book, it's important to remember that Deuteronomy is considered the "second law," not in the sense of being a new law but essentially a reiteration of the "first law" that God originally gave to Moses.[1] Since the original recipients of the law had died in the wilderness, the provisions and blessings of the covenant are repeated to the next generation. Their relationship to God is administered through this covenant. This book recounts the importance of God's law through a series of sermons and poetic charges to both the Israelites and Moses's successor, Joshua.

The book of Deuteronomy records Moses leading the people in *looking back* (a reminder of where they'd been, Deut 1–4), *looking around* (a charge to keep God's commandments in the present, Deut 4–26), and *looking ahead* (a preview of what's to come, 26–34). Due mostly to their disobedience, Israel already failed to enter the Promised Land (Deut 1:19–46). So, in *looking back*, Moses turns Israel's attention to God's faithfulness by

---

[1] Joseph T. Lienhard, *Exodus, Leviticus, Numbers, Deuteronomy*, Ancient Christian Commentary on Scripture, ed. Thomas C. Oden (Downers Grove: InterVarsity, 2001), 276.

highlighting the important connection between God's presence and provision even in response to the people's disobedience. He is gracious and merciful, and God ultimately desires for his people to obey and live holy lives. God's faithfulness in the past should encourage a faithful response in the present.

Next, in *looking around*, Moses reiterates the original commandments given by God at Mount Sinai (5:1–22) and encourages the Israelites to walk faithfully in obedience to God, who will bless them in the Promised Land (vv. 32–33). The beauty of the law presented in Deuteronomy may be best found in the Shema, where Moses begins with an exhortation in 6:4—"Listen, Israel: The LORD our God, the LORD is one." This unique confession explicitly affirms monotheism, that Israel followed one almighty God—quite different from other religions of the time. The Shema proceeds to emphasize the importance of daily obedience and commitment to Yahweh (vv. 4–9)—which will result in great blessing through Israel's receiving abundant life in the Promised Land (vv. 10–12). While God's covenant with Abraham was unconditional, Moses indicates through the second giving of the law that God's covenant with Israel requires faithful obedience and commitment in each generation in order to experience blessing from God in the land.

In *looking forward*, Moses promises that God would send a prophet like him, that is, Jesus (18:15–22). Moses's address informs the people of Israel of the blessings in store for them if future generations maintain covenant faithfulness . . . and the curses they can expect for breaking the covenant (see especially Deut 28–30). Also, Moses promises that God would circumcise their hearts so that they would love God fully (30:6). Finally, Moses shifts their focus to the future when he hands over his leadership to Joshua, who will lead Israel into the land (Deut 31).

Moses's sermons given in Moab, at the doorstep of the Promised Land, serve as a strategic appeal for recommitment and change. Much had happened in the previous forty years since Israel left Egypt—and many had either forgotten the past or were too young to know it. Thus, the second law given here serves as both a reminder of God's covenant and a demand for repentance. It also sets the stage for what follows as God continues to remain faithful to his covenant people in anticipation of their coming Messiah.

START YOUR JOURNEY

- Read slowly through the Shema passage (Deut 6:4–9). Jesus himself quotes from verse 6:5 when asked, "Which command in the law is the greatest?" (Matt 22:36). Consider memorizing this traditional confession of faith in the God of Israel. For each verse of the Shema, write down one or two things you can do to apply its truths about remembering and living God's word in your daily life.

- In modern society, we often have a warped sense of blessing because of rampant entitlement—the feeling that life *owes* us something. As you read Deuteronomy and hear of God's blessings toward the Hebrews, consider how God has blessed you and your family. Make a list of the ways that God has shown himself faithful in your life.

- It's easy to overlook Deuteronomy as a collection of old, irrelevant laws. After all, Christians today aren't held under the law and covenant of the Old Testament. Yet Deuteronomy provides an abundance of clarity about the love and grace of God, whose character hasn't changed between the Old and New Testaments. The God that blessed Israel as they sought to enter the Promised Land is the same God that you and I follow today!

JOSHUA

SNAPSHOT

How could anyone step into the shoes of a towering leader like Moses? By trusting and obeying God for courage. Welcome to the life of Joshua, a man God called to lead a wayward people, often intent on doing things their own way. The book of Joshua records the first steps in the fulfillment of God's promises to Abraham, Isaac, and Jacob to give them a land of prosperity and peace.

ORIENTATION

Date: 15th–13th centuries BC

Author(s):   Joshua (possibly including Eleazar the high priest and possibly Phinehas, his son)

Audience: The nation of Israel

Outline:
1. Prologue—Joshua's Commission (1:1–9)
2. Entering the Promised Land (1:10–5:12)
3. Conquering the Promised Land (5:13–12:24)
4. Dividing the Promised Land (13:1–21:45)
5. Settling the Promised Land (22:1–24:28)
6. Epilogue—Joshua's Death and Burial (24:29–33)

YOU ARE HERE

Episode 3: Promise and Hope

In the English Bible, Joshua is the first of the Historical Books, which follow the Pentateuch both chronologically and in the order of the canon. Joshua begins where Deuteronomy ends, with Israel poised to enter the land of Canaan to begin the conquest of the land God had promised them.

EXPLORING JOSHUA

The Pentateuch ends with Israel camped on the plains of Moab, just east of the Jordan river across from the city of Jericho. In the latter chapters of Deuteronomy, Moses recounted his upcoming death and designated Joshua as the leader who would go before Israel to conquer the land that God had promised. Joshua was the obvious choice for this new role. He had served as Moses's second-in-command throughout the wilderness wanderings. He was a man "who has the Spirit in him" (Num 27:18; Deut 34:9), but we get the sense that Joshua feared his new leadership role and the task set before him.

Moses had challenged Joshua to "be strong and courageous" (Deut 31:7). After Moses's death, Joshua may have felt lost without his mentor, but he wasn't alone. The God of Israel was still present with Joshua and the children of Israel. As God had been with Moses, so now he would be with Joshua. The one condition was that Joshua must follow God's law. In doing so, he would find strength and courage to accomplish what God had called him to do. It's a good reminder to each of us that, unlike the way the world thinks, strength and courage come from obedience and dependence.

The action-packed book of Joshua follows the exploits of the armies of Israel as they cross the Jordan River to enter the land of Canaan—conquering the land's wicked, godless nations—and to divide the land among the tribes of Israel, spanning several decades of Israel's history. It's also a story of contrasts. While God demonstrates his faithfulness in giving the land to Israel as he promised, Israel only partially upheld their end of the bargain—keeping the covenant of the law and showing obedience to the lawgiver without compromise. As a result of their partial obedience, Israel never took complete possession of the land, allowing some of the godless inhabitants to remain. That partial obedience led to Israel's disaffection with God as those whom they had allowed to remain on the land influenced God's people toward infidelity and sin.

Israel's partial obedience constantly reminded subsequent generations how quickly the nation could forget God's faithful provision in keeping his promises. In response, God frequently ordered the people of Israel to establish memorials—reminders, usually constructed of stone—to mark important turning points and victories experienced when they obeyed God's voice. At least eight instances are recorded where God's miraculous intervention in the life of the nation as they took possession of the land God promised them was marked by memorial stones. These were strategically placed to be constant physical reminders to a forgetful nation of God's miraculous power, his faithfulness, his deliverance, his justice, his mercy, and his grace poured out on a nation that didn't deserve it.

The book concludes with Joshua's death and the testimony that Israel worshipped and served the Lord throughout Joshua's lifetime—a fitting epitaph for the man who followed Moses.

START YOUR JOURNEY

- The best way to prepare a study of Joshua is to go back and reread the narrative accounts of Israel's travels in Numbers and Deuteronomy. Remember, the Bible is one grand narrative, not a collection of unrelated short stories. Reading the books in their chronological order will give you the important context for the conquest and division of the land in Joshua.

- A helpful study is to look back at all the places in the Pentateuch that mention Joshua to gain a fuller picture of the man whose life this book follows and for whom the book is named.

- Spend time studying the passages related to memorial stones throughout the book and the circumstances that made them so important in the life of the nation. See Josh 4:8–9, 20–21; 6:20, 26; 7:26; 8:28–32; 10:27; 22:26–27; 24:26–27.

- For the believers who find themselves following in the footsteps of a strong and well-respected leader, a study of the life of Joshua can be an encouraging reminder that it's more about the God one serves than the person one follows. Joshua points forward to Jesus, the perfect and righteous leader.

JUDGES

SNAPSHOT

When reading the book of Judges, you might be tempted to ask: What's a book like this doing in the Bible? Violence is present from start to finish. The worst sins imaginable, including murder, kidnapping, and rape, stain its pages. Yet the book has its purpose. It illustrates what can happen when God's people rebel against him and insist on doing what's right in their own eyes.

ORIENTATION

Date: Between 14th and 11th centuries BC
Author(s): Unknown, traditionally credited to the prophet Samuel
Audience: Ancient Israel
Outline: 1. Prologue: Israel Becomes Pagan (1:1–3:6)
           2. Accounts of Leaders (3:7–16:31)
              a. Othniel: Paradigm of Faith (3:7–11)
              b. Ehud: Man on a Mission (3:12–30)
              c. Shamgar: Philistine Killer (3:31)
              d. Deborah and Barak: Hesitant General and Heroic Woman (4:1–5:31)

YOU ARE HERE

Episode 3: Promise and Hope

As the second of the Historical Books, Judges records Israel's story from the conquest of Canaan to the eve of the monarchy.

EXPLORING JUDGES

Despite, or maybe because of, its disturbing content, the book of Judges makes an important contribution to our understanding of Israel's story. It shows what can happen when God's people disobey him and decide what's right in their own eyes. Everybody loses when that happens, particularly innocent people who become the collateral damage of sin and judgment.

The book's prologue (1:1–3:6) describes how Israel failed to eliminate the Canaanites and instead settled down and intermarried with them. They embraced the Canaanite gods, especially Baal, the Canaanite god of storm and fertility. As Moses had warned Israel generations earlier, idolatry brought God's discipline. The Lord doesn't tolerate rivals, and he handed his people over to their enemies. A pattern developed: Suffering under their oppressive conquerors, they cried out to the Lord for help. In response, the Lord mercifully raised up leaders to deliver his people. But inevitably the people returned to their idolatry and the cycle repeated itself.

The book's lengthy central section (3:7–16:31) gives a more detailed account of this cyclical pattern with specific—sometimes explicit—examples. The Lord used a series of leaders (Othniel, Ehud, Deborah, Barak, Gideon, Jephthah, and Samson) to deliver his people from their oppressors (the Arameans, Moabites, Canaanites, Midianites, Ammonites, and Philistines). Eventually, the people's idolatry escalated to include the gods of all the surrounding nations, not just Baal (10:6). The Lord angrily gave them over to the Philistines and Ammonites. The people confessed their sin, but they discarded only their Baal idols. This time the Lord refused to help them. When they threw away all their idols, the Lord showed them compassion and empowered Jephthah, who defeated the Ammonites. Of course, the people again returned to their sin, and the Lord gave them over to the Philistines. This time they accepted enslavement and didn't cry out for help. Nevertheless, despite their apathy, the Lord mercifully delivered them through Samson.

In this central section, we detect a decline in the quality of Israelite leadership. Othniel and Ehud were courageous deliverers of God's people, but Barak and Gideon were hesitant leaders who, though possessing some faith, didn't measure up to the standards set by their predecessors. Jephthah and Samson lacked foresight and compromised their God-given triumphs through serious personal failure that brought great tragedy in its wake.

The book's epilogue (17:1–21:25), which begins and ends with the observation that Israel did what was right in their own eyes (17:6; 21:25), is particularly alarming. Without competent spiritual leadership, the people were plagued by a corrupt form of religion where greed predominated. The book ends with an account of rape, civil war, and kidnapping. Israel desperately needed the kind of king described in Deut 17:14–20, one who would read God's law as well as model and promote obedience to God. None of Israel's rulers measured up, until Jesus emerged as the perfect king and just judge.

START YOUR JOURNEY

- One must take advantage of the many tools that can help the reader understand the geographical, historical, and cultural background of the Historical Books. These include Bible dictionaries and atlases. Particularly helpful are the *Photo Companion to the Bible* (BiblePlaces .com), *The Baker Illustrated Bible Background Commentary*, and the *Zondervan Illustrated Bible Backgrounds Commentary*.

- The narratives of the Historical Books are true stories that should be read as literature. This means we must pay careful attention to setting, characterization, and plot development.

- When reading Old Testament stories, it's important to ask the following questions: (1) What are the major themes of the story? (2) What does the story teach us about God's character and how he relates to people? (3) Who are the major characters in the story, and what principles and lessons do we learn from their example and experience?

- Fundamental human nature hasn't changed much in the last several thousand years, and Israel's pathetic, repeated cycle (sin, suffering, repentance, deliverance, rest, and a return to sin) is instructive for us today. One indicator of a society's failure to follow God is the treatment of the weak. We can have the hope that one day Jesus, the righteous Judge, will vindicate the oppressed, elevate the downtrodden, and establish his reign of justice on the earth.

- Many believers struggling with besetting sin and their own frailty can relate to this pattern of sinning, saying sorry, then sinning again. We can take comfort in the fact that God is ready and willing to forgive when we repent. Yet Judges warns us of the permanent damage caused by the pattern and the diminishing quality of people's relationship with God as a result of those cycles.

RUTH

SNAPSHOT

Sometimes Ruth is portrayed as a Disney Cinderella character, and Boaz her Prince Charming. However, this sentimental picture completely misses the point. God is the hero of the book of Ruth, and the big idea is the illustration of his loyal love and care, his *hesed*, for women, and their significant place in his Big Story.

ORIENTATION

Date: Uncertain, possibly during King David's reign (11th century BC)

Author(s): Unknown, traditionally the prophet Samuel

Audience: All people of all times

Outline:
1. The Vale of Tears (1:1–5)
2. The Long Walk Home (1:6–22)
3. The Harvest (2:1–23)
4. The Ask (3:1–18)
5. The Obstacle (4:1–12)
6. The Serendipities (4:13–22)

YOU ARE HERE

Episode 3: Promise and Hope

As the third of the Historical Books, Ruth unfolds chronologically during the time of Judges, creating a narrative bridge from the period of the judges to the life of King David.

EXPLORING RUTH

The inspiring account of Ruth begins when a famine in Judah forces the Hebrew Elimelech and his wife Naomi to pack up their family and move to Moab, where he hopes to find work. Tragically, Elimelech dies, and his two sons marry Moabite women. Then both sons die, leaving three widows: Naomi, Ruth, and Orpah.

With the famine subsiding, the distraught Naomi believes God has abandoned her. She decides to go home to Bethlehem. She encourages both daughters-in-law to stay behind and return to their families. However, Ruth refuses, promising to follow both Naomi and her God for the rest of her life. Here we find the oft-quoted words of heartfelt devotion: "For wherever you go, I will go, and wherever you live, I will live; your people will be my people, and your God will be my God" (Ruth 1:16).

Upon returning to Bethlehem, we aren't told how Naomi and Ruth provided a roof over their heads initially, but their lack of food implies that they were trapped in poverty. Perhaps she sold her husband's land to provide temporary shelter for herself and Ruth. However, losing the land came at a high price because the land was the next generation's inheritance. With no prospects of a future son to carry on the family name and inherit the land, the family line and Elimelech's name would disappear forever. In that culture, this amounted to paramount tragedy. If someone in Naomi's extended family didn't redeem (buy back) the land, all hope for the continuation of the family would be lost.[1]

---

[1] Irving L. Jensen, *Judges and Ruth, A Self-Study Guide* (Chicago: Moody, 1987), 89.

In response to their situation, Ruth risks her life by gleaning for grain in the fields surrounding Bethlehem. The Old Testament law commanded landowners, "When you reap the harvest of your land, you are not to reap to the very edge of your field or gather the gleanings of your harvest. . . . Leave them for the poor and the resident alien" (Lev 19:9–10). The author explains in Ruth 2:3, "She happened to be in the portion of the field belonging to Boaz, who was from Elimelech's family." She was, by God's providence, in a field owned by a close relative of Naomi's husband. This "chance" meeting of Ruth and Boaz is significant. To understand why, the reader must grasp Deut 25:5–6, where God provided for widows in a practice known as Levirate marriage: "When brothers live on the same property and one of them dies without a son, the wife of the dead man may not marry a stranger outside the family. Her brother-in-law is to take her as his wife, have sexual relations with her, and perform the duty of a brother-in-law for her. The first son she bears will carry on the name of the dead brother, so his name will not be blotted out from Israel."

As the account continues, Naomi counsels Ruth to go to the threshing floor and petition Boaz to step into the role of their guardian-redeemer (Ruth 3:1–15). Boaz consents, and then we observe how God used Ruth's *hesed* ("loyal love," or "grace") to catalyze *hesed* in Boaz's life and bless them all. The Hebrew word *hesed* is a many-faceted word. The phrases "loyal love" and "unconditional love" come close to its meaning. It's the way God loves people and the way he wants them to love one another. *Hesed* is the outworking of the emotion of loyal love, which results in the deepest and richest kind of sacrificial love-in-action we can experience. We observe *hesed* in thriving long-term marriages and devoted parental love for beloved children, but nowhere is *hesed* better illustrated than in the sacrifice that Jesus made on the cross for us.

The story of Ruth concludes when Ruth bears a son, and the author illustrates God's *hesed* to Naomi, Ruth, and Boaz in a genealogical table that reveals that this child was in the line of one of Israel's greatest kings, David, and ultimately Jesus the Messiah (Ruth 4:22; Matt 1:5–16).

START YOUR JOURNEY

- Jews read the book of Ruth annually during Pentecost, because the feast takes place during the grain harvest, which coincides with the time of Ruth's and Boaz's meeting. Reading it regularly is a good reminder of God's *hesed* in our lives as well.

- As you dig into the book of Ruth, search out ways that Ruth, Boaz, and even Naomi illustrate God's *hesed* in their actions. Then reflect on ways you, too, can show *hesed* in your actions toward others.

- Don't assume that God endorses all the cultural customs regarding women in the Book of Ruth. However, the cultural forms we see in Ruth remind us of an important truth: "God blesses those who act faithfully, even when that faithfulness is expressed within social structures that they cannot change and in which they may be trapped."[2] We all have different opportunities and restrictions based on our social and cultural contexts. Ponder how you can faithfully live out your faith in Christ even amidst your present limitations.

---

[2] Robert B. Chisholm Jr., *A Commentary on Judges and Ruth* (Grand Rapids: Kregel Academic, 2013), 563.

1 SAMUEL

SNAPSHOT

As history lumbers along, change is inevitable. And in God's story, we witness several changes that transform the political landscape of Israel. The book of 1 Samuel gives a detailed account of the major transition from the period of the judges—an era of spiritual and moral decline—to the period of the monarchy, when God prepares Israel for the rise of a king after God's own heart.

ORIENTATION

Date: About 1025–900 BC

Author(s): Samuel (1–24), Nathan, Gad, or Abiathar (25–31)

Audience: The people of Israel in the period of the monarchy (27:6)

Outline:
1. The Choice of Samuel over Eli (1:1–3:21)
2. The Journey of the Ark of the Covenant (4:1–7:1)
3. The Return of Israel to the Lord (7:2–17)
4. The Choice of Saul by the People of Israel (8:1–12:25)
5. The Fall of Saul with the Loss of His Dynasty (13:1–15:35)
6. The Choice of David over Saul (16:1–18:5)

7. The Righteousness of David in His Struggle with Saul
   (18:6–26:25)
8. The Preservation of David and the Death of Saul
   (27:1–31:13)

YOU ARE HERE

Episode 3: Promise and Hope → Episode 4: The Kingdom Rises

As the fourth of the Historical Books, 1 Samuel transitions from the period of the judges to the period of kings and demonstrates the qualities of a king after God's own heart.

EXPLORING 1 SAMUEL

First Samuel begins with a prayer; the prayer of a neglected and childless woman, Hannah. God heard her heartfelt petition and blessed her with a child—Samuel (1:12–20). The birth story culminates in the song of Hannah, which provides the theological outlook of the book. The Lord will sovereignly choose his anointed king to be the horn of salvation for his people (2:1–10).

Samuel was chosen by God to replace the high priest Eli as the prophet-judge of Israel (3:1, 4, 8, 10, 19–20). Eli, with poor eyesight, experienced the demise of his family, the defeat of Israel in battle, and the loss of the ark of the covenant (4:17–22). Israel lost the ark by using it in a way it wasn't meant to be used. The Lord demonstrated his sovereignty by the outbreak of a plague in the major cities of the Philistines. The journey of the ark from Philistia to Beth-shemesh substantiated the sovereignty of Yahweh over Israel and her enemies (6:7–9, 19–21). The return of the ark and the ministry of Samuel brought the hearts of the people of Israel back to the Lord. This resulted in their victory over the Philistines (7:2–4).

The Lord raised up Samuel as a faithful priest and a powerful prophet to rule over Israel (2:35; 3:19–20). Samuel became the kingmaker who anointed the first two kings of his people. Yahweh granted the anointed king the gift of his Spirit (10:6, 9–10). The mission of Samuel was to prepare both the people and their king for the right perspective as a theocratic kingdom (12:19–24). Saul was disqualified because of his disobedience to the command of the supreme king, God (13:13). In place of Saul, David was chosen as a man after God's own heart (13:14; 16:7, 13). The Lord made a way for David by sending an evil spirit upon Saul and a military peril by Goliath (16:14–23; 17:54–18:2). With God's providential working and sovereignty, David rose to become a mighty warrior, a popular hero, and a perceived threat to Saul's authority (18:7–8).

Saul's jealousy led David to flee for his life from the maniacal king. His time as a fugitive shaped David to become a leader of character. David won the respect of his rival, Saul, by demonstrating the qualities of a righteous leader Saul lacked; he even refused to take vengeance against Saul out of respect for his office as king (24:13, 17; 26:21). As a spiritual leader, David sought God's will and empowerment in every critical moment (23:2, 9–13; 30:6). He lived out his mission as God's anointed king before his warriors and people (22:2, 21–23; 25:28–29; 30:21–24). In contrast to Saul, David pleased God as a spiritual, moral, and competent leader. No wonder many believers see David as a kind of foreshadowing of the ultimate King of Israel, the Messiah.

The book of 1 Samuel echoes the theology of Hannah's song that rejoices in the salvation of the Lord (2:8). Yahweh, the supreme king, deposed the arrogant—Eli's delinquent sons and the disobedient Saul. In his providence, God raised up the humble—Samuel and David. The Lord sovereignly delivered his people and judged their enemies by lifting the horn of his anointed king, David (2:10). As such, this historical book ultimately looks forward to the greatest Son of David, Jesus, who will rule Israel as a righteous king forever.

START YOUR JOURNEY

- Set aside time to read through 1 Samuel in one sitting. Try to answer the question of how God led Israel out of the dark ages of the judges by raising up a king after his own heart. Look for indications in the text of God's obvious and not-so-obvious working toward bringing about his perfect plan.

- As you read through the story, note the ways God providentially shapes David's character to lead as a man after God's own heart. In what ways has God used seemingly mundane experiences in your own life to nurture your own gifts for service?

- From the rise and fall of leaders in the book, is there anything we learn about the significance of one's heart for the transformation of our community? What are the character flaws we see in the "bad guys" of the story that led to their decline and defeat? What are the positive examples we see in the "good guys"?

2 SAMUEL

SNAPSHOT

While 1 Samuel portrays the rise of David, 2 Samuel paints a monumental picture of how God nurtures his anointed regent amid adversity. The book emphasizes God's faithfulness to the one he chose, even when David is not faithful to the one who chose him. The covenant God made with David also looks forward to a future king who will fulfill God's ideal for a kingdom.

ORIENTATION

Date: About 1011–900 BC
Author(s): Nathan, Gad, or Abiathar
Audience: The people of Israel in the monarchy period (1 Sam 27:6)
Outline: 1. The Victory of the House of David over the House of
                    Saul (2 Sam 1:1–4:12)
                2. The Establishment of the Davidic Covenant and
                    Kingdom (5:1–9:13)
                3. The Violation of the Covenant in David's Sin with
                    Bathsheba (10:1–12:31)
                4. The Flight of David on account of the Conspiracy of
                    Absalom (13:1–18:33)

5. The Restoration of David and Tension between Israel and Judah (19:1–20:26)
6. The Conclusion of David's Reign in View of God's Redemption (21:1–24:25)

YOU ARE HERE

Episode 4: The Kingdom Rises

As the fifth of the Historical Books and second volume of the account of David's life and career, 2 Samuel demonstrates God's promise and discipline of David as the anointed king of Israel.

EXPLORING 2 SAMUEL

Second Samuel begins with the lament of the deaths of Saul and his son Jonathan (1:17–27). David then moves to Hebron and becomes king of Judah (2:1–4). In the long war with the house of Saul, Abner convinced the elders of Israel to make a treaty with David (3:12–21; 5:1). David's response to the death of Abner and Ish-bosheth wins the heart of Israel (3:31–39; 4:9–12). So, all the elders of Israel come to Hebron to make peace with David and to anoint him king over Israel (5:3). This third anointing becomes the final confirmation of David as the king of Israel after the anointing by Samuel (1 Sam 16:13) and the people of Judah (2 Sam 2:4).

The establishment of David's kingdom is highlighted by the capture of Jerusalem (5:6–10), the building of the royal palace (vv. 11–12), and victories over his enemies (vv. 17–25). Amid his prosperity, David arranges a solemn procession of the ark of the covenant to Jerusalem with 30,000 chosen men of Israel (6:1). The demand of a proper transportation of the ark, the throne of Yahweh, demonstrates the sovereignty of God as the ultimate king over the kingdom (6:12–15; cf. 6:3–7). In fact, the presence of the Lord marks the theological theme of the story of David's ascent.[1]

---

[1] David Toshio Tsumura, *The Second Book of Samuel*, The New International Commentary on the Old Testament, ed. Robert L. Hubbard (Grand Rapids:

The Davidic covenant (2 Sam 7) is a turning point in God's history of redemption. It continues the promise of the Abrahamic covenant to bless all peoples by extending the means of blessing through a line of royal descendants (Gen 17:16; 49:10). The Historical Books develop the theme of Israel's king in the book of the Judges (Judg 17:6; 21:25) and 1 Samuel (1 Sam 13:14). The Davidic covenant itself continues the theme with the promise of a future king, a Son of David, who will reign forever on David's throne (2 Sam 7:13, 16).

David experienced an initial partial fulfillment of the covenant blessings with a great name, a house, the defeat of his enemies, the security of Israel, and a successor to build the temple (7:9–13; cf. 8:1–10:19). Yet, in spite of all of God's blessing, David violated the covenant in his sin against Bathsheba and Uriah (12:7–15; cf. 7:14). Though God forgave David upon his deep, heartfelt repentance (12:13), David and his people reaped severe consequences for his sin. David's sin led to the death of his son (12:15–23), the rape of Tamar by her brother Amnon (13:1–21), and his flight on account of the conspiracy of Absalom (15:1–18:33). The latter part of David's life was surrounded by the disunity of his people (19:40–43), the rebellion of Sheba (20:1–10), the weakening of his strength in battle (21:15–17), and the sin of a census (24:1–17). God had shaped David's character in times of adversity; yet in times of success, David's character slipped. Yet, as an example for all who will fall short in their walk with God, David responded to God's discipline with humility, remorse, and godly repentance (15:27–37; 16:10–12; 24:10–17).

The book of 2 Samuel concludes with a climactic structure of the epilogue (21:1–23:25), which centers on David's song (2 Sam 22) and his last words (23:1–7). Hannah's poem (1 Sam 2:1–10), together with David's final words, constitute an *inclusio* of 1 and 2 Samuel.[2] The song and farewell recap the entire reign of David. In contemplation, David exalted Yahweh as the rock, the fortress, and the horn of salvation throughout his journey as

---

Eerdmans, 2019), 100.

[2] Tsumura, *Second Book of Samuel*, 289.

the king of Israel. David held on to God's covenant at the end of his life. As in 1 Samuel, this book looks forward to the hope of a greater Son of David, one who will reign over Israel in perfect righteousness and wisdom. That future Son will avoid all the vices of his ancestor David while embodying perfectly all his virtues. As such, he will fulfill to the uttermost the covenants with Abraham, Moses, and David.

START YOUR JOURNEY

- Read through 2 Samuel as a story in one sitting. Note the places where you see cracks forming in David's life—cracks that widen into character flaws and result in disastrous decisions. What does this teach us about the "little sins" we overlook in our own lives?
- Think through the essential elements of the Davidic covenant (2 Sam 7) and consider how this is fulfilled in the ultimate Davidic King, the Messiah.
- Meditate on the response of David to God's discipline and consider how he models repentance. What do you learn about repentance from this example? How does this compare to your own seasons of repentance?

Q&A

"Bible Translations"

With Dr. W. Hall Harris III

Dr. W. Hall Harris III (ThM, Dallas Theological Seminary; PhD, University of Sheffield) is a professor of New Testament and translator for several Bible translations. He served as project director and managing editor of the NET Bible, the first Bible to be published on the internet. We thought he'd be a great person to ask about English Bible translations.

Q: You probably get the "what's-the-best-Bible-translation" question a lot. So, we're not going to ask that. Instead, could you fill us in on the *kinds* of approaches to Bible translation that are out there?

A: First, let's think of Bible translations on a spectrum or horizontal scale rather than as unrelated individual points. That means there are two extremes, one at each end of the scale, and a lot of space in between. So, on one extreme you have the "word-for-word literal" (which translators call "formal equivalent"); on the other extreme, you have the "free paraphrase" (called "dynamic equivalent").

Q: Could you give us an example of each of those?

A: Sure. The American Standard Version (ASV, 1901) is often considered the most literal English Bible translation ever done. It comes close to the idea that the same Hebrew or Greek word should always be translated by the same English word wherever possible (this has its problems, as anyone who knows at least one second language realizes). At the extreme other end of the spectrum we have The Message by Eugene Peterson (2002), a paraphrase of the Bible in contemporary English. Every other English Bible falls somewhere in between these extremes.

Q: OK, so avoiding the extremes, what do we see in the middle?

A: Closer to the center of the scale, but a little more formal and literal, is the New Revised Standard Version (NRSV, 1989) and then the New International Version (NIV, 2011), which is somewhat more dynamic (more paraphrase). Some people will prefer a translation that's a little more literal, while others will like one with more paraphrase because they find it easier to understand. Someone who wants a clear, readable translation but would still like to know "what the literal Hebrew or Greek says" might like the New English Translation (NET Bible, 2019), which has a text that often falls between the NRSV and NIV and includes thousands of notes by the translators that explain the choices made.

Q: As a Bible translator yourself, what would you like everyday Bible readers to know about the challenges of that process?

A: A good English translation is a moving target—not mainly because our understanding of ancient Hebrew and Greek changes (though occasionally it does), but because the English language changes. And with the Internet and social media, it changes more rapidly than ever. New meanings are continually added, while older meanings drop out of use. Want a funny example? I had to remind some of my OT translators they could not use the word "booty" to describe the plunder David's men captured in war because of the contemporary colloquial usage (we had to use "spoils of war" or similar instead). I think—and it's just my opinion—that a revision of a modern translation is needed about every twenty or twenty-five years to keep it up-to-date. Another thing readers might not know is how hard

Bible translators work to prevent misunderstanding. In the NET Bible's second beta edition (yes, like software) of 1 Sam 23:7, we had Saul saying about David, "He has boxed himself into a corner by entering a city with two doors and a bar." Obviously, the modern reader might think of a pub or saloon, but that's not at all what Saul meant. To remove that possible misunderstanding, NET now reads "a city with two barred gates." Another challenge is being as clear as possible, avoiding figures of speech that add color and interest but would confuse non-native English speakers, or even British readers compared to American ones. The New English Bible (NEB, 1970) has "mattocks" in Isa 2:4. Who knows what those are? Finally, while we're at it, a Bible designed to be read aloud (as in a worship service) might not be quite the same as a Bible for personal reading and study.

Q: If somebody were to say, "This is the only acceptable translation, and all others are wrong," how would you respond?

A: I would start with a question: Do you speak another language than your native one? Spanish, or French perhaps (North American options). If you do, you'll realize that no translation perfectly mirrors the original. I would also want to know how the person knows this translation is the only acceptable one. Did they arrive at this through personal research and study, or because an individual or a denomination told them so? This is really a philosophical question about how we can obtain certainty in a complex world.

Q: When a preacher or teacher corrects a translation by appealing to "the original Hebrew" or "the original Greek," should we be nervous?

A: Well, that probably depends on whether the preacher or teacher really knows biblical Hebrew or New Testament Greek! Maybe we should be nervous if we think this is an indicator of an authoritarian figure who seeks to control the hearers by claiming the Bible's authority for whatever interpretation they're preaching. I personally don't drop statements like "in the original Greek" into sermons intended for general audiences very often (classes, Bible studies, or other sessions where people can ask questions are a different situation). The reason is that after hearing this mantra of "in the original Hebrew/Aramaic/Greek it says . . ." enough times, some people will begin to think, "I don't see that in my English Bible. My translation must be wrong. If I can't understand it, I may as well not read it." Anytime you convince someone not to read the Bible for themselves, you've done them a major disservice. For centuries common people were not permitted to read the Bible for themselves; it had to be interpreted for them by clergy. Some who were instrumental in getting the Bible translated into English, like William Tyndale, were martyred for doing so—they gave their lives so that others would have the Bible in a language they could read and understand. As my friend the late Dr. Bruce Metzger (who headed the NRSV translation committee) liked to say, "At least now they burn the translation rather than the translator!" Seriously, most scholars and linguists who work on translating the Bible don't do so for personal gain; they do it out of a love for the Bible and a desire to give Christians the best translation possible for the present day. As someone who's worked at this for much of my career—I've worked on the NASB1995 update, directed the NET Bible, and produced the Lexham English Bible (LEB)—that has certainly been the goal of my efforts. I see this as my gift to the church.

1 KINGS

SNAPSHOT

If Solomon was the wisest man on earth, why didn't his wisdom keep him from sin? If Elijah had faith to stop the rain, why did he run from the evil queen Jezebel? First Kings gives more than just a survey of the political and religious history of the divided kingdoms of Israel and Judah. It also shows how God's people can be easily seduced by the world—with disastrous consequences.

ORIENTATION

Date: 6th century BC
Author(s):   Unknown, traditionally attributed to Jeremiah
Audience: Originally the Jews in exile
Outline: 1. Transition from David to Solomon (1 Kgs 1–2)
                 2. Solomon Secures the Kingdom (3–4)
                 3. Solomon Builds the Temple (5–8)
                 4. Solomon's Successes . . . and Failures (9–11)
                 5. The Kingdom Divided (12–16)
                         a. Rehoboam vs. Jeroboam (12–14)
                         b. First Kings of the Divided Kingdom (15–16)

6. Ministry of Elijah (17–22)
   a. Elijah's Miracles (17)
   b. Elijah's Confrontation of Ahab and Jezebel (18–19)
7. The Conflicts and Fall of Ahab (20–22)

YOU ARE HERE

Episode 4: The Kingdom Rises → Episode 5: Division and Judgment

As the sixth Historical Book, 1 Kings recounts the glories of the united kingdom under Solomon due to covenant obedience and the division of the kingdom due to covenant unfaithfulness.

EXPLORING 1 KINGS

The setting of 1 Kings begins with an attempted coup in the last days of King David by his son Adonijah (1 Kgs 1). Nevertheless, Solomon is anointed king in place of David and secures the throne (1 Kgs 2). The narrative of 1 Kings portrays the beginning of Solomon's reign very positively, showing his humility and desire to serve the people with a heart of understanding. God grants him wisdom beyond any human being on earth (3:3–28). The message is clear: wisdom and righteousness—not power and might—are the keys to successful rule.

As predicted in the covenant with David (2 Sam 7), Solomon applies his great wisdom and wealth to build a temple for God and a palace for himself in Jerusalem (1 Kgs 6–7). Solomon's prayer in the dedication of the temple during the Feast of Weeks sets up the reader for what will follow, which is a foreshadowing of things to come—sin, covenant disobedience, division, and exile (1 Kgs 8).

In 1 Kings 10–11, the characterization of Solomon drastically shifts to highlight why Solomon and Israel would fail in the future: Solomon allows his wives to worship foreign gods in the land of Israel, causing Solomon to lose ten tribes of Israel under the reign of his son Rehoboam. Taking foreign wives and accumulating horses, gold, and silver was a fulfillment of what Moses warned would happen in Deut 17:14–20 (1 Kgs 10:26–29). When Solomon dies, he leaves his powerful and prosperous kingdom in a precarious position spiritually and politically (1 Kgs 11).

After the death of Solomon, his son Rehoboam exhibits none of Solomon's wisdom and prudence; he becomes a power-driven ruler who fails to listen to the advice of the past generation. This folly leads to a division of the kingdom. Rehoboam takes over the southern kingdom of Judah, centered in Jerusalem, while Jeroboam establishes the northern kingdom of Israel (1 Kgs 12). To compete with the temple in Jerusalem, Jeroboam even establishes a temple with golden calves to worship in the region of Dan—far north from the legitimate temple in Jerusalem (12:25–33).

The division and disobedience of the kings of Israel and Judah leads to the ministry of Elijah, whose miracle-packed preaching against the kings' wickedness fills the rest of the book of 1 Kings. In the ministry of Elijah, we witness the battle of gods: the true God, Yahweh, and his prophet Elijah vs. the false god Baal and his pagan prophets. In the battle of the gods, Yahweh defeats the rain god Baal by creating the drought, thus suffocating those who worship Baal and those who depend on him for rain. Elijah defeats the prophets of Baal and returns rain to the land, believing that a revival would happen in the land as all the people confess that Yahweh is God (1 Kgs 18:39).

Yet spiritual victory over Baal leads to political retribution. Queen Jezebel, the wife of Ahab, king of Israel, puts a bounty on Elijah's head (1 Kgs 19:1–3). Elijah runs for his life to Mount Horeb, sustained by God's provision (vv. 4–8). God reveals to Elijah that he will bring destruction upon the northern kingdom (vv. 9–18).

START YOUR JOURNEY

- From the life of Solomon, we learn that while wisdom shows you the right path to take in life, it doesn't guarantee a man or woman of God will take it. Consider the overarching course of Solomon's life—how he started out so well and ended so badly. What were the character flaws or bad decisions he made that led him to decline spiritually and morally?

- The book of James names Elijah as an ordinary man who could stop the rain with his great faith (Jas 5:17). As you read through the account of the ministry of Elijah, note the ways in which he reflects normal, frail humanity . . . and how God miraculously uses him in spite of his weakness. Great faith like Elijah's doesn't mean we won't have moments of weakness, as when we run away from our fears. But like Elijah on Mount Horeb, we must face our fears and false expectations and realign our mission with God's mission.

- Though the issue of leadership—political, spiritual, or otherwise—is not the main focus of 1 Kings, some very practical examples and illustrations of good and bad leadership decisions can be seen in the lives of the kings as well as the prophets mentioned in the text. For those in leadership, a fruitful study is to reflect on the leadership priorities and principles from those mentioned in 1 Kings and to glean some wisdom from both their successes and defeats.

2 KINGS

SNAPSHOT

The good, the bad, and the ugly—this sums up the episodes that constitute the story of the kings of Israel and Judah until their spiritual badness and moral ugliness result in divine judgment for both nations. All the while, the imperfect kingdom of David is held as the standard against which all subsequent kings are measured. This book serves as a warning that though God is patient, eventually his hammer of judgment will fall.

ORIENTATION

Date:	6th century BC
Author(s):	Unknown, traditionally attributed to Jeremiah
Audience:	Originally the Jews in exile
Outline:	1. Translation of Elijah and Transition to Elisha (2 Kgs 1–2)
	2. Elisha's Miracles and Message (3–8)
	3. The End of Ahab's Dynasty (9–10)
	4. Covenant Blessing and Death of Elisha (11–14)
	5. Rise of Assyria and Exile of Israel (15–17)
	6. Blessing in Judah under Hezekiah (18–20)
	7. Babylon Rises, Judah Declines (21)

8. Final Revival under Josiah (22–23)
9. Fall and Exile of Judah (24–25)

YOU ARE HERE

Episode 5: Division and Judgment

This seventh Historical Book traces the parallel reigns of the kings of Israel and kings of Judah while prophets call them back to covenant faithfulness until God judges both nations.

EXPLORING 2 KINGS

The book of 2 Kings starts with a bang: Elijah calling down fire from heaven to consume two sets of fifty soldiers of Israel and their captains. This proves once again that Elijah is a true prophet of God (1:9–16). This explosive introduction then transitions to the end of Elijah's ministry when Elijah is swept up into heaven in a chariot of fire, and the mantle of the prophet's authority is placed upon Elisha (2:1–14).

God gives Elisha "two shares" of Elijah's spirit, enabling him to do even more and more astonishing miracles than his mentor (2:9–14). But his ministry isn't a big-tent, signs-and-wonders extravaganza; it's serious spiritual warfare. Elisha's miracles are performed and his message preached against the wicked and idolatrous northern kingdom of Israel (2:15–8:29). Elisha's mission finally ends when the dynasty of the wicked king Ahab is destroyed (9:1–10:31). From here on the narrative focuses on Israel and Judah and how each kingdom follows the sins of Jeroboam and Ahab.

Until Israel is taken in judgment to captivity by Assyria (17:6), the book presents a back-and-forth chronological account of the kings of the northern and southern kingdoms, comparing and contrasting them. The kings are characterized as either good or bad, with David held up as the standard (1 Kgs 11:4; 14:8; 15:3–5, 11; 2 Kgs 14:3; 16:2; 18:3; 22:2). Though David was far from a perfect person or faultless leader, he serves as the model because of his deep devotion to worshipping and serving Yahweh. In this sense, David was a man after God's own heart, in that he did not turn to the left or to the right and follow after other gods. Yes, he sinned grievously and suffered the consequences. But because of his genuine repentance, his life becomes a picture of God's mercy and grace for generations to come.

Although Judah is eventually destroyed along with Jerusalem (586 BC), the book ends on a positive note due to God's irrevocable promises in the Davidic covenant (2 Sam 7:12–16). Though the kingdom is destroyed, God preserves the house and line of David even in exile in Babylon. By the providence of God, the king of Babylon shows favor toward Jehoiachin, who is released from prison and treated like a guest in the palace of Babylon (2 Kgs 25:27–30). What a picture of hope! The lovingkindness promised to David and his descendants in the Davidic covenant concludes a sometimes good, mostly bad and ugly narrative of political conflict, religious apostasy, and spiritual decline. With the preservation of the line of David, 2 Kings implicitly looks forward to the greater Son of David, the ultimate Messiah, who will one day take the throne and rule over Israel and all the earth forever.

START YOUR JOURNEY

- The miracles of Elisha are twice as numerous as the miracles of Elijah, but they mirror them in many ways. In fact, Jesus also mirrors these miracles, which is why many wrongly concluded Jesus was Elijah returned from heaven (Matt 16:14; Luke 9:8). This fact reminds us that the Spirit working powerfully in the life of Elisha is the same Spirit who worked in the life of Jesus and the same Spirit who works in our own lives today.
- As the parade of godly and godless kings of Israel and Judah illustrate, there is no guarantee that our children will follow the examples of godly parents . . . nor do wicked parents prevent God from breaking the cycle and calling forth a godly generation. Though

parents have an impact for good or ill in the lives of children, each child must trust and obey God on his or her own.

- As you read through 2 Kings, cheering for the heroes of faith and jeering at the villains, pay attention to God's tenacious mercy and grace generation after generation. Note the ways God's patience toward both Israel and Judah is evident, even as eventual judgment looms over the horizon. Just as God was so merciful and forgiving to Israel for hundreds of years, so God is patient and forgiving with us today.

1 CHRONICLES

SNAPSHOT

Ever feel disillusioned by current politics? Join the (ancient) club. First Chronicles was written years after a remnant returned to Judah from exile. Their temple? Rebuilt—but nothing like the temple of Solomon. Their topsy-turvy world? Ruled not by a Davidic king, but by pagan nations. What happened to the Lord's promises? First Chronicles provides Israel a reminder of hope by looking back in order to look forward.

ORIENTATION

Date:	4th century BC
Author:	Uncertain, usually referred to as "the Chronicler," traditionally identified as Ezra
Audience:	The remnant population of Jews who had returned from Babylon
Outline:	1. History of Hope: Ancient Genealogies (1–9)
	a. Adam to Israel (1)
	b. Children of Israel (2–8)
	c. Returned Exiles (9)
	2. History of Hope: Saul to David (10–29)

    a. Death of Saul (10)

    b. Life of David (11–28)

    c. Death of David (29)

YOU ARE HERE

Episode 1: The Beginning → Episode 4: The Kingdom Rises

First Chronicles is the eighth of the Historical Books in the English Bible. Both 1 and 2 Chronicles provide hope that the Lord's promises to Abraham and David will still be fulfilled.

EXPLORING 1 CHRONICLES

The first nine chapters of 1 Chronicles detail the longest genealogy of the Bible. There's a reason. The Chronicler crafted this list of names to highlight four themes: rule, blessings, curses, and hope—especially hope in the advent of the Davidic dynasty.

This is why: Judah, the tribe from which David comes, receives primacy of honor. Judah is the tribe of rulers (cf. 5:1–2). The arrangement of David's genealogy ultimately focuses on Solomon, a man of peace. That's important later. David's genealogy concludes with listing sons beyond the last king of Judah, Zedekiah (3:17–24), and a generation or so after Babylon. Note that no Davidic king ascended to the throne after Zedekiah, but keeping the genealogy alive marks 1 Chronicles with a deep longing for a restoration in the future—*that's hope*!

Don't miss the short narrations curated in these chapters. They emphasize covenantal blessings and curses. The message for the generation of readers returning from captivity in Babylon is clear: obedience brings blessings (e.g., 4:10, 38–40); disobedience brings curses, including captivity (5:26; 9:1). Israel and Judah go into captivity, but a remnant of people, including Levites and priests, return to Judah. They begin to reestablish their land and worship (9:1–34)—*that's hope*!

The genealogies end with Saul's heritage (9:35–44), which then transitions the reader from the genealogical sections to narrative sections. Saul's disobedience to the Lord brings death (1 Chr 10). After Saul, the Chronicler includes select events from the life of David and his sons. These events continue to develop themes of rule and hope, but a new theme also emerges: rest—peace that comes from God's protection and provision as well as confidence in God's promises and their ultimate fulfillment. *That's hope!*

The Lord provides David with victories over Israel's enemies, and the people then establish David as ruler over all Israel (1 Chr 11–12). A failed attempt to bring the ark of the covenant to Jerusalem (1 Chr 13) highlights the theme of rest. David defeats the Philistines, and the Lord causes nations to fear David. Consequently, there's rest in Israel (1 Chr 14), and the ark now comes to Jerusalem (1 Chr 15). Peace precedes God's presence (cf. Deut 12:10–11).

At the tabernacle of the Lord, David assigns certain Levites permanent duties (cf. 2 Chr 23:18; 35:15) to invoke, thank, and praise the Lord (1 Chr 16:4, RSV). Don't miss the term "invoke." To invoke the Lord is to ask him to remember the covenant he made with Abraham (vv. 15–20). This covenant is the foundation for trusting that God will gather Israel from nations and restore them (v. 35). David later establishes prophetic musicians at the temple—they give thanks to the Lord (25:2–5) for his everlasting loving-kindness (16:41–43)—*that's hope!*

In chapter 17, the Lord promises David he will set one of his own sons as king over Israel. He will rule forever and ever. This son isn't Solomon. Unlike 2 Sam 7:14, Chronicles excludes any prediction of chastisement. This son points forward—far forward to the ultimate Son of David, the Lord Jesus—*that's hope!*

Before his death, David's rule brings more rest (1 Chr 18–20). After a chaotic event, he purchases land for the temple of the Lord (1 Chr 21), but because David is a man of war, unable to build the temple. Solomon, defined only in Chronicles as a man of peace, will be the one who builds God's temple in Jerusalem (cf. 28:3). Although David prepares the way (1 Chr 22–27),

Solomon must build the temple (1 Chr 28) with the Lord's help (29:18–19). Thus, the book of 1 Chronicles ends with a view toward the immediate future—*that's hope*!

START YOUR JOURNEY

- First Chronicles is more than just a stitched-together patchwork of historical events. The Historical Books—even books filled with lists of names like Numbers and 1 Chronicles—"were written for our instruction" (1 Cor 10:11). Consider how knowledge of the past can have an impact on understanding your present and provide hope for the future.

- Read 1 Chronicles in light of hope in the Lord to fulfill his covenantal responsibilities to Abraham and David. What is topsy turvy will be made right by the Lord. The process may be long and arduous. It may take not years but generations. But God is always at work, moving his plan forward for our good and his glory.

- Take the time to dig for gems in 1 Chronicles. This book is loaded with profound biblical theology, often riveted by phrases like "Give thanks to the LORD, for he is good; his faithful love endures forever" (1 Chr 16:34). As you work through this book, note the ways in which God's character shines through.

- The hope of Chronicles ought to be your hope. The Lord will remember his people. One day soon, maybe today, the ultimate Davidic King, the Lord Jesus Christ—the hope of 1 Chronicles—will return for us—*that's hope*!

Q&A

"Bible Commentaries"

With Dr. John Dyer

Dr. John Dyer (ThM, Dallas Theological Seminary; PhD, Durham University) is a professor of theology, author, coder, and developer of the website www.bestcommentaries.com. Since 2008, that website, known as the "Rotten Tomatoes for Biblical Studies," has helped students of the Bible at all levels make informed decisions about which commentaries to use in their exploration of Scripture.

Q: Some people harbor distrust toward commentaries. They want to avoid commentaries altogether or to consult them only as a last resort. Why would you say incorporating commentaries in Bible study is helpful? Are there any cautions?

A: There is certainly a risk in relying too heavily on commentaries, looking for answers to trivia, rather than allowing the Spirit to move in us through the Word. On the other hand, if we read a translation of the Bible alone by ourselves, we risk missing important details and making the same mistakes that many others have made before us. This is where commentaries can be helpful. They bring together and summarize how many Christians before us have read the Bible and walk us through the various interpretive options they came up with. This is especially helpful for challenging or controversial passages, but also for familiar ones, because they may help us see something we hadn't noticed before, which can draw us into a deeper appreciation of God's wonder, mystery, and majesty.

Q: What are different kinds or categories of commentaries out there?

A: Commentaries range from highly technical, academic works that assume prior training in Greek and Hebrew to more devotional works that focus on the themes, message, and application of the book. There are also many commentaries somewhere in the middle, where the author may discuss the original languages but not assume that the reader is fluent in them. In this middle range, commentary series often have a particular emphasis, such as being designed for those who preach, focusing on the historical background of the book, or drawing out the theology of the texts. Some series also attempt to bring a little bit of everything together to take a reader deeper than a study Bible, without getting overly detailed.

Q: What are your go-to "single-volume" commentaries that cover the whole Old Testament, New Testament, or even the entire Bible?

A: For many years, the *Bible Knowledge Commentary* was a go-to, but I am grateful that newer works like this one offer insights and fresh perspective. On bestcommentaries.com, one of the highest rated single-volume commentaries is the *New Bible Commentary*, edited by four scholars who have written some of the best commentaries of individual books, including Gordon Wenham and D. A. Carson. I would also mention the *Baker Illustrated Bible Background Commentary* for a bit more devotional feel with more images, the *New International Bible Commentary* since it is based on the familiar NIV version, and the abridged *Expositor's Bible Commentary*, which is based on one of the best multivolume series. To widen our perspective of how God is working in the world, it might also be good to consult works like the *Africa Bible Commentary* and *South Asia Bible Commentary*, which feature scholars from around the world.

Q: Don't name names, but any kinds of commentaries to avoid? Any yellow or red flags to look for that tell us to keep our distance?

A: The main two things that come to mind are avoiding commentary authors that don't trust God's word and avoiding commentary series that aren't suited to your needs. A quick way to check for the first is to look for who the commentary author thinks wrote the book of the Bible and when they think it was written. For example, if the author doesn't think Moses was involved with Genesis or offers very late dates (after AD 100) for New Testament books, then they might not be worth your time. Another quick check you can do is see if the commentary uses Greek and Hebrew letters instead of English characters. For example, if it says אֲדֹנָי but doesn't also transliterate that as *Adonai*, you might find it hard to use unless you learn the language first.

Q: Some of your answers make me think that a study Bible might be a kind of running commentary. How might your points about commentaries also apply to study Bibles?

A: Indeed, commentaries and study Bibles share several important features—they usually include background information on the author and setting of the book, an overview of its major themes and overall message, and notes on key words and passages. The main difference between the two is the length and detail of the notes and the goal of those notes. Some study Bibles (and commentaries) are written to be a general help to as many people as possible, but others are written from a particular theological perspective, or emphasize a key theme through the Bible, and others focus more on how to apply the text to your life. Each can be valuable as long as we know its position ahead of time and it aligns with our current goals.

2 CHRONICLES

SNAPSHOT

The books of 1 and 2 Chronicles report historical events like people share pictures on social media—selected and arranged by the author to present a message. Except unlike social media posts, the Chronicler doesn't post just the prettiest, most impressive pictures. Especially in 2 Chronicles, we see image after image illustrating the progressive decline and fall of Judah—with a few bright and hopeful spots along the way.

ORIENTATION

Date: 4th century BC

Author: Uncertain, usually referred to as "the Chronicler," traditionally identified as Ezra

Audience: The remnant population of Jews who had returned from Babylon

Outline: 1. History of Hope, Continued (2 Chron 1–10)
              a. Rise of Solomon (1)
              b. Solomon Builds the Temple (2–7)
              c. Triumphs and Death of Solomon (8–10)
            2. History of Hope, Concluded (11–36)

    a. Rehoboam's Failures (11–12)
    b. Mixed Success in Succession (13–35)
    c. Fall of Judah and Jerusalem (36)

YOU ARE HERE

Episode 4: The Kingdom Rises → Episode 6: Return from Exile

Second Chronicles, the ninth of the Historical Books, continues the narrative begun in 1 Chronicles, inspiring hope of restoration for the exiles returned from Babylon.

EXPLORING 2 CHRONICLES

In the opening chapters of 2 Chronicles, the Lord answers the prayer of David and Solomon, and Solomon's life is nothing short of astonishing. The author depicts Solomon as the embodiment of obedience, peace, wisdom, and resultant blessing, while transgressions against the Lord are passed over. In devotion to God, Solomon builds the temple (2 Chr 1–5), and the Lord moves in (2 Chr 6–7). The Lord blesses Solomon with immense prosperity (2 Chr 8–9). Don't miss several themes that emerge in the middle of Solomon's narrative—permanent presence in Jerusalem (6:6), disobedience bringing curses to the land and people, and repentance bringing forgiveness and healing (7:12–16). These themes are the backbone of the next section.

    The author weaves these themes throughout the book to demonstrate a downward progression: peace gives way to chaos, which leads to captivity. Rehoboam, Solomon's son, is evil and doesn't seek the Lord (12:14). This results in the Lord allowing the king of Egypt, Shishak, to capture some of Judah. Rehoboam's repentance, however, provides relief (12:1–8). A brief pause in the chaos comes when righteous kings like Asa, Jehoshaphat, Hezekiah, and Josiah lead the nation in repentance and reform. Yet even these seemingly bright lights of hope flicker like candles in the wind. Take Hezekiah. Though he brings Israel peace through his obedience, he displays self-aggrandizement (32:27–31). And though King Josiah brings spiritual reform and peace (34:1–18), he picks a fight with Pharoah Neco, fails to heed the word of the Lord, and suffers an untimely death in battle (35:20–27).

Yet those few mostly righteous kings still stand as bright lights compared to the majority of the kings of Judah, who engage in outright disobedience. Despite his involvement in restoring the temple, Joash murders his spiritual father (24:22). In comparison with his predecessors, Ahaz has a more severe degree of unfaithfulness to the Lord (28:22). Manasseh encourages Judah to commit more evil than the nations which the Lord destroyed. As a result, Manasseh is personally taken into captivity. But even in that dark valley of judgment, a beam of God's mercy and grace shines. The wholly wicked Manasseh turns to the Lord from his captivity, and God allows him to return to Judah, where he ends up ruling for a staggering fifty-five years! This demonstrates that God's work of redemption can penetrate the darkest heart.

The lights of righteousness prove to be mere glow-in-the-dark revivals that quickly fade in the darkening spiritual landscape of Judah. The book of 2 Chronicles closes with the four last kings of Judah, who fail to trust the Lord. As a result, the people, the temple, and the land all suffer destruction (36:1–20). The people don't allow the land to enjoy its sabbaths as required by the Mosaic law; therefore, captivity results. The land promised to Abraham, Isaac, and Jacob and entrusted to the family of David is devastated.

Though the book of 2 Chronicles could have ended with the desolation of Judah, the story actually presents a cliffhanger that anticipates return and restoration. The Chronicler reminds us that the Jews' exile to Babylon would come to an end after seventy years, in keeping with the prophecy of Jeremiah (2 Chr 36:20–21). Then, the final paragraph points out that Cyrus, king of Persia, issues a proclamation that frees the people of Judah to return and to rebuild the temple in Jerusalem (36:22–23). Though the story ends abruptly with the decree to return, the following historical book, Ezra, picks up precisely where 2 Chronicles ends—with the decree of Cyrus to return and rebuild (Ezra 1:1–4), instilling hope of restoration for the remnant returned from Babylon.

START YOUR JOURNEY

- In the midst of chaos, confusion, and spiritual blindness, God's word remains. His promises never fail. His faithfulness never wavers. So, with full confidence, we must teach truth in our own crooked generation, regardless of the personal cost, while we wait for our blessed hope, the Lord Jesus.
- People often view God in the Old Testament as cold, cruel, and callous. This is simply untrue. In the approximate 345 years between Solomon's reign and Judah's exile to Babylon, most of the kings who ruled Israel and Judah were wicked, ruthless, and godless. Despite this, the Lord never gives up on his people. Focus on the words and works of the Lord in 2 Chronicles and note what this book teaches you about the God we serve today.
- Take a second look at chapters 10–33. Second Chronicles, as well as the entire Bible, shines with continuous evidence of God's grace. As we seek to live in conformity to the character of God, we should show mercy, patience, and forgiveness toward others. That is, love well. Be eager to follow the example of the gracious God of Judah.

EZRA

SNAPSHOT

Even when you're doing God's work, expect opposition from enemies on the outside and failures among allies on the inside. The book of Ezra illustrates this reality. Here we see the providential hand of God as he orchestrates a physical rebuilding of Jerusalem's temple and initiates a spiritual reformation of his people through Ezra the priest. Though these God-ordained works face stout challenges, God sees his people through.

ORIENTATION

Date: 5th century BC
Author: Ezra
Audience: Jews returning from captivity after the exile
Outline: 1. First Wave of Return under Zerubbabel (1–6)
            a. Rebuilding the Temple Begins (1–3)
            b. Rebuilding the Temple Challenged (4)
            c. Rebuilding the Temple Completed (5–6)
       2. Second Wave of Return under Ezra (7–10)
            a. Ezra's Personal and Political Credentials (7)
            b. Ezra's Companions Return from Captivity (8)

    c. Ezra's Confrontation of the People's Sin (9–10)

YOU ARE HERE

Episode 6: Return from Exile

The tenth Historical Book in the English Bible, Ezra, is the first to detail the return of the exiles from Babylon and the rebuilding of the temple in Jerusalem.

EXPLORING EZRA

After the empire of Media-Persia defeated the Babylonian empire in 539 BC, Cyrus rose as the new king over the region. He issued his famous decree for many of his subjects to return home.[1] The period covered in Ezra is the first return of the captives from Babylon in 538 BC to the second return of the people with Ezra in 458 BC. The text reminds a people struggling with the challenges of returning to a homeland both familiar and foreign that God's providence is with them in their work to rebuild the city.

  The book of Ezra narrates the first return of Judah under Cyrus's proclamation (1:1–4), which includes the return of the furnishings of silver and gold in the temple (vv. 5–11). All who return are listed in a census in chapter 2 (2:1–70). The returnees immediately rebuild the altar of the temple as their first priority in order to resume the sacrifices on the upcoming Feast of Tabernacles (3:1–6). Then they focus on the rebuilding of the foundation of the temple (3:7–13). But the temple construction is opposed by the neighboring enemies of Israel (4:1–23).

  Although the temple construction was halted by opposition (v. 24), it was eventually completed amidst great opposition because the Lord was with Judah, giving them prophets like Zechariah and Haggai (5:1) and leaders

---

[1] James B. Pritchard, ed., *Ancient Near Eastern Texts Relating to the Old Testament* (Princeton: Princeton University Press, 1969), 315–16.

like Jeshua (Joshua) and Zerubbabel (v. 2). Although the work was opposed by Tatennai (vv. 3–17), the Persian king Darius found the Cyrus decree and reissued another decree to continue to rebuild the temple, ironically with full financial support from the opposition of the provinces beyond the river (6:1–13)! The temple was finally completed in 515–516 BC, and the people celebrated the Passover and the Feast of Unleavened Bread (vv. 14–22).

The second part of the book narrates the second wave of returnees from the exile. While chapters 1–6 cover eighty years, the second half of the book covers only one year (7:1–8:36). The recurring theme of God's gracious hand being upon the people is presented in their safe return to Jerusalem (7:6, 9, 28; 8:18, 22, 31). Finally, Ezra starts his spiritual reforms, renewing the covenant and confronting the spiritual leaders, urging them to send their foreign wives away, lest they fall into the same sins of idolatry that had caused the exile to Babylon in the first place (9:1–10:44).

The book of Ezra doesn't present the events in a strict chronological order. In fact, three verses in Ezra 4:5–7 sum up the opposition to the returnees that span three Persian kings and a period of eighty years! The following table provides a tidy reconstruction of the historical events and their recounting in Ezra.[2]

Book of Ezra	King of Media-Persia	Date (BC)	Events
1:1	Cyrus	539–530	First return
4:5	Darius I	522–486	Work on temple and city opposed
4:6	Xerxes I (Ahasuerus)	486–464	Work on city opposed
4:7	Artaxerxes I	464–423	Work on city opposed

6:15	Darius	516	Work approved, temple finished
7:7	Artaxerxes I	458	Second return
7:8		5th month, 1st day	Ezra and returnees arrive safely
8:31		1st month, 12th day	Flashback to departure from Babylon
10:9		9th month, 12th day	Ezra reads the law
10:16		10th month, 1st day	Ezra investigates intermarriages
10:17		457, 1st month, 1st day	Marriages dissolved

START YOUR JOURNEY

- Just as the good hand of the Lord was upon Ezra and Judah (Ezra 7:6, 9, 28; 8:18, 22, 31), we can trust in his providential care as we seek to do his work even in the face of opposition.
- Note the emphasis on rebuilding the physical temple in Jerusalem and recommitting to spiritual revival among the returnees. We, too, must focus on both physical and spiritual renewal. Our external deeds should be accompanied by internal devotion; and our internal faith and love should manifest themselves in external attitudes and actions. The church, the body of Christ, is not a physical temple, but a spiritual temple made of living stones (1 Pet 2:5).
- How easy it is to slip back into old sins that had already done us in! As you read through Ezra and meditate on its message, consider the way in which seemingly mild compromises threatened to lead the generation of Ezra's day down the same path of the previous generation and how Ezra took drastic measures to prevent it. What areas in your own life may need similar radical reform?

NEHEMIAH

SNAPSHOT

Have you ever felt challenged to step out of your comfort zone and tackle a mission or ministry that seemed overwhelming? In a historic moment, Nehemiah resolved to leave a posh lifestyle in a Persian palace and take up a strenuous mission of rebuilding the wall of the city of Jerusalem. The seemingly insurmountable task would put Nehemiah's fortitude, faith, and leadership abilities to the test . . . and inspire us in our own service to God.

ORIENTATION

Date: 5th century BC
Author: Memoir of Nehemiah, Ezra
Audience: Remnant of the second and third returns
Outline: 1. Return to Rebuild the Wall of Jerusalem (1–6)
                    a. Prayer of Nehemiah (1)
                    b. Preparation and Planning of Nehemiah (2–3)
                    c. External Threats and Internal Conflicts (4–5)
                    d. Completion of the Wall (6)
                2. Restoration of the Jewish Community in Jerusalem (7–13)

a. Repopulation for the Security of the City, Part 1 (7)
b. Reformation of the People (8–10)
c. Repopulation for the Security of the City, Part 2 (11–12)
d. Dedication of the Wall (12)
e. Second Reformation (13)

YOU ARE HERE

Episode 6: Return from Exile

As the eleventh Historical Book, Nehemiah documents God's faithfulness to the returned remnant by sending a seasoned leader to rebuild the wall and reform the community.

EXPLORING NEHEMIAH

The book of Nehemiah begins with bad news concerning the city of Jerusalem and its struggling remnant of returnees (1:1–3): the city wall remained in ruins and the people unprotected from threats around them. Nehemiah first reacts with a devotion to prayer and fasting before the God of heaven. He confesses the sins of his people and asks God specifically for a favor according to the promise of his covenant (vv. 4–11). For an extended period, Nehemiah prayed for the divinely appointed moment to get the permission and support of King Artaxerxes for the rebuilding of the wall (2:1–8). God answers his prayer. With complete faith in the good hand of the Lord, Nehemiah returns to inspect the ruins of Jerusalem and to mobilize God's people to act (vv. 9–20).

The building project is characterized by wise division of labor (3:1–32), yet the rebuilding of structures destroyed by the Babylonians requires deep commitment of every heart and hand (3:13, 28). Yet the people prove to be up to the task. Even so, their unified effort enraged leaders of surrounding provinces who posed a threat. Not affected by the intimidation, though,

Nehemiah stationed guards to protect the builders (4:1–23). Meanwhile, a widespread outcry arises from the oppressed people. Nehemiah confronts the injustice of the nobles: charging high interest rates on loans and selling the children of Israel (5:1–13).

With the wall nearly complete, several enemies of God's people—including Sanballat, Tobiah, Geshem—try to entrap Nehemiah by an open letter falsely charging him with revolt. But Nehemiah prayerfully and prudently frustrates their plans (6:1–14). Despite the stout political and personal opposition, the wall of Jerusalem is completed in just fifty-two days (vv. 15–19). Then, Nehemiah wisely chooses faithful men, Hanani and Hananiah, and entrusts them with governance of the city (6:17–7:3).

After the completion of the wall, a new issue arises. The city is spacious, but the inhabitants are few. Nehemiah assembles the nobles and the people (7:4–73), then all the remnant gather in Jerusalem for the reading of the law of Moses, the keeping of the Feast of Booths, and a renewed ratification of the covenant (8:1–10:39). All the leaders and people join with their brothers and swear an oath to walk in God's law (10:28–29). The leaders and one-tenth of the people commit to living in Jerusalem (11:1–12:26).

With the people restored and the defenses in place, the completed wall of Jerusalem is dedicated to the Lord (12:27–43). At last, the provision for the priests and Levites is put in place (vv. 44–47). Then, as an act of repentance, when the people hear the reading of the law, they separate from all those of foreign descent (13:1–3). The book of Nehemiah ends with a second religious reformation (13:25, 30). Nehemiah stays in Jerusalem until the thirty-second year of Artaxerxes (432 BC) and returns to serve the king of Persia only to return once again for a second reformation of the community (vv. 4–31).

This historical account reflects the need for perseverance for a long-term transformation of a community. A thorough reformation demands a leader committed to planning, investigation, mobilization, organization, supervision, modeling, problem-solving, confrontation, and education. Above all, the hope of success lies not just on a leader competent and skillful, but on a godly person committed to faith, hope, and prayer.

START YOUR JOURNEY

- As you read through Nehemiah, preferably in one sitting, reflect on the work of God's hand in the rebuilding project. While acknowledging the human effort that led to success, consider what the Lord did to bring about his will through his people.

- Stepping out of Nehemiah and reflecting on the entire biblical story, consider how the themes of return, restoration, repentance, and recommitment fit in the broader narrative of redemption. How would you explain the place of Nehemiah in God's grand narrative?

- Looking at Nehemiah's example of godly leadership, consider both the skills and character exhibited in Nehemiah's actions. Especially note how he responds to bad news, criticism, complaints, and lies. What lessons can you learn from him in your own realms of influence? Consider how Jesus is the leader who is greater than Nehemiah.

GOING DEEPER

"Nehemiah: The Timeless Traits of Leadership"

— Donald K. Campbell —

The focus of today is leadership. One observer said recently, "The power of leadership seems to be declining everywhere. More and more [of those] coming to the top seem to be merely drifting." There is a crying need for responsible leadership in America and around the world. The need is for individuals to get the job done, not merely fill a position. It was a former president of Columbia University who said, "There are three kinds of people in the world—those who don't know what's happening, those who watch what's happening, and those who make things happen." Christian leaders must fall into the third category. We should be a part of that company that makes things happen.

Many Old Testament figures were outstanding leaders because they got the job done in their generation. There was Joseph, a wise and dynamic administrator and leader in Egypt. There was Moses—we can scarcely tally up all his contributions as a leader of God's people. There were also Joshua, David, Nehemiah, and many more. Nehemiah, a man who made things happen, had qualities we should consider.

First, we see him as a *man of prayer* (chapter 1). Nehemiah's example reminds us to pray, as we read in the New Testament, "without ceasing." Prayer is an essential ingredient of spiritual leadership.

Second, Nehemiah was a *man of vision* (2:1–3). Occupying an official position similar to that of a prime minister, he was always near the king, giving him counsel, and tasting his food and wine. On this particular occasion, Nehemiah was solemn. He had a burden on his heart—a burden that was becoming a vision. He wanted to do something about the ruined city of Jerusalem. But why had no one caught this vision before? Jerusalem had lain waste since its destruction in 586 BC. And for all those years people had said, "It can't be done." But Nehemiah had a vision that seemed an impossible dream. When some people receive bad news about the plight of God's work, they simply weep and mourn. They wring their hands and wonder what can be done about the situation. But Nehemiah was not that kind of man. He wept, mourned, fasted, and prayed. Responsible leadership takes the problem and deals with it decisively.

Third, Nehemiah was also a *man of foresight* (2:5–8). He was a wise planner. It is not unspiritual to make careful plans and organize strategy for the work of God. When the king asked Nehemiah what his burden was, Nehemiah had his answer prepared. I imagine he had written it out and rehearsed it before the mirror, praying that God would give him the opportunity to verbalize his request to the king. That time came, and Nehemiah revealed his intentions. He was thus a man who planned, and well he should have, because before him lay the enormous task of directing the rebuilding of an entire city—a task even today's urban planners would find immensely complex.

Fourth, we see Nehemiah as a *man of caution* (2:11–20). He was not content with a report of the conditions in Jerusalem. He wanted to see for himself. So, while the rest of Jerusalem slept, Nehemiah prowled the ruined walls and confirmed that the situation was desperate. Then he challenged the people and overcame that first obstacle in any work for God—inertia. The response of the people was electric: "Let's start rebuilding" (2:18). Not only could Nehemiah analyze the situation he faced, but he also possessed the ability to make things happen, a characteristic common to all leaders.

Fifth, Nehemiah was a man of *extraordinary organizational skill*. Chapter 3 is one of the most interesting chapters in the book of Nehemiah, although it doesn't make for exciting reading at first glance. The chief value of the chapter is found in what it teaches about organizing a task and getting it done.

Sixth, Nehemiah was also a *man with faith and common sense*. In chapter 4, we find that the enemy was conspiring against the Jews and was ready to fight against Jerusalem and to hinder the work of rebuilding. Nehemiah said, "So we prayed to our God and stationed a guard because of them day and night" (4:9). He didn't just pray, he prayed and set a watch. In the Lord's work, piety and practicality must be wedded. Christian leaders must be models of this.

Seventh, Nehemiah was a *man with compassion for the oppressed* (chapter 5). Poor Jews were oppressed by rich Jews who loaned them money, charged them high interest rates, and took as security their lands, their homes, and even their children. When Nehemiah heard of this, he was infuriated and took action (5:6–7). It should be our prayer that God would keep us from becoming callous to human need—that he will make us persons of compassion and concern. It is a mark of Christian leadership.

Eighth, Nehemiah is clearly a *man of personal integrity*. While he was governor of the land, he did not claim the salary assigned him. He did not engage in land speculation and, in fact, gave liberally of his own resources (5:14–16). Nehemiah's life was an open book. He was therefore in a position to rebuke others who had fallen into wrongdoing.

Ninth, Nehemiah was a *man of impartiality*. He denounced evil wherever it appeared, even when it surfaced among wealthy and influential men who no doubt had made great contributions to the Jerusalem building program. It was not easy, but Nehemiah did what was right, letting the chips fall where they would. Few leaders have this kind of courage.

Finally, Nehemiah was a *man with a sense of mission* (chapter 6). The enemies kept hammering away at him. As construction came to a climax, it seems that enemy attacks intensified. They practiced deceit (vv. 2–3), intimidation (vv. 5–9), and distraction (vv. 10–14). But Nehemiah persisted in his work, retaining his sense of mission and finishing the job in an amazing fifty-two days (v. 15).

God has not called us to mediocrity. He has called us to excellence. And in the life and ministry of Nehemiah, we see a man who achieved that excellence in the work of God.[1]

---

[1] Adapted from Donald K. Campbell, "Nehemiah: The Timeless Traits of Leadership," *Kindred Spirit* 1, no. 2 (spring 1977): 21–23. ©1977 Dallas Theological Seminary.

ESTHER

SNAPSHOT

Do you ever find yourself in situations needing divine intervention, but God seems nowhere to be found? The book of Esther teaches that while God might seem hidden from our view, he never abandons his people. More often than not, God seems to work behind the scenes through the seeming mundane details of life to bring about his blessing in unexpected ways.

ORIENTATION

Date: 5th or 4th century BC
Author: Uncertain, but traditionally attributed to Mordecai
Audience: Originally to the Jews of the Diaspora
Outline: 1. Persian Festival and Ascension of Esther (1–2)
                2. Jews Are Endangered by Archenemy (3)
                3. Mordecai Appeals to Esther to Act (4)
                4. Esther's First Banquet (5)
                5. Unexpected Fall of Haman and Rise of Mordecai (6)
                6. Esther's Second Banquet (7)
                7. Mordecai Appeals to Ahasuerus to Act (8)
                8. Jews Are Victorious over All Enemies (9)

9. Jewish Festival and Ascension of Mordecai (9–10)

YOU ARE HERE

Episode 6: Return from Exile

As the twelfth and final Historical Book, Esther is also the third book of the post-exilic era (Ezra, Nehemiah, and Esther), narrating events of Jews living in exile in Persia.

EXPLORING ESTHER

The book of Esther follows the story of the Jewish maiden named Hadassah, who had been deported and was living in Susa, the capital of Persia. Having lost her parents, she was raised by her uncle Mordecai, who instructed her to hide her Jewish identity and go by the Persian name Esther. His concern hints at a fear of anti-Jewish sentiments in a foreign land—a danger that would soon become very real.

In an unexpected turn of events, Esther (along with other powerless maidens) was taken into the palace. Infatuated by her beauty and unaware of her true identity, King Ahasuerus made her queen. But what could have been a life of privilege was soon disrupted when Mordecai sent her a private message revealing that the king's trusted advisor Haman—the anti-Jewish archenemy of Mordecai—had manipulated Ahasuerus to issue an irrevocable decree of genocide targeting all Jews in the Empire.

Yet in what can only be explained as an example of divine providence, the date set for this fateful event by casting lots (*pûrîm*) was nearly a year away. Sensing God's providence at work, Mordecai appealed to Esther to use her new status to intervene on behalf of her fellow expatriates. Warning that once her true identity was discovered she also would be in danger, Mordecai uttered the most theologically loaded statement in the book: "Who knows, perhaps you have come to your royal position for such a time as this" (4:14).

The once-powerless maiden who had acquiesced in silence to every form of male domination up to now suddenly transformed into a self-confident woman of valor. Instructing her uncle to call on their fellow Jews to fast (and pray) on her behalf, Esther sprang into action with a plan to use her diplomatic skills and feminine charms to persuade the king to intervene for the Jews. Without divulging the plot (WARNING: SPOILER ALERT), a series of unexpected events combine to strengthen Esther's resolve and soften the king's heart, leading to a second royal decree which empowered the Jews throughout the empire to defend themselves, turning the tables on their enemies. In an ironic twist of events, Haman was hanged on the very gallows he had built with the intent of hanging Mordecai. His royal office suddenly evacuated, the king then appointed Mordecai in Haman's place, enabling Mordecai to secure the safety of his fellow Jews. As the story closes, the Jews in Persia celebrate the festival of Purim for the first time, commemorating their deliverance made possible by the fateful result of Haman's lots (*pûrîm*). While the casual reader might simply think the Jews were lucky, the careful reader of the Bible knows, "The lot is cast into the lap, but its every decision is from the Lord" (Prov 16:33).

The book of Esther is one of only two books in the Bible (the other is Song of Songs) in which God is not directly mentioned. Although interpreters explain this anomaly in different ways, its inclusion in the canon seems to imply—if not demand—that we interpret this story in the light of God's hidden providence working behind the scenes to deliver his people. Indeed, the eye of faith can see God's fingerprints on every page and his invisible hand working behind the scenes.

The intentional absence of direct mention of God in the book of Esther also has the intended effect of highlighting the pivotal role of the heroic actions of Esther and Mordecai. Although God was working providentially behind the scenes to provide the opportunities for Esther and Mordecai to intervene on behalf of their fellow Jews, all the divinely open doors would have come to naught if God's chosen instruments (Esther and Mordecai) had not acted. So, the book of Esther also teaches us that God's people must act with courage to do what is right in a hostile world even when divine guidance is not as clear as we might wish. But those who seek God will be given enough wisdom both to discern and to do what is right in difficult situations.

This book is filled with situations in which the opposite takes place from what was expected—and always in a way that benefits God's people in the end. To be sure, life is filled with unexpected events that bring difficulty into our lives, but Esther reminds us that God is always at work, and in the end he will ultimately reverse every wrong.

START YOUR JOURNEY

- Since the story unfolds in nine episodes, consider reading one each day (see outline above). Watch for (1) the way the plot unfolds through unexpected twists and turns leading to the final resolution, and (2) the way the main characters—especially Esther—develop.

- As you read, try to identify the ordinary, seemingly insignificant events God providentially used in significant ways to bring about an extraordinary outcome. Ask God to help you see how he is working in the everyday events in your life as well.

- Observe the crucial role of the human agents (Mordecai and Esther) who not only sensed the presence of divine providence but took bold initiative to act upon the divinely appointed opportunities set before them. Ask God to give you the wisdom to see the divinely appointed opportunities that he is setting before you to serve him as well.

- Recognize the ways that Esther points forward to the deliverance that Jesus brings. In what ways is Esther's role as a deliverer of her people a type of Christ as deliverer?

GOING DEEPER

"Lessons from the Book of Esther: Of Kings and Casseroles"

— Charles R. Swindoll —

Who of us has not longed for a word from God, searched for a glimpse of his power, or yearned for the reassurance of his presence, only to feel that he seems absent from the moment? Maybe even unconcerned. Yet later, we realize how very present he was all along. Though God may at times seem distant, and though he's invisible to us, he's always invincible. This is the main lesson of the book of Esther. Though absent by name from the pages of this particular book of Jewish history, God is present in every scene and in the movement of every event, until he ultimately brings everything to a marvelous climax as he proves himself Lord of his people, the Jews.

Esther was an unknown, orphaned young woman whose life had absolutely no connection with the most powerful man in the Persian Empire. Yet God, in his providential tapestry, was weaving these two unrelated lives together.

The book begins by telling us that the king gave a banquet: "He held a feast in the third year of his reign for all his officials and staff, the army of Persia and Media, the nobles, and the officials from the provinces. He displayed the glorious wealth of his kingdom and the magnificent splendor of his greatness for a total of 180 days" (Esth 1:3–4).

Can you believe that? A 180-day banquet! We're talking six full months of banqueting, which makes today's celebrity blowouts look like stingy potlucks! As if this weren't enough, the king held a second banquet. But then something happened. One of those unexpected but pivotal moments that change everything: "On the seventh day, when the king was feeling good from the wine, Ahasuerus commanded . . . the seven eunuchs who personally served him . . . to bring Queen Vashti before him with her royal crown. He wanted to show off her beauty to the people and the officials, because she was very beautiful" (1:10–11).

By now the king was drunk. And while in his inebriated state, he decided to show off another of his prizes: the physical beauty of his queen. "But Queen Vashti refused to come at the king's command that was delivered by his eunuchs. The king became furious and his anger burned within him" (1:12).

It was never God's design that a wife submit to her husband's evil desires. In King Ahasuerus's case, this sinful act took the form of desiring to display her before those who had nothing in mind but lust. And Vashti refused.

If I may cut to the chase, four words will suffice: Exit Vashti; enter Esther.

What you have to keep in mind is that Esther doesn't have the foggiest idea that any of this is going on; she knows nothing of the events transpiring in the royal palace. She also knows nothing yet about this "royal edict" which will set events in motion that will totally change her own life. Is she in for a surprise!

This is the wonder of God's sovereignty. Working behind the scenes, he is moving and pushing and rearranging events and changing minds until he brings out of even the most carnal and secular of settings a decision that will set his perfect plan in place. Elsewhere outside the palace, God's hand prepares to move the heart of the king like a channel of water. Esther 2:5–6 says, "In the fortress of Susa, there was a Jewish man named

Mordecai son of Jair, son of Shimei, son of Kish, a Benjaminite. Kish had been taken into exile from Jerusalem with the other captives when King Nebuchadnezzar of Babylon took King Jeconiah of Judah into exile."

Mordecai is totally unrelated to the king and the Persian kingdom. He's a Jew living out his years in exile. He's also raising his orphaned cousin, Hadassah: "Mordecai was the legal guardian of his cousin Hadassah (that is, Esther), because she had no father or mother. The young woman had a beautiful figure and was extremely good-looking. When her father and mother died, Mordecai had adopted her as his own daughter" (2:7).

This is the first reference to Esther, and already we've learned two things about her. She was orphaned, and she has grown up to become a young woman of incredible beauty. The original text is colorful, "beautiful in form and lovely to look at." Before long she will hear, "There she goes—Miss Persia." And she will win the lonely king's heart. It will be the classic example of the old proverb "he pursued her until she captured him." But at this point, she knows nothing about palace politics or a lonely king or what the future holds for her. She is simply living out the rather uneventful days of her young life, having not the slightest inkling that she will one day be crowned the most beautiful woman in the kingdom as well as the new queen of Persia. Later as she risks her life to use her influence with the king, God will guide her to save her people. My, how God works!

Woven through the tapestry of this wonderful story, we find at least three timeless lessons.

First, *God's plans are not hindered when the events of the world are carnal or secular.* He is as much at work in the Oval Office as he is in your pastor's study. He is as much at work in other parts of the world, like Iran or China or the Middle East, as he is in North America. To doubt that is to draw boundaries around his sovereign control.

Second, *God's purposes are not frustrated by moral or marital failures.* Isn't that encouraging? Force yourself to imagine the debauchery of that banquet hall. The vulgarity and obscenity of the jokes. The lust in the mind of King Ahasuerus when he wanted to display his wife for the carnal pleasure of himself and his friends. The decision to divorce Vashti because she wouldn't cooperate. Yet, in spite of all that, God's purposes were not frustrated. And neither are they in your life. How do I know that? Because he is a God who applies grace to the long view of life.

Third, *God's people are not excluded from high places because of handicap or hardship*. Esther was a Jewish woman exiled in a foreign land. She was an orphan. She was light-years removed from Persian nobility. Yet none of that kept God from exalting her to the position where he wanted her.

Where are you today in your journey? Are you discounting the significance of your days? Sighing rather than singing? Wondering what good can come from all your struggles? The kids you can't handle? A marriage that lacks harmony? Pressures that seem to have no purpose? God's hand is not so short that it can't save, nor his ear so heavy that he can't hear. He is at work in your life this very moment. He specializes in turning the mundane into the meaningful. He not only moves in unusual ways; he also moves on uneventful days. He's just as involved in the mundane events as he is in the miraculous. As one of my friends used to say, "God moves among the casseroles."

In the midst of our usual days, we must remain pure and committed to the things of God and his work in our lives, even as we remain sensitive to his hand moving in carnal, secular, even drunken places. Only then can we bring to our broken world the hope it so desperately needs. Esther does that, but equally important, you can do that too. Starting today, this no-big-deal day that seems so mundane, so commonplace, so full of, well . . . casseroles.[1]

---

[1] Adapted from Charles R. Swindoll, "Lessons from the Book of Esther: Of Kings and Casseroles," *Kindred Spirit* 23, no. 1 (spring 1999:12–14.). © 1999 Dallas Theological Seminary.

JOB

SNAPSHOT

Are you going through trials? Facing a chronic disease? Have you lost your possessions in a disaster? Or—worse—lost a loved one? These real-life struggles can make us question God's goodness, power, and wisdom. We may be tempted to find some cause-and-effect explanation for our suffering . . . or blame God for it all. The book of Job may not answer all your "Why" questions, but it will give you deeper insight into the one we can trust through it all.

ORIENTATION

Date: Likely by the 6th century BC

Authorship: Unknown

Audience: Unspecified, but application to all people throughout history.

Outline: 1. Prologue: God Allows Satan to Afflict Job (1–2)

                   2. Job Laments and Wishes for Death (3)

                   3. The Speeches: The Friends' Accusations and Job's Rebuttals (4–31)

4. Elihu's Speech concerning Sanctification in Suffering (32–37)
5. The Yahweh Speeches (38–42)
6. Epilogue: God Rebukes the Three Friends and Praises Job (42)

YOU ARE HERE

Episode 3: Promise and Hope

As the first of five books of Wisdom literature, Job presents its profound message on the real human struggle with suffering in the styles of narrative, poetry, and dialogue.

EXPLORING JOB

The book of Job starts with an introduction that characterizes Job as "a man of complete integrity, who feared God and turned away from evil" (1:1). Then the antagonist, Satan, appears in the angelic meeting in heaven, where God questions Satan regarding his activities (vv. 6–12). The implication is that Satan had been searching for someone to devour. The plot thickens when God suggests Satan consider how upright is his godly servant, Job. Satan claims that the only reason Job fears God is because God has a hedge of protection around him and has blessed him materially (vv. 9–11). So, God allows Satan to test Job by taking all that Job has, including his children. Despite all this, Job doesn't sin. Instead, he praises God with the famous phrase: "The Lord gives, and the Lord takes away. Blessed be the name of the Lord" (v. 21). This verse raises one of the most challenging interpretive issues in the book. God didn't take anything away from Job, Satan did—with God's permission. So, how should we understand God's relationship to the problem of evil and unjust suffering in the world?

The book of Job isn't really given to answer the question, Why does God let bad things happen to people? It's really about continuing to trust in the goodness and greatness of God even in the midst of deep pain and unanswerable questions. Job represents "every" believer who has struggled to stay afloat in a quagmire of questions. Job teaches us that we worship God because of who he is, not because of material health or wealth (Job 1–2).

In chapter 3, Job laments over his suffering, not knowing why God is allowing him to go through it all. In chapters 4–29, Job's three friends show up and, one after another, they engage in a series of poetic discourses basically trying to explain why it is that Job is suffering these things. Remember, none of them know the behind-the-scenes reality of Satan's hand in the matter, and neither does Job. And none know God's overarching plan. These friends, then, represent human attempts at theologizing in the face of the problem of evil. The first friend, Eliphaz, states that Job is reaping what he sowed. The second, Bildad, says Job is suffering because his children had sinned (8:4). The third, Zophar, accuses Job of concealing secret sin (11:13–14): if Job would just admit it and repent, God would restore his health (vv. 15–19). When a fourth figure, Elihu, shows up, his discourse wrestles with how suffering leads to our sanctification (Job 32–37).[1]

Finally, as if he's had enough hearing mortals wax eloquently in half-truths and ignorance, God shows up. He reminds Job and his friends that God alone has the power and wisdom to know and do what is good. Job isn't qualified to demand a trial with God. In fact, real wisdom is recognizing you can't know everything (Job 38–41). Job sees God in his power and glory and realizes his error (38:1–3; 40:3–5; 42:1–6). And Job's friends, despite their rousing reasoning, are rebuked by the Lord, who says, to Eliphaz, "I am angry with you and your two friends, for you have not spoken the truth about me" (42:7).

In the end, God never does answer the people's questions—our questions. He never submits to the interrogation of Job or provides a bullet-point solution to the "problem of evil." Instead, he vindicates his own

---

[1] Larry Waters, "Elihu's Categories of Suffering from Job 32–37," *Bibliotheca Sacra* 166, no. 664 (Oct–Dec 2009): 405–20.

power, wisdom, and goodness and restores Job's health and prosperity (Job 42:7–17). In the story, Job never really learns why he was suffering, but he is content to know that God is great, God is good, and he is with him through his suffering (vv. 1–6). In the course of the book, we also catch glimpses of important theological themes: forgiveness (14:16–17), resurrection (19:26–27), and a day of judgment when a redeemer will appear on the earth (19:25). Many see these as pointing forward to God's ultimate answer to the problem of evil: the person and work of Jesus Christ.

START YOUR JOURNEY

- Beware of retribution or compensation theology—sometimes referred to as "karma." Quite often we experience suffering and loss simply because we live in a fallen world. And even though God, in his vast wisdom, allows these things in our lives, we may never know precisely why. We must learn to trust him in the midst of the storms of life.

- Be careful not to rest your theology too heavily on the words of Job's friends, as God declares later that they "have not spoken the truth" about him (42:7). Scripture reports faithfully what people say, but what mere humans say is not always completely true. Focus your attention on God's words in Job. As you study the book of Job, summarize what they reveal about his power, purposes, and personality.

- Though Rom 8:28 affirms that "all things work together for the good of those who love God," this doesn't mean those "things" will be pleasurable or good. Nor does it mean we will always understand exactly how they work together for good. Nor does it rule out the possibility that we will not experience the good in this life. The book of Job teaches that the righteous will one day be vindicated, but its future hope also reminds us that the day of vindication may not come until resurrection and reward at Christ's return.

GOING DEEPER

"Why Does a Good God Allow Suffering?"

— Kenneth O. Gangel —

The headlines screamed out at me from the front page of the *Dallas Morning News*: "Rescue Teams Search Tornado Debris." Subtitles reminded readers of the "23 still missing in Central Texas," "Death toll at 30," and "Survivors hang on every scrap of news." Details of the tragedy in Jarrell, Texas, captured the spotlight in the national news for more than a week. Where fifty homes once stood on the flat Texas prairie, none remained. Nearly 10 percent of the town's citizens lost their lives.

If God is good, why would he allow a tornado to level Jarrell?

Millions have pondered that kind of question as they faced other natural disasters, family tragedies, and personal despair. Years ago, Rabbi Harold Kushner leaped to fame with his book *When Bad Things Happen to Good People* by emphasizing that we have only two options to explain such events. Either God is not good and our Judeo-Christian theology has been sadly misinformed, or God is good but quite incapable of handling events in a world gone mad. Kushner opts for the second choice, holding on to God's love while dethroning his power. He asks, "Are you capable of forgiving and loving God even when you have found out that He is not perfect, even when He has let you down and disappointed you by permitting bad luck and sickness and cruelty in His world, and permitting some of those things to happen to you?"[1]

But Christians who know their Bibles cannot wander down the Rabbi's trail, as attractive as it might seem in times of tragedy. Indeed, few Christians lack an intellectual sense of God's power and presence. The difficulty comes in trying to transfer that knowledge into practical and emotional reality during times of crisis.

None of that explains why God allows suffering, pain, and heartbreak in a world he claims to control. Natural disasters and personal tragedy defy explanation, particularly when we stand in the quagmire of grief. Most of them contain riddles we cannot answer until we get to heaven. But one principle stands firm to those who believe God's Word: through every tragic experience God calls us to look up and trust him with the outcome, however bizarre it might seem at the time.

But what about prayer? Didn't Hezekiah ask God for a longer life, a request honored with fifteen more years (2 Kgs 20)? Yes. But we may also assume that James cried out to God in prison (Acts 12) only to die at the hand of King Herod. For reasons we often do not understand, God sometimes chooses to heal or save his people on the basis of prayer . . . and sometimes he chooses not to.

Perhaps the financial blood drains out of a business and a Christian goes bankrupt. A believer may lose her job or get sued. Marriages break up, or children take drugs. Why does God allow such things to happen? Perhaps the Joseph epic in the last fourteen chapters of Genesis can help us remember the struggles of life, even when maliciously caused by other people (or by our own stupidity), cannot thwart God's ultimate goals. Solid believers hold on to the doctrine of God's sovereignty, which simply means, "God knows what he's doing and he's doing it."

It may help us to realize our Lord faced terrible personal grief before he was nailed to the cross, even though his perfect understanding of

---

[1] Harold S. Kushner, *When Bad Things Happen to Good People*, 20th anniversary ed. (New York: Schocken, 2001), 198.

God's will surely had all the pieces of the Father's plan well in place. Mark tells us, "He began to be deeply distressed and troubled. He said to them, 'I am deeply grieved to the point of death'" (Mark 14:33–34). The possibility of facing death horrified Jesus Christ.

Why does God allow pain and suffering?

Though we too often utter the words as a cliché, biblical truth assures us that God's plan for our lives may at times seem incomprehensible and desperately painful, but it will always work out for our own good. Jesus's sorrow in the Garden of Gethsemane turned into his death on a cross. But that awful tragedy gave way to resurrection and glory, defeating Satan and opening the doors of heaven to all who trust Christ for salvation.

The people of Jarrell, Texas, struggled with the loss of property but genuinely grieved over the loss of life. Contrary to what some contemporary experts suggest, death is not a normal part of life, it is an enemy destined for ultimate destruction by the King of life. In the deepest darkness of the "last enemy" (1 Cor 15:26), when we face the death of a loved one or even find ourselves on the precipice of eternity, we must grab hold of Jesus's words: "I am the resurrection and the life. The one who believes in me, even if he dies, will live. Everyone who lives and believes in me will never die" (John 11:25–26).

Where is God when we need him?

Precisely where he always has been—in his heaven taking complete charge of everything that happens in his world (Ps 103:19) and present with us in our suffering by his Spirit (Heb 13:5). We don't have to understand God's plan, for it often may not make sense to our limited, finite, human logic. In tragedy, our response to the omnipotent King of heaven must echo the attitude of those brave young men in the book of Daniel: Our God is able to deliver us from any suffering. But even if he chooses not to, we will still serve him.[2]

---

[2] Adapted from Kenneth O. Gangel, "Why Does a Good God Allow Suffering?," *Kindred Spirit* 21, no. 3 (fall 1997): 4–5. © 1997. Dallas Theological Seminary.

PSALMS

SNAPSHOT

When we think about the elements of modern worship, many things come to mind—instruments, choirs, raised hands, voices singing in harmony, projected words on a screen, and, sometimes, a worn hymnal in the seatback pocket of the pew. Worship throughout the ages has taken many forms. But if we were to imagine ancient worship in book form, we'd capture the essence of the 150 poetic songs and prayers collected in the Psalms—the *original* praise and worship.

ORIENTATION

Date: Most psalms were written at the time of David, Asaph, and Solomon (about the 10th century BC), but the book spans close to 1000 years, between the time of Moses to Ezra.

Authors: As a collection of 150 poems and songs, this book is one of the few to name multiple authors. The most prominent are David (73 psalms), Asaph (12 psalms), Solomon (1–2 psalms), and Moses (Psalm 90).

Audience: Original Israelite worshipers

Outline: 1. Book 1 (Psalms 1–41)

2. Book 2 (Psalms 42–72)
3. Book 3 (Psalms 73–89)
4. Book 4 (Psalms 90–106)
5. Book 5 (Psalms 107–150)

YOU ARE HERE

Episode 4: The Kingdom Rises → Episode 6: Return from Exile

One of the largest books of the Old Testament, Psalms is the second of the five books of "Wisdom" and is organized into five books.

EXPLORING PSALMS

As soon as we step into this book, it's important to remember that the collection was written by a diverse group of authors across many centuries—with about half of the songs written by King David. As such, the psalms contain a variety of historical, theological, and practical truths about the work of God and condition of his people as well as the mysterious nature of his inherent power, majesty, wisdom, and grace. The most basic Old Testament truths are found scattered through the hymnbook, including elements of monotheism (Psalms 81–83, 86), creation (Psalms 8, 19, 139), sin/fall (Psalms 19, 66) God's covenant (Psalms 25, 78, 89, 105), and future hope (Psalms 22, 24, 51, 78). The book of Psalms contains much more than fancy poetry and songs of praise, as it truly reflects deep theological truth!

The book presents a wide variety of psalms, with some being set to music and others taking a more poetic tone. Some of the more common types of psalms are

- **Psalms of Lament:** circumstances in which the worshipper cries out to God during a very difficult, overwhelming situation.
- **Psalms of Praise:** hymns of celebration and joy, sometimes in response to God's character or actions.

- **Psalms of Thanksgiving:** personal or corporate gratitude for God's blessing and work in the life of the author or community.
- **Psalms of Wisdom:** often containing themes from the other books of Poetry—Job, Proverbs, Ecclesiastes, and Song of Solomon.
- **Psalms of the Messiah:** pointing forward in hope to the coming Messiah, the descendant of David, and his divine rule as the fulfillment of God's promises.
- **Psalms of History and Law:** remembering past events or reflecting on God's laws, which gives assurance of God's faithfulness, protection, and provision.

The psalms were often used by the early church to teach people how to pray, worship, and give glory to God through song.[1] And many churches today have set the psalms to music and use them in their worship. This makes sense, because the collection of these songs and poems stands as a constant reminder that we worship a faithful and mighty God. In fact, this collection should drive believers to their knees in personal prayer and worship in light of God's goodness and power, grace and mercy. In both good and bad days, we're called as believers to worship our faithful God, and the wide variety of psalms present us with many different ways to approach God today. Though each psalm represents a different context, desire, intention, author, and conviction, readers today will find solace and comfort through these powerful hymns and poems.

Many of the psalms are directly messianic, meaning they look forward to the coming Messiah. Others are indirectly prophetic of the Messiah, often having direct application to the life of the writer but also pointing toward the ultimate King. Yet all the psalms should be understood in light of the person and work of Christ. Since Jesus experienced the full range of

---

[1] Craig A. Blaising, "Prepared for Prayer: The Psalms in Early Christian Worship," in *Forgotten Songs: Reclaiming the Psalms for Christian Worship*, ed. C. Richard Wells and Ray Van Neste (Nashville: B&H, 2012), 55–56.

human emotions, he embodied the theology of the psalms. And since he is the coming King, the messianic psalms point forward to him.

START YOUR JOURNEY

- The twentieth-century German theologian Dietrich Bonhoeffer wrote, "If we want to read and to pray the prayers of the Bible, and especially the Psalms, we must not, therefore, first ask what they have to do with us, but what they have to do with Jesus Christ."[2] Bonhoeffer advised reading one psalm per day, which he called "praying the psalms."[3] As you read and reflect on the words, pray the psalm as an act of worship, reflecting on what it teaches about God, about humanity, and especially about how this shines light on the God-man, Jesus Christ.

- Jesus used the psalms in his life and ministry. In fact, Christ's last words, "My God, my God, why have you abandoned me?" (Matt 27:46) and "Father, into your hands I entrust my spirit" (Luke 23:46) are direct quotations from the psalms (Ps 22:1 and Ps 31:5). In your darkest and most glorious moments alike, take comfort and solace in this powerful book of prayers.

---

[2] Dietrich Bonhoeffer, *Psalms: The Prayer Book of the Bible*, trans James H. Burtness (Minneapolis: Augsburg Fortress, 1970), 14.

[3] Bonhoeffer, 17.

GOING DEEPER

"When God Is Silent"

— Roy B. Zuck —

A little boy prayed, "Lord, please make Boulder the capital of Colorado."

His friend asked, "Why did you pray that?"

"Because," the boy answered, "that's the answer I put on my exam."

Obviously, God might not answer that prayer. But what about legitimate prayers? Sometimes we make requests we think are in line with what God wants, but he seems silent. He seems to ignore us. We feel he has gone off and left us. He is distant, far off, unconcerned, and has abandoned us—or so it seems.

David prayed, "My God, my God, why have you abandoned me? Why are you so far from my deliverance? . . . My God, I cry by day, but you do not answer" (Ps 22:1–2). Many Christians feel that way today:

> "Why doesn't he heal me?"
> "Why doesn't God bring back my wayward son?"
> "Why did God take my spouse to heaven?"

When we feel like that, Psalm 22 offers us a guide through the dark.

Since some of the verses in this psalm seem like they are referring to Christ, some say all of it is prophetic of Christ. Yet it seems better to see the psalm as referring first to David's experiences, with many of the statements then being *applied* to Christ. In other words, the psalm is recording primarily the experience of David, who was suffering at the hands of wicked men. The psalm shows us a progression of response to physical and emotional pain. These are steps David took, and they are also steps Jesus took.

Tell God your problem (vv. 1–2; 6–8; 11–18). Twice in the first verse David asked, "Why?" Yet three times in the first two verses he said, "My God." Even though he wondered why God seemed absent, he voiced his problem to the Lord. On the cross Jesus would voice these same words. He felt forsaken by God the Father as he "bore our sins in his body on the tree" (1 Pet 2:24). And Isaiah wrote, "The LORD has punished him for the iniquity of us all" (Isa 53:6).

David expressed in vivid, graphic terms the reasons he felt abandoned by God (vv. 1–2; 11–18), many of which apply to Jesus's suffering as well. David was brutally honest in telling God that it didn't seem as if his prayers were being heard. Yet, though he felt abandoned by God, David did not denounce his Lord. We, too, should tell God our problem, even telling him that he seems remote and aloof.

Remember God's faithfulness (vv. 3–5, 9–10). Though God seemed distant, David knew God is holy and can be trusted. Though God was silent, he is still sovereign. In verses 3–5, David used the word *you* six times in referring to God. This shows that in his agony David focused on God and his holiness. Though puzzled, he still praised him. David mentioned that his own "fathers" (ancestors) put their trust in God, and so he wanted God to help him, too. "You didn't forsake them, so why forsake me?"

Then David reminded the Lord that he had nurtured David right from the moment of his birth; so why should be abandon him now? "Lord, you were faithful in the past, so be faithful now" (cf. vv. 9–10).

Keep praying (vv. 19–21). David went on to voice several requests to God. He asked God to be not far off from him, to help him, to deliver him, to rescue him, and to save him. In referring to dogs, lions, and oxen, he reversed the order of these three animals from the order in which he mentioned them in verses 12–13 and 16.

Praise Him (vv. 22–31). Determined to praise the Lord (v. 22), David called on Israel to praise, fear, and revere God (v. 23). David was sure that God does see those who are suffering and he hears their cry for help (v. 24). He said he would worship the Lord (v. 25), and then he called on the poor and the rich to praise him (vv. 26–29), including all the families of the earth (v. 27). Even people not yet born would praise him (vv. 30–31).

In a storm at sea, apparent disaster was ahead. The son of the author Robert Louis Stevenson was on board. So he went to the captain's cabin and asked if something could be done about the bad situation. Just then the pilot turned and smiled. Stevenson's son went back to the men and said, "I have good news."

"What do you mean?" they asked.

He said, "I've just seen the pilot's face, and that's enough."

We, too, have seen the face of our heavenly pilot, and it tells us enough to know all will be well.[1]

---

[1] Adapted from Roy B. Zuck, "When God Is Silent," *Kindred Spirit* 36, no. 1 (Spring 2012): 4–5. © 2012 Dallas Theological Seminary.

PROVERBS

SNAPSHOT

Caught in an ethical dilemma? Torn by competing voices of practical advice? Not sure where to turn for direction along life's twisting, turning path? The book of Proverbs is like an always-on navigation system of practical living for the people of God. Its clear, memorable sayings lead readers to live wise, godly lives while avoiding the pitfalls of folly and sin.

ORIENTATION

Date: Spanning 11th–7th centuries BC

Authors: Numerous authors, including Solomon (Prov 1:1–22:16; 25–29), Agur (Prov 30), Lemuel (Prov 31), anonymous "wise ones" (Prov 22:17–24:34)

Audience: All people of all times

Outline: 1. The Preface (1:1–7)
2. The Words of Solomon on Wisdom's Value (1:8–9:13)
3. The Proverbs of Solomon (10:1–22:16)
4. The Sayings of the Wise Ones (22:17–24:34)
5. The Proverbs of Solomon Collected by Hezekiah's Men (25–29)

6. The Words of Agur (30)
7. The Words of Lemuel (31:1–9)
8. The Noble Wife (31:10–31)

YOU ARE HERE

Episode 4: The Kingdom Rises → Episode 5: Division and Judgment

As the third book in the section of Scripture called the Poetical Books, Proverbs shares a lot in common with Job, Psalms, Ecclesiastes, and Song of Songs in both themes and structure.

EXPLORING PROVERBS

As soon as we step into this book, we encounter a sort of signpost pointing readers to seven purposes of Proverbs:

1. To know wisdom and teaching (1:2)
2. To discern sayings of understanding (1:2)
3. To receive instruction in wise behavior, righteousness, justice, and fairness (1:3)
4. To give prudence to the unlearned and unskilled (1:4)
5. To give knowledge and discretion to novices and youth (1:4)
6. To increase the learning and counsel of the experienced and knowledgeable (1:5)
7. To aid in grasping the significance of proverbs, parables, and life's puzzles (1:6)

The profound-but-pithy statements in the book of Proverbs are among the most practical—and sometimes most puzzling—of the Bible. The book begins with Solomon addressing his son regarding the desperate need for wisdom—underscoring the need for passing practical instruction from one generation to the next (1:8–7:27). Then the author personifies Wisdom as a virtuous woman beckoning people to accompany her on life's journey

(8:1–9:18). To join her is to avoid the woman of folly, whose end is destruction. Then the collections of proverbs—collected from far and wide—fill the rest of the book (10:1–31:31). In some way, all the proverbs in the book contrast wisdom and folly, righteousness and wickedness, the way of life and the way of death. The reader is called to choose the right and avoid the wrong.

The sayings in Proverbs should be regarded as general principles or guidelines, not as absolute promises. Applying the wisdom of Proverbs will not guarantee a life without hardship or calamity, but it will protect a person from a lot of the conditions and situations that lead to preventable pain. And living in line with its wisdom will make the troubles of this life easier to bear. One commentator writes:

> As brief maxims, the verses in Proverbs are distilled, to-the-point sentences about life. They boil down, crystallize, and condense the experiences and observations of the writers. The brief but concentrated nature of the maxims cause [*sic*] their readers to reflect on their meanings. They tell what life is like and how life should be lived. In a terse, no-words-wasted fashion, some statements in Proverbs relate what is commonly observed in life; others recommend or exhort how life should be lived. And when advice is given, a reason for the counsel usually follows.[1]

In the New Testament, Jesus Christ—God the Son made flesh—is Wisdom incarnate. Not merely adorned with wisdom or characterized by virtue, Jesus is the standard of wisdom. As such, he embodies everything the book of Proverbs exhorts. And beyond this, the Spirit of Wisdom who indwells believers also empowers them for virtuous living. In this way, the Proverbs point us to Christ as the ultimate "wise one" while Christ himself exemplifies ultimate wisdom living.

---

[1] Sid S. Buzzell, "Proverbs," in *The Bible Knowledge Commentary: An Exposition of the Scriptures*, ed. John F. Walvoord and Roy B. Zuck, vol. 1 (Wheaton: Victor Books, 1985), 904.

START YOUR JOURNEY

- It may appear the various proverbs are thrown together at random, but isn't that how life is? We never know what obstacles we'll face on life's journey. Sharpening our wisdom in a variety of areas will prepare us for whatever may come.

- Because Proverbs has thirty-one chapters, many have committed to reading about a chapter a day in order to read through the book once a month as part of their daily devotional reading.

- Don't rush through these proverbs. Think through them. They're not meant to be read as a code of laws to obey, but as general truths about life to ponder—often best understood through experience.

- Try studying through Proverbs with a mixed group of older, more experienced believers, and younger believers starting out in the Christian life. Adding the dynamic of life experience to the discussion will lead to much fruit.

ECCLESIASTES

SNAPSHOT

Like an unquenchable thirst, the attainment of satisfaction and meaning in this life often seems just out of reach. The wise teacher of Ecclesiastes takes his readers on a journey through a barren landscape draped in shadow—a life oriented to wisdom, work, and pleasure as ends in themselves. An occasional oasis points to a reality beyond the devastation and despair that surround us, but we will find true satisfaction and meaning only in our Creator.

ORIENTATION

Date: 10th century BC
Author: Unnamed, but traditionally attributed to Solomon
Audience: The nation of Israel, or more generally, humanity
Outline:
1. Everything is Meaningless (1:1–11)
2. Searching for Meaning (1:12–2:26)
3. Meaning and Time (3:1–15)
4. Injustice and Oppression (3:16–4:16)
5. Humility and Riches (5:1–6:12)
6. Wisdom vs. Folly (7:1–8:17)
7. The Harsh Reality of Death (9:1–18)

8. Practical Wisdom (10:1–20)
9. The Journey Home (11:1–12:7)
10. The End of the Matter (12:8–14)

YOU ARE HERE

Episode 4: The Kingdom Rises

As the fourth book in the section of Scripture called the Wisdom books, Ecclesiastes shares a great deal in common with Proverbs in its form and structure.

EXPLORING ECCLESIASTES

Solomon spends the bulk of his words in the book of Ecclesiastes exploring the human search for satisfaction and meaning outside of God. However, Solomon ultimately concludes that human beings will find real meaning and satisfaction in life only through their Creator.

The book's twice-repeated theme serves as a pair of gloomy bookends: "'Absolute futility,' says the Teacher. 'Absolute futility. Everything is futile'" (1:2; 12:8). This melancholy cry leads immediately into the book's classic and poetic opening (1:3–11), a series of images largely drawn from nature that highlight life in a never-ending hamster wheel of despair: sun up, sun down; tide in, tide out; has been, will be.

The opening poem sets up the bulk of the book's contents, as Solomon describes a fruitless search for meaning in diverse areas of human existence. Over and over again, the author seeks satisfaction in some human experience, ultimately encountering only emptiness every time. While he grows great in wisdom (1:16) and wisdom is better than folly (2:13), the result is meaningless (v. 15). He pursues pleasure through consumption and achievement (vv. 3–9), but the result is meaninglessness (v. 11). The wise man also seeks satisfaction in work (v. 24), justice (3:16–22), and riches (5:8–20), only to find emptiness, oppression, and affliction. And what's the end result of this search? *No human pursuit provides ultimate satisfaction for human beings.*

In the midst of this harrowing journey through human failure, Solomon mercifully includes multiple oases along the way—moments that remind us of a reality that transcends the shadows and despair of fruitless, human-centric searches for meaning. The most substantive of these oases appears in chapter 3 and happens to be the book's most famous passage. Solomon places the events that occur in our existence within a broader framework: "There is an occasion for everything, and a time for every activity under heaven" (3:1). As Solomon lists experience after experience, he makes clear that life doesn't consist of a random series of events, but that God has set everything in its proper time and place. God doesn't offer a blanket endorsement of all events, as Solomon reminds us that "God will call the past to account" (v. 15, NIV). God will judge evil, even as his good creation will endure forever (v. 14).

After a restatement of the theme in 12:8, Ecclesiastes concludes with an epilogue that shines brightly against the shadows that stretch across the rest of the book. Solomon affirms that wise words such as those we find in Ecclesiastes come from the one Shepherd (12:11). That Jesus takes on this title for himself (John 10:11), draws our thoughts to the source of wisdom, the Word of God through whom we come to know the Father (1:1–18). Thus, as Solomon concludes with "Fear God and keep his commands" (Eccl 12:13), we recognize no greater way to accomplish this than by laying down our lives for others, just as our Good Shepherd has done for us.

START YOUR JOURNEY

- Slowly read through Ecclesiastes a chapter at a time. As you go, spend a bit of time writing down impressions and questions for further reflection. Understanding the details of this difficult book requires mastering the big picture and flow of the teacher's argument. Be patient with yourself as you seek to understand the parts in light of the whole . . . especially on this book.

- Find the oases that dot the landscape of Ecclesiastes by listing every mention of God or the Creator. With each reference, reflect on what God provides for us or requires of us as we live in a fallen world.

- Ecclesiastes focuses on the despair that comes from seeking satisfaction in the things of this world rather than in God himself. List the exploits of the teacher in his own attempt to find peace and satisfaction "under the sun." Then consider what kinds of pursuits people embrace today in order to find satisfaction or meaning.

SONG OF SOLOMON

SNAPSHOT

Do you ever wonder about God's view of the romantic relationship between a man and a woman? While Gen 2:18–25 reveals that marriage was God's idea from creation, the Song of Solomon puts the divine stamp of approval on courtship and marriage as a gift from God to be celebrated!

ORIENTATION

Date: Most likely around the 10th century BC

Author: While some today regard the author as an anonymous female poet, Song of Solomon is traditionally attributed to King Solomon, as the title suggests

Audience: Originally, young women and men of ancient Israel, applicable to all

Outline: 1. Opening and Closing Love Lyrics (1:1–2:7; 8:1–14)

                2. Journey to the Countryside (2:8–17; 7:11–13)

                3. Seeking and Finding (3:1–5; 5:2–8)

                4. Introductory Query: "What Is He/She?" (5:9–6:3; 6:13–7:10)

5. Introductory Question: "Who Is This?" (3:6–11;
   6:10–12)
6. The Man's Description of Her Beauty: "You Are
   Lovely!" (4:1–5:1; 6:4–9)

YOU ARE HERE

Episode 4: The Kingdom Rises

In the traditional Christian canon, Song of Solomon (aka "Song of Songs"
or even "Canticles") is the last of five Wisdom books.

EXPLORING SONG OF SOLOMON

Many early interpreters in the church and synagogue felt uncomfortable with
the romantic tone and suggestiveness of the Song of Solomon. Assuming
Scripture focuses primarily on God, many read it as an allegory of Yahweh's
relationship with Israel or typology of Christ's relationship with the church.
However, the Song is most naturally read as divinely sanctioned love poetry
that celebrates God's gift of marriage given to humanity (Gen 2:18–25).

Some interpreters suggest the Song is a melodrama involving three
characters: a country maiden, her shepherd lover, and Solomon, the notori-
ous womanizer. According to this approach, the king abuses his power by
forcing the maiden into his harem, where she pines away for her true love.
After failing to win her affections, the king reluctantly allows the maiden
to return to the countryside where she reunites with the simple shepherd.
Others suggest the Song is a poetic narrative involving two characters: the
country maiden and King Solomon. According to this approach, the maiden
was his one true love before he later fell into polygamy. The Song traces
the development of their love story from courtship (1:2–2:17), betrothal
(3:1–5), wedding day and night (3:6–5:1), marital conflict (5:2–6:3) and
reconciliation (6:4–8:4), closing with an epilogue describing how it all
began (8:5–14).

The better view, though, suggests the Song is a collection of love lyrics consisting of both courtship and wedding songs. Rather than developing a narrative in linear fashion, the individual poems are arranged symmetrically. The opening and closing lyrics are courtship songs, while the central sets of lyrics are wedding songs of various kinds. This is reflected in the following:

A: Opening Love Lyrics—How It All Began (1:1–2:7)
B: Journey to the Countryside—the Courtship (2:8–17)
    C: Resolute Maiden Seeks and Finds—Betrothal Decided (3:1–5)
        E: Ascension of the Bride: "Who Is This Coming Up?" (3:6–11)
        F: Groom's Wedding Song—Part 1: "You Are Lovely!" (4:1–5:1)
    C: Pensive Bride Seeks but Does Not Find—Nuptials Delayed (5:2–8)
    D: Guests Prompt Her Praise: "What Is He that You Adjure Us?" (5:9–6:3)
        F: Groom's Wedding Song—Part 2: "You Are Lovely!" (6:4–9)
        E: Elevation of the Bride: "Who Is This Gazing Down?" (6:10–12)
    D: Guests Prompt His Praise: "What Is She that You Gaze on Her?" (6:13–7:10)
B: Journey to the Countryside—the Honeymoon (7:11–13)
A: Closing Love Lyrics—How It All Began (8:1–14)

The Song reminds us that marriage is blessed by God and is not a lower state of spirituality than celibacy. It celebrates the depth of intimacy that a man and woman who cherish one another may enjoy with God's blessing. While the Song is not embarrassed about sex, it handles it in a discreet manner. It suggests that sexual fulfillment is not the goal of marriage, but the result of treasuring one's spouse in a relationship of mutual respect, commitment, and appreciation. Compared to ancient Near Eastern love poetry,

the Song of Songs is tame and restrained. Although the couple long to consummate their love (e.g., 1:2–4; 8:1–2), they wait until their wedding night
(4:1–5:1). In fact, she thrice exhorts the "young women of Jerusalem" (who
function as literary surrogates for the readers) not to "awaken" love before
the proper time (2:7; 3:5; 8:4).

In contrast to poetic narrative, the Song consists entirely of poetic
speech. In contrast to ancient society, in which the male voice dominated
public speech, we hear the female voice most often throughout the Song,
poetically validating a woman's right to speak and be heard in courtship
and marriage. We hear her voice in dialogue with her beloved (e.g., 1:7–8,
12–14, 16–17; 2:1, 3), in soliloquy expressing her feelings (e.g., 1:2–4; 8:1–
2), in reports of her experiences (3:1–4; 5:2–7), and in admonitions to her
friends not to rush love (2:7; 3:5; 8:4). We also hear the young man's voice
praising her beauty, expressing his desire for her, as well as inviting her to
spend time with him (1:8–10, 15; 2:2, 10–14; 4:1–15; 5:2b; 6:4–9; 7:1–8).
Thus, rather than depicting sexual activity, the Song focuses primary attention on emotional intimacy.

START YOUR JOURNEY

- Resist the urge to spiritualize the Song by trying to make it merely
  an allegory of God's love for his people. Rather, read it as it wants
  to be read, as poetry of divinely sanctioned love. The Old and New
  Testaments do use marriage as an illustration of God's relationship
  with his people; and in that sense, Song of Solomon can inform
  our understanding of that spiritual relationship; our relationship to
  Jesus is pictured as a marriage, which means both the single and the
  married are in view in this song.

- As you read the Song, if married, think about how your own courtship or marriage can be transformed if you follow its example by
  cultivating an atmosphere of warmth, cherishing your partner,
  engaging in loving conversation, and spending time treasuring one
  another's presence.

GOING DEEPER

"What About the Apocrypha?"

— Michael J. Svigel and John Adair —

T he books known as "the Apocrypha" are additions to the Old Testament writings. They include Tobit, Judith, Wisdom, Sirach, Baruch, and 1 and 2 Maccabees as well as additional material in Esther and Daniel. Several of these works provide helpful historical information and contain inspiring stories. Thus, most Christians throughout history—including Protestant Reformers—considered the Apocrypha as worthy to be read. But should they be treated as inspired Scripture to be preached from the pulpit? This question has divided Christians for almost two millennia.

In the early Christian period (c. 100–500), the Christian Old Testament often included the books of the Apocrypha—sometimes regarded as inspired, sometimes not.[1] The reason for their inclusion in the libraries of early Christians was that Greek-speaking Gentile believers—who usually knew no Hebrew—used the Greek translation of the Old Testament known as the Septuagint. The Septuagint translation included not only the books regarded as inspired by the Jews but

---

[1] J. N. D. Kelly, *Early Christian Doctrines*, 5th rev. ed. (New York: HarperOne, 1978), 53.

also books regarded as "religiously edifying" though not inspired.[2] These books are what we call today the "Apocrypha" or "deutero-canonical" writings. When Gentile Christians received the Old Testament in their Greek translations, they also received these "extra" writings that Jews would have regarded as secondary sources. Some church leaders in this early Christian period were well informed regarding the history of the Septuagint's translation and its relationship to the Hebrew Old Testament. Around the year 170, the bishop Melito of Sardis (c. 110–180) reported that he had traveled to the Holy Land and there "learned accurately the books of the Old Testament."[3] The canon reported by Melito matches the Protestant Old Testament in content, with one exception—it lacks the book of Esther.[4] Melito's well-researched Old Testament canon did not include the Apocrypha.

Another example of the early Christian view of the Apocrypha is found in the *Catechetical Lectures* of Cyril of Jerusalem (c. 313–386). His list of Old Testament books matches that of Protestants, with the exception of the exclusion of Esther and the inclusion of the apocryphal Baruch, which was included as part of Jeremiah along with Lamentations. The rest of the Apocrypha were not included.[5] Melito and Cyril are not minority reports among the Eastern church fathers. The view among prominent fathers such as Athanasius of Alexandria (290–374) and Gregory of Nazianzus (330–390) "was that the deutero-canonical books should be relegated to a subordinate position outside the canon proper."[6]

It seems, though, the farther away churches were from the Holy Land and the original canon preserved by the Jews, the more likely church leaders were to embrace the Apocrypha. The Western churches, which

---

[2] Kelly, *Early Christian Doctrines*, 53.

[3] These words of Melito of Sardis come to us in quotations from Eusebius, *Church History* 4.26.14 (*NPNF*[2] 1:206).

[4] See F. F. Bruce, *The Canon of Scripture* (Downers Grove: InterVarsity, 1988), 70–71.

[5] Cyril of Jerusalem, *Catechetical Lectures* 4.35–36.

[6] Kelly, *Early Christian Doctrines*, 54–55.

eventually coalesced into what we call the Roman Catholic Church under the papacy, tended to regard the Apocrypha as canonical Scripture. However, Jerome (c. 347–420), who was responsible for the Latin Bible translation known as the Vulgate, spent considerable time in the Holy Land to learn Hebrew in service of his translation efforts. As a result, he came to the same conclusions as many Eastern fathers: "Books not in the Hebrew canon should be designated as apocryphal."[7] Yet Jerome's contemporary Augustine of Hippo (354–430) embraced the Apocrypha. F. F. Bruce notes, "Augustine's ruling supplied a powerful precedent for the western church from his own day to the Reformation and beyond."[8] Following Augustine, the Roman Catholic Church deviated from the original Jewish canon, and many Catholics seemed unconcerned by the hesitancy of many early fathers regarding the Apocrypha.

Throughout the medieval period, then, many in the Roman Catholic Church regarded the Apocrypha as authoritative Scripture. So did, with less dogmatism, the Eastern Orthodox churches—though East and West differed on which additional books should be included. This general acceptance grew without the support of a universal church council and without early, widespread, and consistent testimony of the early church fathers. Nevertheless, "a continuous succession of the more learned fathers in the West maintained the distinctive authority of the Hebrew Canon [without the Apocrypha] up to the period of the Reformation."[9] Those who rejected the Apocrypha as inspired Scripture included Pope Gregory the Great (540–604), the Venerable Bede (673–735), Hugh of St. Victor (1096–1141), William of Ockham (1288–1348), Cardinal Thomas Cajetan (1469–1534), and numerous others who "repeat with approval

---

[7] Carol A. Newsom, "Introduction to the Apocrypha/Deuterocanonical Books," in *The New Oxford Annotated Apocrypha: New Revised Standard Version*, ed. Michael D. Coogan et al., 5th ed. (Oxford: Oxford University Press, 2018), 5.

[8] Bruce, *Canon of Scripture*, 97.

[9] Brooke Foss Westcott, "Canon of Scripture, The," in *Dr. William Smith's Dictionary of the Bible*, vol. 1, rev. and ed. by H. B. Hackett and Ezra Abbot (New York: Hurd and Houghton, 1877), 363.

the decision of Jerome, and draw a clear line between the Canonical and Apocryphal books."[10]

Along with most of the Reformers, Martin Luther (1483–1546) sided with Jerome for historical and theological reasons.[11] However, Luther's German translation of the Bible as well as several other Protestant translations included the books in a separate category clearly marked as "Apocrypha."[12] Like the Jews and many Christians in the early church, the Reformers regarded the Apocrypha as informative and inspiring, but not as authoritative and inspired.

In direct response to the Protestants, the Roman Catholic Church's "Counter-Reformation" at the Council of Trent (1545–1563) established the Apocrypha as part of their Old Testament canon. The council decreed the Latin *translation* to be the final source of appeal in matters of doctrine, not the original Hebrew and Greek texts. Trent sided with Augustine rather than Jerome in the matter of the Apocrypha. Westcott notes, "This hasty and peremptory decree" was "unlike in its form to any catalogue before published."[13] That decree, on April 8, 1546, included Tobias, Judith, Wisdom of Solomon, Ecclesiasticus ("Wisdom of Sirach"), Baruch (an addition to Jeremiah), and 1 and 2 Maccabees.

In light of their content and the history of their use by Christians, the Apocrypha can and should be read as helpful for historical insight into the period between the Old and New Testaments. On the one hand, Bible-believing Christians should avoid a radical rejection of these writings; on the other hand, the Apocrypha should not be embraced as inspired Scripture.[14]

---

[10] Westcott, "Canon," 363.

[11] Euan Cameron, *The European Reformation*, 2nd ed. (Oxford: Oxford University Press, 2012), 165.

[12] Bruce, *Canon of Scripture*, 102–4.

[13] Westcott, "Canon," 363.

[14] This essay was adapted from John Adair and Michael J. Svigel, *Urban Legends of Church History: 40 Common Misconceptions* (Nashville: B&H Academic, 2020), 175–81. Used with permission.

ISAIAH

SNAPSHOT

When studying the Bible, it's easy to get lost in the many details of a passage. However, it's always necessary to keep the big picture in view. Of all the books in the Bible, the prophecy of Isaiah, perhaps more than any other, presents the big picture. It tells us about God's plan for Israel and the nations and has much to say about the Messiah's role in the outworking of God's purpose for the world.

ORIENTATION

Date: 8th century BC
Authors: Isaiah son of Amoz
Audience: Judah and Israel (including the future exiles)
Outline:
1. The Lord Purifies His Covenant People (1–12)
2. The Lord Judges the Nations of Isaiah's Time (13–23)
3. The Lord Establishes His Worldwide Rule over the Nations (24–27)
4. The Lord Judges and Restores His Covenant People (28–35)

5. Deliverance from Assyria and a Prophecy of Exile (36–39)
6. Isaiah Calls a Future Generation to Covenant Renewal (40–66)

YOU ARE HERE

Episode 5: Division and Judgment

The first of the Major Prophets, Isaiah gives a panorama of God's plan for the world, extending from his own time to the coming kingdom.

EXPLORING ISAIAH

The message of Isaiah can be summarized as follows: the Lord will fulfill his ideal for Israel by purifying his people through judgment and then restoring them to a renewed covenant relationship. He will establish Jerusalem (Zion) as the center of his worldwide kingdom and reconcile the once-hostile nations to himself.[1]

For the prophet, the Lord is first and foremost the "Holy One of Israel," a title that appears twenty-five times in the book and is rooted in Isaiah's vision of the holy God in his temple (6:1–13). The title and vision depict God as the transcendent Lord who rules from heaven and possesses moral authority over all people. His very character provides the standard for right and wrong, and he has the authority to demand that people live in accordance with this standard.

The first major section of the book encompasses chapters 1–39, in which Isaiah addresses his contemporary audience and discusses the threat posed by the Assyrian war machine. The Lord accuses his people of violating the Mosaic covenant by worshipping idols, mistreating one another, and

---

[1] Robert B. Chisholm Jr., "A Theology of Isaiah," in *A Biblical Theology of the Old Testament*, ed. Roy B. Zuck (Chicago: Moody, 1991), 305.

placing their trust in foreign alliances. The Lord will purify the covenant community through judgment by implementing the covenant curses (see Deut 28) and sending the people into exile.

But that's not the end of the story or the end of Israel. God will some-day restore his people to their land and establish an ideal Davidic king as ruler. This king's royal titles (Isa 9:6) depict him as an extraordinary military strategist who will be able to execute his plans because of divine enablement. His military ability will ensure the security and prosperity of the covenant community. The Lord's Spirit will enable him to rule wisely, and his reign will be characterized by justice and peace (11:1–9).

The Lord will demonstrate his sovereignty over the nations, especially the powerful Assyrian and Babylonian empires. He will judge all nations for their violation of God's universal laws (24:1–13) and the "everlasting cov-enant," possibly referring to the Noahic covenant (v. 5 KJV). Then, he will rule over all the world from Jerusalem. The nations will no longer go to war and will look to the Lord for guidance as they enjoy peace (2:2–4).

In chapters 40–66, the prophet, having predicted the exile (39:6–7), speaks to the future exiles as if present with them. He assures them that the Lord is infinitely superior to the false idol-gods of the nations and will deliver them from Babylon through the instrumentality of the Persian king Cyrus.

The Lord will also make provision for the sinful nation's spiritual res-toration through the atoning sacrifice of the suffering royal servant, who will mediate a new covenant with Israel. In fact, that Suffering Servant will embody a new, permanent covenant (55:3) to such a degree that God can say to him, "I will appoint you to be a covenant for the people" (49:8). He will also take the light of salvation and justice to the Gentiles, reminding us that the scope of God's redemptive work, even in the Old Testament prophets, goes well beyond Israel to the nations who will come to know the Lord.

The original audience of Isaiah had no name for this Suffering Servant who would one day be the Davidic king, and many Jewish readers had con-flicting understandings of that messianic figure. However, in the progress of revelation, we discover that Jesus the Messiah emerges in fulfillment of the ideal Davidic king of Isaiah 1–39 as well as the Suffering Servant and coming King of Isaiah 40–66.

START YOUR JOURNEY

- Many of Isaiah's prophecies pertain to the nations of his time and have already been fulfilled. So, it's important to know the history of the period, which is covered in most commentaries, study Bibles, and in histories of Israel.[2] Familiarizing yourself with this history will help you understand both the near and far fulfillments in Isaiah's prophecies.

- Isaiah contains many prophecies about Jesus the Messiah. Spend some time studying Isaiah's servant songs (42:1–9; 49:1–13; 50:4–11; 52:13–53:12) and then find where the New Testament quotes these passages. What do we learn about Jesus's ministry from these songs? Without using the New Testament, what can you say about the coming Messiah based on Isaiah?

- When reading Isaiah, it's important to ask the following questions: (1) What does the prophet teach us about God's character and how he relates to his people? (2) What does the prophet teach us about God's relationship to the nations?

---

[2] See, for example, Eugene H. Merrill, *Kingdom of Priests: A History of Old Testament Israel*, 2nd ed. (Grand Rapids: Baker Academic, 2008).

JEREMIAH

SNAPSHOT

Does your life sometimes feel like it's heading toward a hopeless catastrophe? Or that obeying God only draws ridicule? You might want to spend some time with the prophet Jeremiah, who ministered during a devastating time for the people of Israel. Even as he carried out his God-given calling, Jeremiah was ridiculed and persecuted. Yet in the midst of his message of dreadful judgment, we find great hope to help us navigate troubling times.

ORIENTATION

Date: 7th–6th centuries BC

Authors: Traditionally attributed to the prophet Jeremiah and his scribe Baruch.

Audience: Originally people of Judah prior to the exile to Babylon in 586 BC.

Outline:
1. Calling of Jeremiah (1)
2. Prophecies to the People of Judah (2–33)
3. The Fall of Jerusalem (34–39)
4. The Beginning of the Exile (40–45)
5. Prophecies to the Nations (46–51)

6. Recounting the Fall of Jerusalem (52)

YOU ARE HERE

Episode 5: Division and Judgment

Jeremiah is the second book in the "Major Prophets," and his prophecies address the people of Judah prior to their exile, extending beyond to a period of near- and far-future restoration.

EXPLORING JEREMIAH

The opening of Jeremiah sets the tone for the entire book. It begins with the calling of Jeremiah (1:1–19)—one of the most personal callings in all of Scripture. God tells Jeremiah that he was known, consecrated, and appointed as a prophet to the nations before he was even born.

Despite this seemingly great encouragement, Jeremiah resisted this call out of fear that he wasn't up to the challenge. God responds to this self-doubt with further encouragement, assuring Jeremiah that he will indeed be with him and that he doesn't need to be afraid. The rest of the chapter involves God further building the confidence of Jeremiah for what would surely be a very difficult ministry.

Following this personal and special calling of Jeremiah, no time is wasted before he jumps into his prophetic role. Jeremiah begins an extended section outlining the sins of Judah and the resulting impending judgment at the hands of Babylon (Jer 2–33). Throughout these chapters, Jeremiah repeatedly confronts the people for betraying God and breaking his covenant law . . . and he is repeatedly mocked and punished for his message. Jeremiah is sometimes referred to as the "weeping prophet" because throughout the book he is devastated by how he personally suffers and is in agony as he witnesses the unspeakable suffering of his people.

Despite all of Jeremiah's warnings, the leaders of Judah don't heed his message. The nation is invaded, Jerusalem attacked, the glorious temple of

Solomon destroyed, and the people taken into exile to Babylon (Jer 34–39). The fall of Judah was a slow and gruesome process. The events are horrifying to read when we pause to imagine what it might have been like to endure them.

Besides the stern warnings of judgment, as well as periodic glimmers of hope through the promise of future restoration, God also gave Jeremiah prophecies for Judah's neighbors. His prophecies directly addressed the nations of Egypt, Babylon, and others. The basic message? God has seen their evil and idolatrous ways, too, and their own judgment is coming. Though Judah was in a special covenant relationship with God, all people and nations are accountable to him for their actions. The book of Romans tells us that all people have sinned and therefore have fallen short of God's standard (Rom 3:23). We see this powerfully revealed in the book of Jeremiah. God is serious about sin. The consequences of sin are dire and devastating. A natural response to the judgments found in Jeremiah would be one of great fear. This awareness offers a powerful foundation for understanding our desperate need for the Savior who can deliver us from such judgment.

START YOUR JOURNEY

- Don't let the size or apparent complexity of Jeremiah overwhelm you. It's okay if you don't know all the names, events, and locations. You can use a good study Bible, commentary, or history of Israel to help fill in some of those details. However, as you read, focus on repeated themes that can help you better understand the bigger picture of what God was communicating in Jeremiah's day and what he wants us to learn about him through those words.

- Take note whenever God specifically critiques Israel or the nations. God's will and desire for his covenant people—and for people in general—hasn't changed. The Lord's critiques can be very insightful regarding God's heart and what matters most to him. What are the things for which they are being condemned? How do our current governments, politicians, and social influencers land on these matters?

- While Jeremiah is a book marked by much pain and heartache, it bears the gift of helping us see how hopeless and devastating life is apart from God. To choose obedience and faithfulness to God is truly to choose life. It's also a reminder that those who are called to teach and preach truth in the midst of a society that doesn't want to hear it are likely to be castigated as fools or ridiculed as "on the wrong side of history." In the end, though, God's truth will prevail and his people will be vindicated because of the coming King Jesus.

LAMENTATIONS

SNAPSHOT

Jeremiah was not only a storming prophet, but also much abused by his own people because of his unrelenting condemnation of their sin and warnings of coming judgment. However, it was out of profound care for the people that he preached and is known as the "weeping prophet." In the book of Lamentations, he cries out in anguish for his disintegrating nation yet finds refuge in the promises and character of his Lord.

ORIENTATION

Date: 6th century BC

Author: Jeremiah

Audience: The people of Jerusalem

Outline: 1. First Lament: The Devastation and Sorrow of Jerusalem (1)

2. Second Lament: The Destruction of Jerusalem (2)

3. Third Lament: The Lament and Prayer for Jerusalem (3)

4. Fourth Lament: The Description of the Siege of Jerusalem (4)

5. Fifth Lament: The Petition for Restoration of
    Jerusalem (5)

YOU ARE HERE

Episode 5: Division and Judgment

Though small, Lamentations is a companion volume to Jeremiah and is therefore counted among the Major Prophets. The book is about abiding hope amid heartbreaking disaster and distress.

EXPLORING LAMENTATIONS

The Bible pulls no punches. It doesn't shy away from realistic portrayals of catastrophe. It doesn't smooth over the ragged edges of reality. It doesn't airbrush portraits of imperfect people. And it doesn't sugarcoat human emotions, however seemingly negative they may be: anger, frustration, fear, and sadness. The lamentations of Jeremiah, too, treat the realities of the siege and destruction of Jerusalem with sobering seriousness. Its what-you-see-is-what-you-get approach presents an almost too-raw recollection of the horror of Jerusalem's fall and the suffering felt by its people. And it pulls out all the stops with regard to Jeremiah's deep anguish over the city.

The book of Lamentations is composed of five lament poems. Poems 1–2 and 4–5 are each twenty-two verses, beginning with a successive letter of the Hebrew alphabet. Chapter 3 has sixty-six verses grouped in units of three verses and each beginning with a successive letter of the Hebrew alphabet. In form, it's a literary masterpiece, perhaps constructed to facilitate memorization. The center of the book and focal point of its message is chapter three—the expression of hope amid the crisis.

In the first poem, the prophet laments the cause of Jerusalem's downfall. "Jerusalem has sinned grievously. . . . Her downfall was astonishing" (1:8, 9). In the second poem, Jeremiah personally grieves over the destruction of the city, detailing the plight of her inhabitants: "My eyes are worn out from weeping; I am churning within. My heart is poured out in grief because of the destruction of my dear people" (2:11).

Poem 3 is regarded as one of the most wonderful chapters in the Bible, as it relates to the expression of personal pain and hurt, as well as confidence and trust in God. The depth of the perception of loss and disappointment is only matched by the prophet's rousing trust in the Lord's faithfulness and love. "I call this to mind, and therefore I have hope: Because of the LORD's faithful love we do not perish, for his mercies never end. They are new every morning; great is your faithfulness!" (3:21–23). Though afflictions are many, comfort comes through trust in the character of God and his promises of ultimate restoration. His personal reflections have the effect of calling his people to repentance.

The fourth poem describes the circumstantial sufferings and hardships of the people besieged in the city. "Those slain by the sword are better off than those slain by hunger, who waste away, pierced with pain" (4:9). The final poem is a prayer for the nation's restoration. The prayer begins with the words, "LORD, remember what has happened to us. Look, and see our disgrace!" (5:1). It ends much the same way: "Lord, bring us back to yourself, so we may return; renew our days as in former times" (5:21).

START YOUR JOURNEY

- How can we have peace and hope during times of tremendous adversity, grave disappointment, and grievous suffering? By remembering the character of the God we serve. You can find solace in troubling times by turning your thoughts toward God. As you read Jeremiah's stout words in Lamentations, don't lose sight of the hopeful words in chapter 3, especially verses 22–23. In life circumstances that seem almost too unbearable to survive, return to those words for comfort and encouragement.

- Comfort, like distress, is found in what occupies your mind and thought life. You simply cannot think about opposites at the same time. What you choose to focus on will determine your behavior as well as your degree of peace. While Jeremiah dwelled for a season on the effects of judgment and the heart-wrenching effects of sin, he didn't stay there. When reading through Lamentations, mark the passages that acknowledge the goodness of God, hope, and longing for restoration.

- The book ends with a prayer that should be on all our lips. "LORD, bring us back to yourself, so we may return; renew our days as in former times" (5:21). That is a needed prayer, as just as Jeremiah turned his readers' attention from the tragedy in front of his eyes to the hope of glory, so we, too, must turn our attention Godward, beyond the lamentable circumstances of this present age. Ponder Paul's words: "For I consider that the sufferings of this present time are not worth comparing with the glory that is going to be revealed to us" (Rom 8:18), which will be fulfilled when Jesus returns to resurrect the dead and redeem all creation (Rom 8:21).

EZEKIEL

SNAPSHOT

Imagine the most horrible and unthinkable act of terrorism has been committed against your home and country. You've lost your dwelling, the people you love, and all hope for recovery. Then you learn that all this happened because you and your whole nation had rebelled against God. In other words, *it's your fault*. Facing that truth can be quite painful. Most would probably resist it, seek some other explanation rather than take responsibility. Yet Ezekiel's message to the people of Israel attempts to get them to face the music so they can be led to repentance and restoration.

ORIENTATION

Date: 6th century BC
Author: Ezekiel
Audience: The people of Judah and Israel now in exile.
Outline: 1. Calling of Ezekiel (1–3)
                2. The Fall of Jerusalem (2–24)
                3. Prophecies to the Nations (25–32)
                4. Future Restoration of Israel (33–48)

YOU ARE HERE

Episode 5: Division and Judgment

Ezekiel is the fourth book in the section of Scripture called the "Major Prophets," and his oracles primarily address conditions during and immediately after the exile.

EXPLORING EZEKIEL

Ezekiel is in many ways a dark and painful book. The deep emotion of both God and the people of Israel is profoundly apparent throughout. God's pain shows up in his rejection of Israel by delivering them into the hands of Nebuchadnezzar for exile in Babylon. The pain of the people of Israel is a result of their realization of the devastation of life apart from God.

After centuries of grace, patience, and warnings, God finally allowed his people to experience what they thought they wanted—freedom from God and from his laws. Israel and Judah had rejected God in favor of foreign gods over and over for generations. They almost entirely ignored the warning cries of prophet after prophet. Ultimately, God withdrew his glory from the temple (11:22–25). He would no longer allow himself to be defamed in the presence of the idols and the wickedness to which Israel had turned.

Ezekiel recounts all these tragedies. He tells of the great sins of the people of God. We learn about how they desecrated the temple of God and defaced the land he had given them. The prophet gives special attention to the leaders of Israel and their cumulative failure to shepherd and care for their people. Instead of leading the people back to God in repentance, they abandoned their leadership responsibilities. This led to the nation falling deeper and deeper into idolatry and wickedness.

Life without God was horrifying. The temple was demolished, Jerusalem burned to the ground, and the people were slaughtered, scattered, or exiled. The lesson for the people of Israel and Judah as well as the nations—and anyone reading this book today—is that to choose God is to choose life and to reject God is to choose devastation and death.

The judgment of God was not for Israel alone. God also addresses the nations and holds them accountable for their pride and idolatry. A key theme is the phrase "Then they will know that I am the LORD" (6:14; 7:27; 12:16, etc.). Israel and the nations of the world had rejected the Most High God, and that would not be tolerated. When God was finished, there would be no question who reigned and who was worthy of all worship and glory.

While Ezekiel is marked by struggle, it's not all bad news. The book ends with prophecies related to the restoration of Jerusalem, the temple, and the people of Israel. The judgment of God was not the end of the story. The judgment would give way to ultimate restoration.

Through Ezekiel we see the consequences of rejecting God. A life of rebellion may appear tempting, but Ezekiel reminds us that it only and always leads to death. As followers of Jesus, we can find great hope and encouragement knowing that he has suffered the judgment of God in our place. May this compel us to extend our great gratitude and love toward God through a life of faithful obedience.

START YOUR JOURNEY

- As with the other Major Prophets, don't let the size or apparent complexity of Ezekiel overwhelm you. It's okay if you don't know all the names, events, and locations. Study Bibles or commentaries can help with that. Instead, focus on repeated themes that can help you better understand the bigger picture of what God is communicating.

- Take your time with this book. Don't rush through it. Ponder it and pray over it. Sometimes aggressive Bible-reading plans can force us to fly over what needs to be walked through . . . or even wrestled with. And if we rush, we'll miss some nuggets of wisdom and insight.

- Take note whenever God specifically critiques Israel or the nations. These critiques can be very insightful regarding God's heart and what matters most to him. For what things are they condemned? What sins of commission or omission? What might that tell you about his pleasure or displeasure with the world today?

DANIEL

SNAPSHOT

One of the most captivating and puzzling books in the entire Bible, the book of Daniel has the tensions and plot twists of an epic drama, the suspense of a thriller, the stunning visual effects of a fantasy or science fiction blockbuster, and even the frightening images of a horror film. But unlike that Hollywood eye candy, the adventures, visions, dreams, and prophecies of the book of Daniel present divinely revealed truths about the past, present, and future.

ORIENTATION

Date: 6th century BC

Author: Daniel

Audience: Hebrews living in Babylon during the Babylonian captivity

Outline: 1. The Life of Daniel and Friends in Babylon (1–6)

                a. Daniel and Friends Deported (1:1–7)

                b. Daniel and Friends in the King's Court (1:8–21)

                c. Nebuchadnezzar's First Dream: The Statue (2:1–49)

                d. Nebuchadnezzar's Golden Image and the Fiery Furnace (3:1–4:3)

       e. Nebuchadnezzar's Second Dream: The Large Tree and the Stump (4:4–37)

       f. Belshazzar's Feast and the Writing on the Wall (5:1–31)

       g. Daniel and the Lion's Den (6:1–28)

   2. The Visions of Daniel Concerning the Nations (7–12)

       a. The Vision of the Four Beasts (7:1–28)

       b. The Vision of the Ram, Goat, and Little Horn (8:1–27)

       c. The Vision of the Seventy Weeks (9:1–27)

       d. The Final Vision (10:1–12:13)

YOU ARE HERE

Episode 5: Division and Judgment

The book of Daniel is the fifth book of the Major Prophets, written during the exilic period when Judah was taken into captivity to Babylon.

EXPLORING DANIEL

The book of Daniel is composed of two primary literary genres: 1) historical narrative, and 2) prophetic literature. The twenty-first century mind often thinks linearly or chronologically, but Daniel didn't arrange his material in such a straight line. Rather, his content is organized around the two previously mentioned genres. The first chapters contain historical narrative (Dan 1–6), and the second group of chapters are composed of prophetic material (Dan 7–12).

One of the most important recurring themes in the book of Daniel is the sovereignty of God, which is evident at both a personal and a global level. At a personal level, we see God's sovereign hand at work when God sees to it that Daniel and his friends' faithfulness to Mosaic dietary laws make them healthier than those who ate from the king's table (1:15).

God provides them with an unusual aptitude to learn (v. 17), making them advisors to the king (v. 19). He gives Daniel the correct interpretations of dreams (2:19; 4:19–27; 5:13–30) and sends Daniel visions about the rise and fall of future Gentile nations (7:1–28; 8:1–27; 9:24–27; 11:1–45). God's sovereignty is also evident in promoting Daniel during the reign of Nebuchadnezzar (2:48–49), Belshazzar (5:29), Darius (6:1, 28), and Cyrus. God protects Daniel's friends in the fiery furnace (3:17), and preserves Daniel in the lion's den (6:26–28). God also reveals his sovereignty when he turns the most powerful world ruler into a subhuman beast (4:33) then later restores him once he humbles himself (4:36). His sovereignty is also evident when he mysteriously reveals to King Belshazzar that his kingdom will be removed and given to the Medes and the Persians (5:28).

Beyond sovereign acts in the lives of individuals, the book of Daniel exhibits God's sovereignty over his chosen people as well as over all the nations of the world. He raises up and tears down empires according to his plans and purpose. He predicts, through dreams and visions, that several great empires would emerge, one after the other (2:1–45; 7:1–28; 8:1–27). This was prophetic at the time and was fulfilled with great specificity by the Babylonian, Medo-Persian, Greek, and Roman empires from Daniel's day to the time of the coming of Christ. Just as those kingdoms fulfilled the prophecies of Daniel, the final kingdom, instituted by the Son of Man (7:13–14), will also be fulfilled. This kingdom will be global and eternal (2:44; 4:3; 4:34–35; 6:26; 7:13–14; 7:27).

The book of Daniel is one of the most important Old Testament books as it relates to the study of "last things" or "end times." Daniel explains that at the end of the tribulation (12:13) and reign of a fierce world ruler the likes of which the world has never seen, God will establish his kingdom, as predicted in the dream of Nebuchadnezzar (2:44). This kingdom, unlike the long succession of Gentile kingdoms, will never be destroyed. We know from the vantage point of the New Testament that this eternal, perfect kingdom will be established by Jesus Christ himself (7:13–14). During this eternal kingdom, humanity will finally accomplish what God created them to do—to rule and reign as those created in his image (Gen 1:26–28). Only at that time, the perfect image of God, Jesus Christ, will exercise perfect and complete sovereignty over all creation, whose kingdom will have no end.

START YOUR JOURNEY

- As you read through the book, imagine yourself in the shoes of Daniel and his three friends, ripped from their homeland and hauled off to a nation with a culture and language they don't understand. Imagine the emotions and challenges they experience as they seek to be faithful to their God in that strange world. Their firm stance as lights in the darkness can encourage us to stand strong in our own changing culture.

- It's easy to get lost in the prophetic details of the book of Daniel. There's certainly a time and place to explore its connection to doctrines about the end times, especially its connection to the book of Revelation and other New Testament passages like Matthew 24 and 2 Thessalonians 2. However, as you read through the prophetic section, summarize each chapter in one or two sentences that capture the "big picture" of what's being communicated. Then, as you work through details, keep that big picture in mind.

- As you read this book, notice the sovereignty of God on a personal level (in the lives of Daniel and his friends) and on a global level (using kings and empires to accomplish his purposes). What lessons can you learn about God's interactions with (and sometimes intrusion into) individual lives and whole nations? How do you see God doing the same thing in the world today and in your own life?

GOING DEEPER

"Major on the Minors"

— Robert B. Chisholm —

The Minor Prophets are twelve relatively short, often neglected books at the end of the Old Testament in the English Bible. These books span three hundred years, from the eighth century BC to the fifth century BC. In these books God warns sinners of impending judgment, but he also provides a vision of a glorious era that follows the dark days of divine discipline.

Hosea and his eighth-century contemporaries **Amos** and **Micah** warned Israel and Judah of invasion and exile due to their rebellion against God. Hosea denounced Israel's idolatry, while Amos and Micah exposed the economic injustice perpetrated by the royal bureaucracies of Israel and Judah. Yet beyond judgment, they also foresaw a messianic kingdom where God's ideal for his people would be realized (Hos 3:5; Amos 9:11–15; Mic 5:2–9).

The seventh-century BC prophet **Habakkuk** faced the coming invasion of Judah with faith and courage, confident that God's loyal followers would be sustained by their faithfulness (Hab 2:4; 3:16–19). His contemporary **Zephaniah** also anticipated the dawning of a new era beyond the smoke of judgment accompanying the day of the Lord.

The Minor Prophets remind us that God is the King of the entire world, not of just his own people. In **Jonah**'s mission to Nineveh in the eighth century, we see God's mercy toward the evil, but repentant, Assyrians.

But the seventh-century prophet **Nahum** announced the fall of the Assyrian Empire, which had returned to its old ways with unprecedented cruelty. In the aftermath of Judah's exile, **Obadiah** anticipated God's vengeance on the hostile Edomites, who had hit God's people when they were down.

After the return from exile, in the sixth and fifth centuries, the prophets **Joel**, **Haggai**, **Zechariah**, and **Malachi** challenged the people to recommit their lives to God and promised that God would fulfill his ancient promises because of his commitment to them. Joel looked forward to a day when God would pour out his Spirit on his people, while Haggai spoke of a time when the Lord's kingdom would displace earth's kingdoms. Zechariah foresaw the arrival of God's chosen king and a time of national repentance. Malachi anticipated the day of the Lord, which would be announced by the return of Elijah.

Some Christians tend to bypass or ignore the Minor Prophets. In doing so, they miss a vital portion of God's Word. The Minor Prophets are extraordinarily relevant to us today in three important ways:

- *To a wicked, fallen world*, the Minor Prophets proclaim God's passion for righteousness and justice.
- *To religious people* who emphasize outward expressions of piety, the Minor Prophet remind us that God wants devoted hearts, not merely pious actions.
- *To people groaning* under the consequences of sin, the Minor Prophets bring promises of comfort and hope for all who will turn from their sin and follow God.[1]

---

[1] Adapted from Robert B. Chisholm, "Major on the Minors," *Kindred Spirit* 28, no. 1 (spring 2004): 7 (updated by the author). © 2004 Dallas Theological Seminary.

HOSEA

SNAPSHOT

Imagine marrying your spouse with the full certainty that he or she will betray you. This was precisely Hosea's commission! His broken marriage was meant to picture God's relationship with his people. Through his life and message, Hosea confronts Israel's spiritual adultery, alternating between caution of God's imminent judgment and comfort of his future restoration.

ORIENTATION

Date: 8th century BC
Author(s): Hosea
Audience: Israel (northern kingdom)
Outline:
1. Hosea's Allegory (1:2–2:1)
2. Israel's Adultery (2:2–3:5)
3. God's Accusation (4:1–6:3)
4. Israel's Allegiance (6:4–11:11)
5. Hosea's Appeal (11:12–14:9)

YOU ARE HERE

Episode 5: Division and Judgment

One of only two prophets primarily addressed to the northern kingdom of Israel, Hosea is the opening book of the "Minor Prophets," the final section in the Old Testament.

EXPLORING HOSEA

The prophet's oracles are organized in five sections, juxtaposing threats of imminent punishment with promises of future restoration. Hosea not only speaks for God (Hos 4–14), but he also embodies his message (Hos 1–3). First, God uses Hosea's family as an *allegory* to picture his relationship with Israel: just as Gomer is physically unfaithful to Hosea, Israel is spiritually unfaithful to God. With Hosea's children's names, God declares a fracture in their covenant relationship, resulting in his coming judgment (1:2–9). However, in the future, God's covenant promise to Abraham will be realized, reversing the present judgment and restoring their broken relationship (1:10–2:1).

Second, God charges his people with spiritual *adultery*: Israel was offering his material blessing as sacrificial gifts to idols. Thus, he promises to bring retribution to facilitate repentance and restoration (2:2–13). In the future, Israel will be changed from unfaithful to faithful, and God will turn from correction to care, restoring his covenant with them (vv. 14–23). Israel's restoration is pictured in Gomer's redemption, at great cost and with great expectation of devotion (3:1–5).

Third, God expounds on his *accusation*, bringing a covenant lawsuit against his people for breaking his law—both the priests and the people. Their sin is plain, and their punishment is imminent. God is depicted as a lion tearing apart his enemy as prey (4:1–5:15). Only repentance can bring about reversal of the judgment. The prophet's prayer models what God desires (6:1–3).

Fourth, God desires to heal his people, but Israel lacks *allegiance* in relationship with God and man, shown in their spiritual idolatry and social injustice. Israel has rejected God's covenant and will reap the fruit of their sinful deeds, resulting in their coming exile (6:4–11:7). Yet, rather than overthrow Israel, God's heart is overthrown with mercy. He won't completely destroy the nation but will reverse his judgment. He won't tear them apart like a lion but will recall them from exile; and they will return as a dove, not gullible but quick in flight (11:8–11).

Finally, God restates his covenant lawsuit against the people for their idolatry and injustice, urging them to learn from Jacob's life: God desires dependence on him alone, or the disobedient will face divine judgment, ending in exile and destruction (11:12–13:16). Hosea *appeals* to Israel to repent, promising that God will heal their wayward hearts and return his covenant blessing (14:1–8).

In the New Testament, the apostle Paul builds on Hosea's metaphor of marriage as a picture of God's relationship with his people, ultimately fulfilled in the bond between Christ and the church (Eph 5:22–24). Therefore, Hosea's picture of Israel's unfaithfulness and God's faithfulness anticipates the coming of Christ, through whom God offers to redeem and restore a repentant humanity based on his commitment to his covenant promises, not based on what they deserve.

START YOUR JOURNEY

- Hosea focuses on Israel's spiritual adultery in idol worship. Think about our own cultural context. In what ways do things/people in our world similarly vie for our allegiance? For what idols might you, personally, need to repent?
- Since Hosea is structured in five sections (1:2–2:1; 2:2–3:5; 4:1–6:3; 6:4–11:11; 11:12–14:9) combining God's judgment and restoration, try reading one section each day for a week. By reading each section in one sitting, you will better see how God's justice

and mercy work together to serve a single purpose—bringing his unfaithful people back into a faithful relationship with him.

- Create a list of Hosea's different portraits of God. While these various portraits may seem at odds with one another, consider how each section above combines contrite penitence (humanity) and covenant promises (God), reconciling his justice and mercy.

JOEL

SNAPSHOT

What happens when you turn your back on God? For the people of Judah, they received judgment from God's hand—first by locusts, then by an invading army. The book of Joel warns Judah of imminent judgment for their rejection of God and refusal to return to him. Yet even at the brink of judgment, if they repent, God is willing to turn his wrath away from them and toward their enemies, offering forgiveness, mercy, and restoration.

ORIENTATION

Date: Uncertain: as early as the 9th century BC to the 2nd century BC; perhaps 6th century is a good median

Author: The prophet Joel

Audience: The inhabitants of Judah and Jerusalem, before or after the exile

Outline:
1. Judgment against Judah (1:1–2:17)
2. Judgment against the Nations (2:18–3:21)

YOU ARE HERE

Episode 6: Return from Exile

Joel is the second book of the "Minor Prophets" and a standard source for vivid "day of the Lord" imagery.

EXPLORING JOEL

If you've spent any time in the Bible for very long, you've likely encountered the phrase the "day of the Lord." It sounds so ominous! The book of Joel is an example of why this phrase carries so much heaviness. The "day of the Lord" carries the idea of God exercising his right to rule. This may be expressed in the form of judgment but also deliverance. When God steps into time and space, he uses various natural or supernatural means to accomplish his purposes. Such a period is called "the day of the Lord," which demonstrates that he alone is God, he has ultimate control of the world, he alone is worthy of worship and obedience.

Joel begins by describing a devastating invasion of locusts that previews greater judgments to come. This plague of locusts serves as a forerunner of the judgments prophesied to the nations surrounding Israel. While the prophecies of Joel invoke great fear at the calamity of their future fulfillment, they are infused with grace as they appeal to the goodness of God.

In chapter 1:13–14, Joel appeals to his audience to cry out to the Lord that he might relent and alter the course of his impending wrath. This theme is emphasized even more clearly in Joel 2:12–13, where the prophet appeals to God's character as a reason his people should repent and turn to him: "Even now—this is the LORD's declaration—turn to me with all your heart, with fasting, weeping, and mourning. Tear your hearts, not just your clothes, and return to the LORD your God. For he is gracious and compassionate, slow to anger, abounding in faithful love, and he relents from sending disaster" (cf. Exod 34:6–7).

This passage goes on to implore the audience to consecrate a fast, call a solemn assembly, weep and cry out to God that they may be spared (Joel 2:15–17). In other words, even as the nation is dangling by a thread over the fires of coming judgment, they can escape through true repentance.

The day of the Lord is not judgment for judgment's sake. The people of Judah and the surrounding nations are on a path rushing toward doom and disaster due to their rejection of God. The prophecies of Joel are meant to make it clear to everyone that there's only one God and the worship of any other cannot be tolerated—especially when it comes to his covenant people, who ages ago had vowed fidelity to that one God. The prophecies were also meant to give people the chance to turn or return to God and avert the coming calamities.

Joel not only discusses judgment, though. As is common for the biblical prophets, the hope of future restoration is also presented (3:1, 17–21). Joel 3:18 tells us, "In that day the mountains will drip with sweet wine, and the hills will flow with milk. All the streams of Judah will flow with water, and a spring will issue from the LORD's house, watering the Valley of Acacias."

The prophecies of Joel remind us that to reject God is to choose devastating judgment. That was true during the time of Joel, and it's true today as well. Joel pleads with the people to turn back to God and to accept his offer of mercy. Today, the Bible carries the same message: turn to God and receive the grace and forgiveness extended to us through the death and resurrection of Jesus.

START YOUR JOURNEY

- The prophecies of Joel are not given simply for the sake of pronouncing judgment. They offer grace and the chance of restoration if the people turn to God prior to the fulfillment of the prophecies. It's never changed. Though "God's wrath is revealed from heaven against all godlessness and unrighteousness of people" (Rom 1:18),

God always extends his offer of grace and mercy to those who believe and repent.

- The phrase "the day of the LORD" (Joel 1:15) can be joined with the phrase "then you will know that I am the LORD your God" (3:17) to help unite the meaning of the prophecies of Joel. The people of God had rejected him. The surrounding nations had rejected him. These acts of rebellion led to unspeakable evils . . . and justice was demanded. It was time to make it clear who God was and why he was worthy of worship and obedience. We sometimes balk at a God who judges, forgetting that justice against evil is good. If God left wickedness unaddressed, what kind of world would this be?
- Note that the prophecies of the judgments of God are frequently followed by prophecies of restoration. God wants what's best for the people, and he knows that *he* is what's best for the people. To serve lesser gods is to choose death and the merciful God of Israel wants to invite the peoples of the world into life. Don't ever be tempted to trade God in for anything less than him.
- Peter quotes Joel 2 on the Day of Pentecost (Acts 2:16–21) as evidence that the Spirit has come and a new age has dawned. Reflect on the promises God has made in the new covenant and the ultimate fulfillment in the new creation.

AMOS

SNAPSHOT

Are material and economic prosperity signs of God's blessing? Is God concerned about justice? Will God allow societal injustices to go unpunished? Amos prophesies to Israel during a time of peace and prosperity and warns that God's concern for justice will result in judgment of the nations and of Israel. This coming day of the Lord's judgment will be a devastating period of darkness and death, but the end of the story is restoration to blessing.

ORIENTATION

Date: 8th century BC
Author(s):   Amos
Audience: Israel (northern kingdom)
Outline: 1. Prologue (1:1–2)
            2. Judgment Against the Nations (1–2)
            3. Reasons for Judgment (3–6)
            4. Results of Judgment (7:1–9:10)
            5. Restoration after Judgment (9:11–15)

YOU ARE HERE

Episode 5: Division and Judgment

Amos is the third of the twelve "Minor Prophets," prophesying sometime before the destruction of Israel by Assyria and exile.

EXPLORING AMOS

Amos identifies himself as a shepherd from Tekoa who received this vision from God when Uzziah was king of Judah and Jeroboam king of Israel— two years before the earthquake in 760 (1:1). His first oracle promises judgment on Israel's neighbors, "for three crimes, even four" (1:3, 6, 9, 11, 13, 2:1). Judah, too, is threatened judgment (2:4) and then Israel (Amos 2:6). The oracle against Israel is significantly longer and more detailed than the others, calling out her injustice, oppression, sexual immorality, and idolatry. God warns, "I am about to crush you in your place as a wagon crushes when full of grain" (2:13).

In the next section, Amos outlines in great detail and strong language the offenses for which Israel will be judged. For example, he calls the people "cows of Bashan" who "oppress the poor and crush the needy" (4:1). He declares, "The days are coming when you will be taken away with hooks, every last one of you with fishhooks" (4:2). The Lord forewarns plagues like he sent on Egypt (4:10).

Particularly sobering is Amos's description of the coming day of the Lord. After a scathing condemnation of the people's injustice and oppression of the innocent and the poor, he paints a series of sharp contrasts, rebuking the people who believed they were safe because they were on the Lord's side. Amos declares, "Pursue good and not evil so that you may live, and the LORD, the God of Armies, will be with you as you have claimed. Hate evil and love good; establish justice at the city gate. Perhaps the LORD, the God of Armies, will be gracious to the remnant of Joseph" (5:14–15). Unless there is repentance, judgment is coming: "There will be wailing in all the public squares; they will cry out in anguish in all the streets" (5:16).

To those who might be inclined to celebrate the coming judgment, Amos announces, "Woe to you who long for the day of the LORD! What will the day of the LORD be for you? It will be darkness and not light" (5:18). People of mercy and compassion should not desire God's wrath but God's blessing upon his people. But God's blessing follows genuine repentance of the heart, not focusing on outward festivals, assemblies, and offerings. Instead, Amos proclaims, "Take away from me the noise of your songs! I will not listen to the music of your harps. But let justice flow like water, and righteousness, like an unfailing stream" (5:23–24).

The message of Amos is not limited to coming judgment, as central as that is to the book. Rather, God promises to restore his people in the land. The book ends with a picturesque description of prosperity and blessing: "Look, the days are coming—this is the Lord's declaration—when the plowman will overtake the reaper and the one who treads grapes, the sower of seed. The mountains will drip with sweet wine, and all the hills will flow with it. I will restore the fortunes of my people Israel. They will rebuild and occupy ruined cities, plant vineyards and drink their wine, make gardens and eat their produce" (9:13–14). The good news is that God's long-term faithfulness to his people is not dependent upon their obedience but his character. Long and prosperous life in the land of Israel has been promised to his people.

START YOUR JOURNEY

- The message of Amos is a strong warning against Christians regarding their nations of citizenship as exceptionally superior to others. It urges us to consider how we can practice good citizenship while avoiding the idolatry of a kind of nationalism that ends up neglecting the needs of other nations and peoples or even gloating over their misfortune.
- The "day of the Lord" is a time of judgment (see special feature on pages 198–99). Amos warns against longing for judgment. How can Christians look forward to the day of judgment while avoiding taking pleasure in the destruction of the wicked?

- The prophets, including Amos, present us with a tension in which we must live and make decisions: How can we practice justice and mercy in relationships with others while also recognizing their personal responsibility to hold themselves and people around them accountable for practicing justice?

OBADIAH

SNAPSHOT

"O Bad Edom" is a handy device for recalling Obadiah's message, which dooms Edom for rejoicing over Judah's defeat. Believers should be reminded that vengeance belongs to the Lord!

ORIENTATION

Date:	Uncertain: either 9th century or 6th century BC
Author:	Obadiah
Audience:	The Edomites
Outline:	1. The Destruction of Edom (vv. 1–16)
	2. The Deliverance of Israel (vv. 17–21)

YOU ARE HERE

Episode 5: Division and Judgment

As the fourth book of the "Minor Prophets," Obadiah warns Edom of coming judgment.

EXPLORING OBADIAH

Obadiah is the shortest book in the Old Testament, but don't be fooled by its size. This one-chapter book is powerful and relevant today. We know nothing about the prophet Obadiah except his name (v. 1), which means "servant of Yahweh." The invasion of Jerusalem gives us a context for the message of the book. The Edomites had joined the enemies of Israel in the sacking of the city. The proud Edomites returned to their home in the cliffs of Petra to gloat over the defeat of their distant blood relatives.

Because of their delight in the suffering of Jerusalem, Obadiah appears and prophesies the devastation of Edom (v. 6). In verse 15, "the day of the LORD" is mentioned, generally referring to any one of several periods of God's judgment mediated through earthly means. Here it indicates a period of judgment upon Edom for their wickedness.

The pivot of the book is verse 17. From this point until verse 21, Obadiah declares the deliverance of Israel. Yes, Edom may gloat now in its short-term victory of God's city, but eventually the tables will be turned. In that future day, the people of Israel will be restored, the Lord will rule from Zion (Jerusalem), and the kingdom will belong to the Lord. As in Obadiah's day, so in ours: we are not to seek retaliation for wrongs done to us, but to rest in the truth that "Vengeance belongs to me; I will repay, says the Lord" (Rom 12:19).

START YOUR JOURNEY

- The Edomites were descendants of Esau, the twin brother of Jacob. When Esau sold his birthright to Jacob for some red stew, his name was changed to Edom, which means "red." The fact that the Edomites were blood relatives with Jacob made their celebration of Jerusalem's defeat all the more heinous. The lesson for us? "Pride comes before destruction, and an arrogant spirit before a fall" (Prov 16:18).

- Because Obadiah is a short book, only one chapter, try reading it through every day for a month. This exercise will help to solidify the powerful message of the justice of God (to the unbelieving Edomites) and the grace of God (to believing Israel). And it will also serve as a great template for understanding the basic message of the Old Testament prophets.

GOING DEEPER

"What Is Meant by 'the Day of the Lord'?"

— Michael J. Svigel —

B y the end of the Old Testament period, the phrase "day of the Lord" (Hebrew *Yōm Yhwh*) had already been functioning as a technical term for centuries. Other terms, like "day of wrath," "day of judgment," and "tribulation"—as well as common language and imagery like fire, darkness, smoke, sword, pestilence, vengeance, and warfare—would have been associated with the "day of the Lord." So common and colloquial was the phrase "day of the Lord" that if a person stood in a crowded street in Jerusalem in the year 50 BC and just uttered the words "day of the Lord," everybody would have a dreadful picture.

Vander Hart sums it up this way: "The Day of YHWH in the Old Testament prophets . . . has something of a dual character, with the clear emphasis being on judgment—sometimes on Israel, sometimes on the nations. Thus it is a day of darkness, mourning, desolation, fear, cosmic shaking and plague. It can also issue in a time when the covenant people are blessed and raised high before the other nations."[1] This "day of the Lord" would have been generally thought of as God "showing up" in

---

[1] Mark D. Vander Hart, "The Transition of the Old Testament Day of the Lord into the New Testament Day of the Lord Jesus Christ," *Mid-America Journal of Theology* 9, no. 1 (1993): 8.

judgment of the wicked and deliverance of the righteous. Depending on specific circumstances, the object of that judgment could be God's people, Israel, which would usually result in exile, or the enemies of Israel, resulting in the protection, rescue, or deliverance of his people. As such, there has not been only one "day of the Lord" in Israel's history but many "days of the Lord."

Aernie and Hartley summarize the varied use of "day of the Lord" this way:

> The prophets refer to the day of the Lord from different vantage points: (1) The day is described in retrospect by referring to past events where the Lord has previously rendered punishment (e.g., exile). The prophets want their audience to interpret those past incidences as a warning to later generations regarding the future judgment. (2) Judgment may be more imminent in that the Lord will send foreign nations as his agents to carry out retribution on his people. (3) Judgment may be specifically eschatological in nature, looking forward to the consummate day when Yahweh renders the final verdict on all the nations of either divine judgment or divine blessing.[2]

In all cases, "day of the Lord" never refers to a single day, nor is it primarily conceived of as occurring in the afterlife or spiritual realm. The term is used to describe a usually prolonged period of divinely orchestrated and providentially controlled judgment against a nation or nations in this world. The actual historical manifestation of these judgments would usually be seen in natural means: famine, flood, storms, locusts, disease, earthquakes, military campaigns, or sieges. Past manifestations of the day of the Lord, then, might serve as types of future days of the Lord, which themselves would forewarn the world of an ultimate end-times day of the Lord.

---

[2] Matthew D. Aernie and Donald E. Hartley, *The Righteous and Merciful Judge: The Day of the Lord in the Life and Theology of Paul*, Studies in Scripture and Biblical Theology (Bellingham, WA: Lexham, 2018), 38.

JONAH

SNAPSHOT

Is Jonah the story of a God who controls the weather and provides a fish to swallow and spit out a man alive? Or is it about a missionary who runs from God, reluctantly goes where he's told, then resents his own success? Or is it about a gracious God who cares about outsiders as much as his own covenant people? It's all of the above, but it also stands as a rebuke to Israel for caring only about themselves instead of being concerned about the souls of the people of Nineveh.

ORIENTATION

Date: 8th century BC

Author: Jonah

Audience: The Ninevites, Israel, and Judah

Outline:
1. Jonah Disobeys God (1)
2. Jonah Repents of His Disobedience (2)
3. Jonah Obeys God (3)
4. Jonah Is Angry with God (4)

YOU ARE HERE

Episode 5: Division and Judgment

Jonah, the fifth book of the "Minor Prophets," is the "prequel" to the later prophecy against Nineveh in the book of Nahum.

EXPLORING JONAH

Though the book of Jonah ends with the prophet pouting because God spared Israel's enemies in Nineveh when they repented (Jonah 4), the fact that the book of Jonah exists demonstrates that even that brooding prophet eventually came to his senses. The book is written from the perspective of a man who recognized his own folly and sinful attitudes, pointing out the absurdity of his rebellious flight from God (Jonah 1), God's relentless pursuit (Jonah 1–2), and his eventual preaching and grumbling (Jonah 3–4). Because of some of the seemingly fantastical and exaggerated elements of the narrative, some have tossed it into the category of "fiction" or "allegory" or "fable." Yet 2 Kgs 14:23–29 describes the prophet Jonah prophesying in the reign of Jeroboam II, king of Israel. And in Matt 12:40, Jesus takes the most incredible part of the story as historical fact when he says, "As Jonah was in the belly of the huge fish three days and three nights, so the Son of Man will be in the heart of the earth three days and three nights." Further, Jesus declares that this is the only sign his hearers will receive (Matt 12:39). Jesus is greater than Jonah.

Almost everybody knows the story. If you don't, you can read through it in one sitting and experience the drama, the satire, and the somber, ponderous conclusion yourself. Then consider how this book speaks to each of us today in specific ways. First, it reminds us that God is able to work in supernatural ways to accomplish his purposes. He controlled the weather in this book, and he spoke to the big fish twice. He even softened the hearts of the infamously brutal and wicked Ninevites to be responsive to Jonah's message. Second, since God is so powerful, there is no point in trying to resist his will. We can run from him, but we can't outrun him. We can't hide where he can't find us. Third, Jonah is more like us than we would like to admit. Even though his behavior towards the Ninevites is not what we would like to see in a missionary, we have to admit that we aren't perfect in our love for lost people, and only God knows what's in their hearts.

But Jonah is also a warning to us about "playing God." Jonah was playing God by presuming to know what was in the hearts of the Ninevites, and he was totally wrong about them. He also presumed to know God's plans, assuming God wanted to do what Jonah wanted God to do. In his conversation with the Lord after Nineveh repented and was spared from judgment, Jonah says, "Please, LORD, isn't this what I said while I was still in my own country? That's why I fled toward Tarshish in the first place. I knew that you are a gracious and compassionate God, slow to anger, abounding in faithful love, and one who relents from sending disaster" (Jonah 4:2). In that passage, Jonah quotes almost exactly from Ps 86:15 or Exod 34:6. Jonah's theology was right; but that didn't mean he knew how and when God's plan was going to play out. Who was Jonah to say that the Ninevites would or wouldn't repent at his preaching?

Even though the Ninevites responded to Jonah's preaching with repentance (Jonah 3), that revival was short-lived. As we see in the sequel, Nahum, eventually Assyria backslides into its own ways of wickedness and injustice. And though God is "slow to anger," he does not leave the wicked unpunished (Nah 1:2–6). In fact, having once received the grace and mercy of God, it may have become easy for the Ninevites to presume upon that grace. Or perhaps they got the notion that Jonah's preaching of coming judgment was actually untrue, that because nothing happened, maybe they were tricked, rather than believing that they were spared because of their repentance. Whatever the case, the relationship between the books of Jonah and Nahum reminds us that God wants an ongoing lifestyle of repentance from his people, not just a moment of contrition.

START YOUR JOURNEY

- Even Christians can be guilty of Jonah's attitude of self-righteous prejudice. Just look at how divided our churches are today— politics, racism, tribalism, and other sins have taken priority over sanctification and holy living. What kind of repentance is still needed in our own hearts to avoid the sin of Jonah?

- If God asked you to do something that required you to change your direction and move out of your comfort zone to a place you fear, toward people you don't really know or particularly like, to do something you don't want to do . . . would you do it? Consider a scenario in your own life that might be similar to what Jonah was asked to do.

- Are you ever displeased with the outcome of something God clearly told you to do, like giving a gift, or sharing the gospel, or choosing to serve behind the scene rather than up front in the spotlight? Our egos can cause us to be angry when our plans are blocked by God. As you read through Jonah, put yourself in his place and at each pivotal moment in the drama, consider how he could have responded better.

- Read the story of Jesus asleep in the boat (Matt 8:23–27) and notice how Jesus is greater than the prophet Jonah.

MICAH

SNAPSHOT

As the saying goes, "After darkness comes light!" Even after just discipline, God will fulfill his promises. That's good news for us today and for the people of Judah to whom the prophet Micah wrote. Because of his promises, God will not abandon his children. In response to God's grace, the people of Judah showed ingratitude, which led to disobedience, despite God's magnificent promises and provisions—protection, guidance, and material prosperity.

ORIENTATION

Date:	8th century BC
Author:	Micah, a "country prophet" from the Judean countryside and a contemporary of Isaiah
Audience:	Primarily Judah, the southern kingdom
Outline:	1. Introduction (1:1)
	2. Message One: The Justice of Impending Judgment (1:2–2:13)
	3. Message Two: The Promise of Deliverance (3:1–5:15)

    4. Message Three: The Declaration of Future Restoration
       (6:1–7:20)

YOU ARE HERE

Episode 5: Division and Judgment

Micah is the sixth of the Minor Prophets, a contemporary of the prophet
Isaiah, prophesying prior to the exile.

EXPLORING MICAH

The Book of Micah is composed of three messages delivered by the prophet;
each is introduced by the word "listen" or "listen now" (1:2, 3:1, 6:1) and
each ends on a positive note. The first message is addressed to both kingdoms—Israel in the north and Judah in the south. At the time of that first
message, Israel had not yet been taken captive by the Assyrians (722 BC).
The message is clear: because of their sin, judgment is inevitable (1:2–7).
Rather than delighting in judgment, the prophet expresses deep sorrow
(vv. 8–16). The causes of the disaster are enumerated (2:1–11), yet the message ends in hope—the regathering of the people under the leadership of a
king, who is Lord (vv. 12–13).

    Micah's second message begins with a declaration of the causes of
the coming judgment: 1) the wickedness of their rulers (3:1–4), 2) the
deceptiveness of their prophets (vv. 5–8), and 3) the general corruption of
their authority figures (3:9–12). However, the real focus of the message is
regathering and restoration (4:1–5:15). First, the kingdom will be restored
through a returning remnant in Jerusalem under the rulership of a righteous Lord (4:1–8). Second, while judgment is emphasized as a "done deal"
(4:9–5:1), the promise of restoration stressed even more the certainty of gracious and merciful deliverance (5:2–15). The origin of the future redeemer
who will effect this great deliverance is both human and eternal: "Bethlehem
Ephrathah, you are small among the clans of Judah; one will come from

you to be ruler over Israel for me. His origin is from antiquity, from ancient times" (v. 2). This ruler will regather, protect, and exalt his people (vv. 3–9), all as a result of his victory over all his enemies (vv. 10–15). In the New Testament, this prophecy is, of course, applied to the birth of Jesus, who, though born in Bethlehem, is both human and divine, his ultimate origin from eternity past (Matt 2:6).

The third message of Micah consists of two parts: a formal indictment by the Lord (Mic 6:1–16) and a reply by the prophet (7:1–20). First, the Lord, through the prophet, reiterates his great faithfulness to Israel (6:2–5), states what the Lord requires of his people (vv. 6–9), discloses the reasons why the coming judgment is just (vv. 10–12), and ends with a description of the character of that judgment (vv. 13–16). Second, the prophet rehearses the morally bankrupt state of his nation (7:1–6), describes a wonderful restoration to come (vv. 7–17), and concludes with a beautiful description of the character of God (vv. 18–20)—his willingness to pardon, show love, extend compassion and forgiveness, and demonstrate faithfulness. Micah ends with a word play on his own name by raising a question, "Who is a God like you?" (v. 18). Micah's name, being a shortened form of his Hebrew name, *Mikayahu*, means "Who is like the Lord?"

START YOUR JOURNEY

- Micah reminds us that God's great love doesn't cancel justice in judgment. But it also teaches that God's judgment doesn't cancel his great love in forgiveness, mercy, and grace. As you read through Micah, reflect on the character and perfections of God's holiness, justice, mercy, and grace.
- What does the Lord require of us, those delivered from bondage to sin and death by grace and mercy? Take time to reflect on each element of that classic verse, Micah 6:8, which sums up the kind of life the Lord wants from each of us. Consider how you are living out each of those in your own life.

- Like the other prophets, the darkness of looming judgment is always pierced by rays of hope, but hope is only as dependable as the one who makes the promises. The coming of the Messiah, through whom all darkness will be done away, seals God's promise and draws our hearts and minds forward to a future restoration of all things (Acts 3:21). Nothing in our lives is too dark for the beams of hope in Christ to break through.

NAHUM

SNAPSHOT

Once condemned by God—then quickly pardoned (see Jonah)—the powerful, wicked, and terrifying city of Nineveh faces another, and this time irrevocable, decree of destruction. Nahum, an obscure prophet, delivers this vivid, blistering pronouncement. Though brief, Nahum's oracle communicates three key theological themes: God's supremacy over every earthly power, God's vow to punish his enemies, and God's faithfulness to rescue his people in spite of disobedience.

ORIENTATION

Date: 7th century BC
Author: Nahum, from the town of Elkosh
Audience: The people of Judah are the intended recipients. The city
                of Nineveh and the king of Assyria are addressed directly,
                though likely only rhetorically.
Outline: 1. Terse Introduction of the Subject and Author (1:1)
                2. Announcement of Nineveh's Destruction and Judah's
                    Deliverance (1:2–2:2)

3. Chilling Description of Nineveh's Coming Destruction (2:3–13)
4. Inventory of Sins Justifying Nineveh's Judgment (3:1–6)
5. Far-reaching Repercussions of Nineveh's Fate (3:7–19)

YOU ARE HERE

Episode 5: Division and Judgment

As the seventh of the Minor Prophets, Nahum prophesies against the Assyrian city of Nineveh after the events of Jonah and prior to Nineveh's fall in 612 BC.

EXPLORING NAHUM

Nineveh enjoys a particular emphasis as the solitary subject of God's judgment in two prophetic books, Jonah and Nahum. Each features a divine declaration of the city's impending destruction. Though both prophets declare the Lord as "slow to anger," each portrays a distinct theological perspective on the nature of God's wrath against his enemies.

The pronouncement of Nineveh's judgment in Jonah concludes with a display of God's overwhelming mercy in response to immediate repentance by the city and the Assyrian king. The theological reasoning appears in Jonah's frustrated response: "I knew that you are a gracious and compassionate God, slow to anger, abounding in faithful love, and one who relents from sending disaster" (Jonah 4:2).

In contrast, in the opening lines of Nahum's prophesy (Nah 1:2–8), "slow to anger" is couched in language of vengeance, wrath, fury, and anger against wicked enemies. As such, God was castigating the Ninevites for squandering the profound grace and mercy he showed in the ministry of Jonah; in a short span they had returned to their wicked ways. So he reminds his readers, "The LORD is slow to anger but great in power; the

LORD will never leave the guilty unpunished" (1:3). As the opening discourse narrows to address Nineveh directly, signaling its day of judgment has come, Nahum's forewarning of the impending, unrelenting, justified, and complete doom of Nineveh commences.

The remainder of the first chapter affirms this coming of the sudden, swift, and sweeping demise of the city, its king, and the Assyrian empire. The second chapter poetically, graphically, and tragically details the surprising attack which will decimate Nineveh and end Assyria's prideful and misguided quest for global domination and her threat to Judah. The final chapter summarizes the crimes of Assyria, articulates consequences corresponding to her sins, and surveys the ramifications of God's judgment. The proleptic scenes depicted in Nahum's unfolding portrait of Nineveh's coming devastation provide not only testimony of God's sovereignty and power with hopeful encouragement to the oppressed in Judah; they also evoke chilling images of what the wicked will face on the day of final judgment (cf. 2 Pet 3; Rev 5–19).

Juxtaposed to the prophecy of judgment against God's enemies are brief calming assurances of deliverance for God's people. Embedded in the opening decree is the reminder that God is "a stronghold in a day of distress" who "cares for those who take refuge in him" (Nah 1:7). Yet the words of encouragement and hope depend on faith and obedience. The reminder that God "punished" Judah through the yoke and shackles of Assyria (vv. 12–13) and the call for Judah to celebrate their festivals and fulfill their vows (v. 15) couple words of deliverance with warnings for the disobedient of Judah to repent. In short, what happens to Nineveh because of their wickedness can happen to Judah too!

The meaning of the promise "the LORD will restore the majesty" of Jacob and Israel (2:2) draws the eyes of faith to a distant hope. It lifts the reader's perspective from the near events of Nineveh's judgment and Judah's impending destruction of the temple and exile to Babylon. Both the opening oracle (1:2–7) and this promise of restoration provide glimpses of a glorious future. With the return of Christ, God's people will witness the promises of the final judgment of all God's enemies and the establishment of an eternal kingdom under the perfect, just King.

START YOUR JOURNEY

- The book of Nahum reminds us why it's important for Bible readers to have a working knowledge of the overall history of Israel—especially prior to the destruction of Israel in the north (722 BC) and Judah in the south (586 BC)—as well as familiarity with geography of the ancient Near East. Spend a little time in your Bible's maps and timelines to better understand how Nahum fits within the broader story of God's program of judgment and restoration.

- An apparent theological contrast of God's intentions for Nineveh in the books of Jonah and Nahum warrants careful analysis. Are the two theological perspectives including the phrase "slow to anger" in concert or in opposition? How would you explain the character of God exhibited in each of these books? How does that relate to our understanding today of the reality of Christ returning to this world as Judge as well as Deliverer?

- Nahum's prophecy of the downfall of Nineveh and Assyria was fulfilled in history in 612 BC. Sometimes Old Testament prophecies exhibit a near fulfillment, reminding us of the dependability of God's words. Nahum also foresees prophecies yet to be fulfilled in the distant future. Consider how the historical fulfillment of short-term prophecies informs our understanding of the fulfillment of the future prophecies. How does this contribute to the dependability of God's prophetic word?

Q&A

"The Bible in Light of Archaeology and Ancient Literature"

With Dr. Gordon H. Johnston

Dr. Gordon H. Johnston (ThM, ThD, Dallas Theological Seminary) is professor of Old Testament studies at Dallas Theological Seminary, author of numerous articles in scholarly journals, and coauthor of *Jesus the Messiah*. Known for thorough research and meticulous detail, his research and teaching interests include Wisdom literature and biblical theology.

Q: OK, I'm going to ask this right out of the gate. Does archaeology "prove" the Bible?

A: In the first half of the twentieth century, many archaeologists had a single goal: to demonstrate (if not prove) the historicity of biblical narratives. While conceived in good faith, this quest too often resulted in exaggerated claims and suspicion that this kind of approach lacked objectivity. Today, archaeologists define their goals in more broad and less biased terms. Archaeologists now strive to adopt a stance of detached neutrality, allowing the evidence to speak for itself. They also seek a better dialogue between broader cultural concerns of sociological studies and narrower historical concerns of biblical studies. Even if somebody sought to prove the Bible from archaeology, the discipline could not accomplish this. The most that archaeology can provide, for example, is evidence that a particular site was destroyed at a particular time; however, it can't prove that the Israelites were the agents of destruction, much less that God had empowered the Israelites to destroy that site at that time. So, while it's legitimate to note occasions in which archaeological discoveries synchronize with biblical narratives, it's more balanced to say that archaeology helps us better understand the world of the Bible. I like to describe my own archaeological research as a quest to better understand the Bible and to discover the historical basis of ancient Israel's faith.

Q: Well, then, how about the opposite? Does archaeology "disprove" the Bible?

A: Just as "maximalists" often claim that archaeology has proven the Bible, "minimalists" typically claim that archaeology has disproven the Bible. The reality is more nuanced. Since no archaeological artifact is self-interpreting, any discovery must be interpreted by someone, and this is where one's biases enter the equation (often on a subconscious level). An archaeologist inclined to treat the Bible as historically reliable will tend to see synchronisms that are often dismissed by an archaeologist inclined to view the Bible with suspicion. Archaeologists who adopt a more balanced approach present their discoveries in an objective way by simply describing what they have unearthed without weighing in on questions of how their discoveries impact one's view about the Bible.

Q: What, in your estimation, are three or four of the most important archaeological discoveries for helping us better understand the Old and New Testaments?

A: Any list of the most important archaeological discoveries must include the following: 1) the victory stele from year 5 of the Egyptian king Merneptah (composed ca. 1208 BC), which includes the earliest known reference to "Israel," here identified as a nomadic people residing near the Jordan River; 2) the Khirbet Qeiyafa ostracon (composed ca. 1000 BC), the earliest known Hebrew inscriptions, which mentions the "king" and preserves the admonition, "defend the orphan and the widow," suggesting the Israelite monarchy and a Mosaic-like ethic were already in place; 3) an Aramaic victory stele (composed ca. 850 BC) discovered at Tel Dan (aka the "Tel Dan Inscription") that refers to "[Jeho]ram son of [Ahab] king of Israel" and to "[Ahaz]yahu son of [Joram king] of the House of David," revealing that the Davidic dynasty was known by a foreign king about a century after David would have ruled; 4) a Moabite victory inscription (aka "Moabite Stone") commissioned by Mesha King of Moab (ca. 850 BC) that refers to "the vessels of YHWH [= Yahweh]," which the Moabite king plundered from a sanctuary dedicated to the national deity of Israel.

Q: Sometimes we hear people say, "The Bible is nothing special. It's just like all the other literature of the ancient Near East or Roman world." So, what about ancient literature outside the Bible?

A: Some 500+ archives and libraries have been discovered throughout the ancient Near East, dating from ca. 3200 to 300 BC, preserving hundreds of thousands of inscribed clay tablets (and some papyri). These texts represent a variety of genres (e.g., law codes, treaties, king lists, royal annals, poetic epics, myths and legends, hymns and prayers, cultic rituals, incantations, omens, Wisdom literature). Comparative studies reveal both continuity (comparisons) and discontinuity (contrasts) with the literary genres of the Bible. While the Bible reflects many literary conventions of the ancient culture in which the biblical authors lived, it stands out by dramatic contrast in proclaiming that Yahweh is the one and only living God who has intervened in history to create the cosmos and redeem the faithful.

Q: What are a couple important ancient texts that shed light on the Old Testament especially? And where might a novice find translations of those?

A: For a standard translation of hundreds of ancient Near Eastern texts related to the Old Testament, see William Hallo and K. Lawson Younger Jr., eds., *The Context of Scripture*, 3 vols. (Leiden: Brill, 2003). For example, tablet 11 of the Gilgamesh Epic preserves an ancient Mesopotamian tradition of a massive flood that destroyed five cities in the Tigris-Euphrates flood plain (ca. 2900 BC); the Genesis Flood narrative seems to represent the biblical Hebrew version of this event that destroyed "the world" that the ancients knew. The Law of Eshnunna (ca. 1930 BC) and Law Code of Hammurabi (ca. 1750 BC) belong to an ancient legal tradition which provides the cultural context that helps us better understand the case-laws in the Law of Moses (Exod 20–23; Lev 18–25; Deut 12–26). Collections of Wisdom literature from all corners of the ancient Near East provide insight into biblical Wisdom literature (Proverbs, Ecclesiastes, Job), showing how God provides wisdom for daily living to anyone who opens his eyes and heart to the ethical patterns which he built into the way the world works.

Q: Short of going on an actual archaeological dig, is there a resource or two you'd recommend on the Bible and archaeology for beginners?

A: A great way to whet one's appetite is the *NIV: Archaeological Study Bible* (Zondervan), which features about 500 color photographs with accompanying essays discussing archaeological discoveries tied to selected Old and New Testament passages. Two excellent e-newsletters that provide brief summaries of current archaeological work and research throughout the ancient Near East are *AGADE* (contact listserv@unc.edu for a free subscription) and *Ancient Near East Today* (contact membership@asor.org for a free subscription).

HABAKKUK

SNAPSHOT

There are times when life is tough, so you pray and ask God for relief. Instead, things get even worse! This experience was exactly what happened to the prophet Habakkuk. The short book of Habakkuk—a dialogue between the prophet and God—helps us to understand God's providence and purpose, even when things seem to be falling apart.

ORIENTATION

Date: 7th century BC
Author: Habakkuk
Audience: Jerusalem and the southern kingdom of Judah
Outline: 1. Habakkuk's Lament: Why Is Judah's Injustice and Violence Tolerated? (1:1–4)
                2. Yahweh's Plan: God Is Raising up the Babylonians in Response (1:5–11)
                3. Habakkuk's Complaint: How Can God Use the Evil Babylonians? (1:12–2:1)
                4. Yahweh's Deeper Plan: He Will Punish Babylonian Wickedness (2:2–20)

> 5. Habakkuk's Prayer: The Sovereignty of God Restores
> His Faith (3:1–19)

YOU ARE HERE

Episode 5: Division and Judgment

Habakkuk is the eighth book of the twelve "Minor Prophets," unique in that it presents its message in the form of a back-and-forth dialogue between the prophet and God.

EXPLORING HABAKKUK

Habakkuk serves as a good entrée into the problem of evil, because so many of its features are introduced. The prophet lamented the hiddenness of God (1:2). Yahweh's startling answer reflects the truths of what has often been called "the free will defense." Evil is present in the world because God permitted humans, like the Babylonians (and the Hebrews), to make real choices (1:4, 7). These sinful actions don't contradict divine providence; instead, God uses them to bring about his purposes. This hard truth was a stumbling block for Habakkuk (vv. 12–13), but eventually he came to understand God's ultimate goals. In 3:2, he implores Yahweh, "In your wrath remember mercy!" The beautiful conclusion of the book portrays the restored faith of Habakkuk as he waits patiently for God's plan to unfold and rejoices, despite trials (3:16–19).

Habakkuk's concerns were appeased, in part, because of the distinction between discipline and punishment. God used Babylon to *discipline* Judah so they would return in faith to him (1:12). But the wicked and unbelieving Babylonians will be *punished*, as seen in the five "woes" of chapter 2 (vv. 6, 9, 12, 15, and 19). God is chastening the people of Judah with the Babylonians (3:13), but for the Babylonians, a day of judgment ("distress," 3:16) is coming.

The pivotal passage in Habakkuk is 2:2–4. The prophet declared that he would stand watch to wait for God's answer (2:1). The answer is that the revelation will come at its proper time: "Though it delays, wait for it, since it will certainly come and not be late" (v. 3). This revelation is the Word of God, his own Son, who will put an end to all sin and injustice. The ultimate answer to the problem of evil is the grace which is found in the atoning work of Jesus. The right response—for those in Habakkuk's time as well as our own—is faith. The climactic expression, "the righteous one will live by his faith" (v. 4), is cited three times in the New Testament (Rom 1:17; Gal 3:11; and Heb 10:38). Habakkuk grasped the key insight to the problem of evil. We must trust in a good and powerful God who is working to bring all the faithful to himself, who will one day defeat evil through the resurrection of the dead.

The conversational format of the book highlights the indispensable nature of prayer. Renz writes, "Maybe more so than other books in the Bible, Habakkuk suggests that thoughtful, engaged prayer, informed by Scripture, can help us to discern what is truly going on in a situation. . . . The mature posture towards God is firm hope in his future coming, trusting that God's deeds must ultimately speak of his justice and compassion because God cannot be made known in random acts of aggression."[1]

START YOUR JOURNEY

- The dialogical nature of the book is reminiscent of others who talked with God, like Abraham, Moses, and Job. This style reveals the deep emotion and frankness with which God's people in the Bible speak with God . . . and how God relates personally and intimately with his people.
- Habakkuk demonstrates that we can confidently share our deepest concerns, questions, and even complaints with the Lord. In this way, Habakkuk functions like a lament, like Lamentations and

[1] Thomas Renz, *The Books of Nahum, Habakkuk, and Zephaniah*, The New International Commentary on the Old Testament (Grand Rapids: Eerdmans, 2021), 218–19.

various psalms. Jerome (fourth century AD) thought Habakkuk's complaint was not respectful toward God. Some readers may agree, but a study of biblical lament reveals that God invites his people to cry out with their deepest concern. The practice of lament is actually an act of faith.

- It is appropriate to put oneself in Habakkuk's place and to present to God our fears and unanswered questions. It is essential to remember that God's most important response (sending Jesus to bear our sins and to rise from the grave) has already occurred. The righteous still live by faith today, in hope of our resurrection at the return of his Son.

GOING DEEPER

"Getting into the Word"

— Howard G. Hendricks —

In my judgment, the greatest problem in evangelicalism today is that we have an increasing number of Christians who are *under* the word of God but who are not *in it* for themselves. Being under the word of God should be a stimulus, not a substitute, for getting into it for yourself. The Bible is still the best-sold book—and also the most neglected. Now if you were interested in teaching people how to study the Bible, you need to ask and answer one basic question: Why study the Scriptures? I want to give you three reasons. The first reason is found in 1 Pet 2:2—"Like newborn infants, desire the pure milk of the word, so that by it you may grow up into your salvation." Just as the baby grabs for the bottle, you ought to grab for the book. The first reason is that the Scriptures are the primary means for spiritual growth. Just think of it, God wanted to communicate with you in the twenty-first century, and he wrote his message in a book. There's no growth apart from that book.

The second passage is in Heb 5:11–14. The writer says, "We have a great deal to say about this, and it is difficult to explain, since you have become too lazy to understand. Although by this time you ought to be teachers, you need someone to teach you the basic principles of God's revelation again. You need milk, not solid food. Now everyone who lives on milk is inexperienced with the message about righteousness, because he is an infant. But solid food is for the mature—for those whose senses have been trained to distinguish between good and evil." Please note the reason for the rebuke. The reason is not the difficulty of the revelation but the density of the reception. He says, in effect, you've got hearing loss. The important phrase to underline in that paragraph is the little phrase in verse 12: "by this time you ought to be teachers." These were not recent converts. At least from the standpoint of the author, sufficient time had elapsed that these people ought to be going into the college department, yet they've got to return to the kindergarten and learn their ABCs all over again. When they should be communicating the word of God to others, they need to have someone teach them. Then he adds this interesting note: "Now everyone who lives on milk is inexperienced with the message about righteousness, because he is an infant. But solid food is for the mature—for those whose senses have been trained to distinguish between good and evil" (5:13–14). The highest mark of spiritual maturity is the ability to take the word of God and relate it to your life. So, you ought to study the Bible not only because the Scriptures are the primary means of spiritual growth, but also because the Scriptures are the only means of developing spiritual maturity.

The third passage is in 2 Tim 3:15–17. Look at verse 16: "All Scripture is inspired by God and is profitable for teaching, for rebuking, for correcting, for training in righteousness." *All* Scripture is profitable. That includes 2 Chronicles. I've said that and heard the response, "I didn't even know there was a first Chronicles." *All* Scripture is inspired by God, and it is *profitable*. No book has been included which should've been excluded; no book is excluded that should've been included. It's profitable for *teaching*. It'll structure your thinking. It's profitable for *rebuke*; it'll show you where you're out of bounds. It's like the umpire in a baseball game who says "Out!" or "Safe!" And it's profitable for *correction*. It will not only show you you're out of bounds; it'll also correct your life. And it will give you instruction in righteous living. Look at the overall purpose: "So that the man of God may be complete, equipped for every good work" (3:17). That's the third reason why you need to study the Bible. The Scriptures are the essential means of becoming an effective servant of Jesus Christ. These three reasons conspire to build a convincing case that personal Bible study is not an option, it's an essential.

I'd like to share with you a three-stage model for personal Bible study. The first stage in Bible study is *observation*, where we ask and answer the question, What do I see? The psalmist prayed, "Open my eyes so that I may contemplate wondrous things from your instruction" (Ps 119:18). He was praying for the powers of observation. He was asking the Spirit of God to tear the bandages from his eyes so that he might see with spiritual insight into the truth, which God had revealed. The moment you come to read the Scripture, you assume the role of a biblical detective. You are looking for clues, and no detail is trivial.

The second stage in the process we call *interpretation*. That's where you ask and answer the question, What does it mean? Too much Bible study begins and ends in the wrong place. People open the Bible, read a statement, and ask, "I wonder what that means?" In fact, they don't even know what it said! Because it begins with observation, most people are derailed in the process. Too many begin and end with interpretation. The moment they say, "Now I understand what this passage teaches," they feel they can wash their hands and move on. The purpose of the Word of God is not to make you a smarter sinner, it's to make you like Jesus Christ; it's not to satisfy your curiosity, it's to change your life.

That leads us to the third stage in our model: *application*. This is where we ask and answer the question, How does it work? Please note, we don't ask, *Does* it work? I think I'll scream the next time I hear somebody get up in a pulpit or in a teaching situation and say, "We're going to make the Bible relevant." If the Bible is not relevant, nothing you do will help. The Bible is relevant because it's revealed. It's a return to reality and no matter how it appears to you, this is the way it is.[1]

---

[1] Adapted from Howard Hendricks, "Getting into the Word," Hendricks Center/Dallas Theological Seminary, https://hendrickscenter.dts.edu/media-post /getting-into-the-word/. © 1995 Dallas Theological Seminary.

ZEPHANIAH

SNAPSHOT

The book of Zephaniah stands as a stark warning to powerbrokers in Judah and the surrounding nations of God's fierce judgment against their oppression, lawbreaking, and pride. Even still, God plans a future for the faithful in Judah and the nations.

ORIENTATION

Date: 7th century BC
Author: Zephaniah
Audience: Judah and the nations
Outline: 1. Superscription (1:1)
                2. Judgment on Judah and the Nations (1:2–3:8)
                3. Change is Coming (3:9–20)

YOU ARE HERE

Episode 5: Division and Judgment

As the ninth book in the section of Scripture called the "Minor Prophets," Zephaniah warns Judah and her neighbors of the coming "day of the Lord."

EXPLORING ZEPHANIAH

Zephaniah, a prophet with royal blood (he was the great-great grandson of King Hezekiah), directs his message of judgment to the elites of society: princes, judges, prophets, and priests (3:3–4). After decades of serving Assyrian powers under the wicked kings Manasseh and Amon, the culture of Judah had devolved. Rather than serving the Lord and his people, Judah's leaders answered to foreign gods and earthly rulers (1:4–5). Even as the Lord dwelled in the center of the city, the people embraced injustice (3:5). Judah refused the Lord's guidance, choosing its own oppressive way and devouring its own people.

But Zephaniah also turns his attention to many of Judah's traditional enemies: Philistia, Moab, Ammon, Ethiopia, and Assyria (2:4–15). In each case, the nation in question will become desolate. The faithless will be moved out while God's faithful people will move in (v. 7). Judgment scatters, but redemption gathers.

After the devastation wrought by these "day of the Lord" judgments (1:2–2:3), God will redeem his people from among both Judah and the nations. God's vision of future redemption incorporates people from "beyond the rivers of Cush [Ethiopia]" (3:10) in addition to the people of Israel and Judah (v. 14). Rather than oppressing God's people, this new people will be changed: "meek and humble" (v. 12), turning away from injustice and lies (v. 13), and dwelling with the Lord (v. 15).

START YOUR JOURNEY

- Since it's so short, read Zephaniah in a single sitting to experience both the judgment and redemption of the book together (this should take about ten–fifteen minutes).
- As you read through Zephaniah, list out the sins of the people: In what ways do these mirror sins today? Where are you personally implicated by God's warnings through the prophet?
- Memorize Zeph 3:9–20, and praise God for his redemptive work!

HAGGAI

SNAPSHOT

How often do we start well but finish poorly? Or fail to start at all? The prophet Haggai had some choice words for the returned exiles who neglected their call to rebuild the temple.

ORIENTATION

Date:	6th century BC
Author:	Haggai
Audience:	Zerubbabel and Joshua, leaders of the remnant of Judah returned from captivity
Outline:	1. The First Message: Build the Temple! (1)
	2. The Second Message: Build up Spiritually (2)

YOU ARE HERE

Episode 6: Return from Exile

Haggai is the tenth book of the "Minor Prophets" and the second shortest of the Old Testament.

EXPLORING HAGGAI

The book begins with a problem. The resettled exiles invested themselves in their "paneled houses," which suggests luxury, while God's house—the temple—"lies in ruins" (1:3–4, 9). The people had dragged their feet on rebuilding the temple while prioritizing their own comfort (v. 2). God responded by withholding the productivity of the land (vv. 5–11). When they recognized God's chastening, "the people feared the Lord" and "began work on the house of the Lord" (1:12, 14). Convicted by the preaching of the prophet, the people are encouraged to "be strong" because God is with them (2:4); because God's Spirit is present among them, they need not fear (v. 5).

Judah's past points forward to God's future. God will "shake all the nations," then give the world what it desires—the peace of God's presence (2:7, 21). The second chapter of Haggai calls the people to reflect on their own trust in God and holiness of heart and life (vv. 10–19). The people must "think carefully" about the purity of their worship, or their injustices would impoverish the land again (2:14–19). The book emphasizes the priority of the glorious presence of the Lord more than the grandeur of his "house" (vv. 6–9). On the day of the Lord's blessing, God used Zerubbabel to supervise the construction of the post-exilic temple. The governor's "signet ring" will validate the Persian decree to rebuild Jerusalem and the temple and guarantee that the Lord's promises to Israel are the hope of the world (v. 23).

START YOUR JOURNEY

- God castigated the people for focusing on themselves and their own material comfort in building paneled houses while God's temple needed to be rebuilt. How easy it is for us to focus on our own material things, creature comforts, and entertainment or luxuries when so much of God's work—including helping others—is neglected!

- Haggai repeatedly emphasizes the need to be strong. As you read through this book, note all the exhortations to courage and strength. Where does such strength come from? Where do you need that strength in your own life today?

ZECHARIAH

SNAPSHOT

In a world of revolving national powers, cultural conflicts, political polarities, and spiritual decline, where can we find genuine hope? Will the world ever know that God is real and that his way is right? Can we really trust God's promises for the future? These questions weighed on the returning captives from Babylon, and they burden people today as well. Enter the prophet Zechariah, whose fascinating visions give a glimpse into realities beyond the present world.

ORIENTATION

Date: 6th century BC

Author: Zechariah, from one of the priestly families returning from Babylon

Audience: People of the post-exilic community of Israel living in Jerusalem

Outline:
1. Introduction (1:1–6)
2. Eight Night Visions (1:7–6:8)
3. Symbolic Coronation of Joshua, the High Priest (6:9–15)

4. Four Messages (7:1–8:23)
5. Two Burdens (9:1–14:21)

YOU ARE HERE

Episode 6: Return from Exile

The eleventh of the "Minor Prophets" and second of three post-exilic prophets, Zechariah preached a message that urged the people on to persevering faith and hope.

EXPLORING ZECHARIAH

The book opens (1:1–6) with a call to learn the lessons of history and repent and return to the Lord. God is jealous for his people and for Jerusalem. If God's Word proved true in their disciplinary exile, his promises of a glorious future kingdom ruled by the Messiah can also be trusted. The book consists of eight visions, four messages, and two burdens, which represent three different kinds of prophetic writings: visionary, ethical, and purely predictive. The presence of an angelic interpreter and the symbolic and cosmic imageries are clues to the presence of visionary literature.

The eight visions (1:7–6:8) are recorded in a literary form called a "chiasm," in which the outer sets (vision 1 and vision 8) form a paired set, with subsequent sets working inward toward the central set, visions 4 and 5. The first outer set of the first and eighth visions deal with the Lord's concern for the nations at large. While they have been used as agents of judgment, they themselves will be judged as well in contrast to the promised blessings of restoration for Israel.

The second and seventh visions reveal how God sovereignly uses Gentile nations as tools of his discipline and objects of his judgments. God reveals that what appear to be independent world powers are his servants for accomplishing his purposes. The personification and future localization of wickedness in Babylon show God's ability to fully and finally judge the rebellion that has been against him throughout the history of the world.

The third and sixth visions concern the future of God's people. While the Lord will one day come to dwell in a rebuilt Jerusalem as the glorious and protected center of his kingdom, Israel, as well as those from other nations, will need to be cleansed of their sin if they are to enjoy such blessings.

The centerpieces of the fourth and fifth visions deal with both the cleansing and power needed for godly leadership. God's defense of Joshua against Satan's accusations and his clothing symbolize the individual and national forgiveness of sin to be provided by the coming branch—the King-Priest Messiah. As was true for Joshua and Zerubbabel, both near and far off mountains of impossibility are only overcome by the power of the Spirit and not human might or methods.

The coronation of Joshua the high priest (6:9–15) symbolizes the ultimate roles of king and priest that the Messiah will fulfill. The names "branch" and "servant" depict the humility and lowliness of character with which he will function in those offices.

Four major messages (7:1–8:23) are laced together with formulas of divine utterance for the ethical prophetic exhortations to the people. The first is a message of rebuke for superficial religious rituals without a heart of righteousness. The second is a call to obedience by learning the lessons of previous generations that disobedience always results in judgment. The third is a prospective view when devastation is replaced with restoration for Israel and other Gentiles when the Lord as the Davidic King comes to reign in Jerusalem. The last message is an expectation of joy when fasting will be replaced by feasting, when truth and peace will find their rightful place, and Israel will fulfill their purpose as a witness to the nations.

Two burdens or oracles finish the book. The first is an oracle (9:1–11:17) against the nations opposed to Israel. The King who comes to judge and to save will come humbly. Those scattered of both Israel and Judah who follow the leadership of the Messiah will be joined again as a single flock, while those opposing will be judged accordingly. The second oracle

(12:1–14:21) details Israel's repentance prompted by the Holy Spirit and the refinement of a remnant through the pressures of international persecution and the protection of the Lord. Climaxing this oracle and the book as a whole is the judgment on the nations, the deliverance of a remnant, and the Lord's return to the earth with the accompanying blessings of a righteous reign.

START YOUR JOURNEY

- Read through the book and make a list of all the predictions of future events. Zechariah has been called "the book of Revelation of the Old Testament" because it gives a fairly detailed account for the future conversion and restoration in preparation for the messianic kingdom.
- Zechariah is the most quoted prophet in the passion narratives of the suffering, death, and resurrection in the Gospels. Consider what can be learned about Jesus from the following messianic prophecies: 3:8; 6:12, 13; 10:4–11; 11:12, 13; 12:10; 13:7; 14:4.
- Over fifty times, the title "Lord of Armies" (or, in some translations, "Lord of Hosts") is used to highlight God's infinite power and authority. Why would that title for God be so important for the post-exilic community? How does that title encourage you today?
- Zechariah, whose name means "God remembers," reminds the people of his purpose to restore Israel and Jerusalem along with the temple to a place of unprecedented glory. Not to be missed in this book is the fact that such promises are renewed even after the disciplines of the Babylonian exile. Just as God can be trusted to keep his Word to Israel, he can be trusted to keep his promises to us.

MALACHI

SNAPSHOT

Imagine your worst betrayal. How would you respond? How would you right the wrong done? The book of Malachi describes God's reaction when his people break their covenant with him. Shockingly, God remains loving and loyal to his promises, graciously warning those who do harm, sparing those who remain faithful, and predicting the nations will come to honor his name.

ORIENTATION

Date: 5th century BC
Author: Malachi
Audience: Israel, contemporary Jewish listeners in that day
Outline: 1. God's Selection of Israel (1:1–5)
　　　　　　　　　2. God's Objection and Warning to Faithless Priests
　　　　　　　　　　　(1:6–2:17)
　　　　　　　　　3. God's Promise of the Lord's Return to Purify (3:1–5)
　　　　　　　　　4. God's Call for Israelites to Return (3:6–15)
　　　　　　　　　5. God's Solace for the Faithful (3:16–18)
　　　　　　　　　6. God's Final Warning and Promise (4:1–6)

YOU ARE HERE

Episode 6: Return from Exile

After Haggai and Zechariah, the book of Malachi, last of the "Minor Prophets," was written in the post-exilic period after temple worship had been restored (1:7–14; 3:10).

EXPLORING MALACHI

The book of Malachi begins and closes with the bookends of God's divine prerogative of election, beginning with the selection of Israel and ending with God's unwavering commitment to distinguish good from evil (1:2–5; 3:18). God is unlike any other being in the universe: uncreated, self-existent, independent, pure, trustworthy. God doesn't cheat, deceive, or change—which preserves humanity (3:6).

Moreover, the world is God's possession, and God's mission—that his name will be known and honored—is the goal. The nations will know and respect his name, and everywhere the aroma of proper offerings to God will rise (1:11, 14). God dispossessed other nations for their evil practices, yet he promises that those who honor his name will form God's "treasured possession" (Deut 9:1–5; Mal 3:16–18 NIV). God leads with love to communicate his ways; however, judgment is also his just method (1:2; 3:1; 4:1). The repeated title "Lord of Heaven's Armies" emphasizes God's authority, power, and preeminence.

Malachi contains a chilling warning to religious leaders. God had appointed those from the tribe of Levi to lead the people to live in right relationship before him. They instead dishonored God's name, breaking sacrificial laws and naming as acceptable what is unholy (1:6–8; 2:17). God calls the priests to honor him and warns of the consequences of ignoring him (2:1–4). God recounts the myriad ways the priests have shown faithlessness, such as in their false teaching, partiality, and marriages (vv. 8–17). God will remain faithful to Israel by purifying the priesthood and bringing righteousness on earth (2:4; 3:1–6; 4:1–2).

The Israelites understood what human kings and governments rightly demand, yet they cheated God of the same (1:6, 8). They pretended to be self-possessed, presuming they could determine their reality apart from God's law. This stiff-necked turning is reminiscent of a toddler resisting with their whole body the direction a parent provides (3:7). A conversational question-and-answer interplay ensues between God and his people (vv. 6–15) as it did between God and his priests (1:1–14). God entertains their defenses, and in answering them, the Jewish readers are reminded of the truth. Their protests, commonplace in our time, include the following:

"How have you loved us?" (1:2)

"How can we return?" (3:7)

"How do we rob you?" (3:8)

"What have we spoken against you?" (3:13)

"What have we gained" by serving the Lord? (3:14)

This contrast between the respect due God and human rejection pervades the book. Ignoring their dependence on him, the people profane God's name and ways.

Through Malachi, God mercifully declares that despite how Israel has misrepresented his image (beckoning their return), his name will light the nations (1:11; 3:7). "The day" is coming when those who do evil will be judged (Mal 4:1–5; Joel 2:30–31; Amos 5:18; Obad 15; Rev 22:11–13). God's people are reminded to remain faithful by remembering his law and to look for the Messiah's forerunner, who will turn their hearts back to God (Mal 3:1; 4:5).

START YOUR JOURNEY

- Guard against a self-confident sense of independence from God. Our shallow holes dug defiantly in the sand will be swept away with the evening tide. We must disabuse ourselves of the notion, the lie, that we have a right to claim ownership over ourselves or others. All is given. Offer yourself to God.

- Listen to your conscious or unconscious back-talking toward God. About what do you protest? Does it align with God's view (3:5)?
- For those in ministry, ask yourself: How have you shown contempt for God? Are you cutting corners, calling good what is evil, or showing partiality (1:6–14; 2:6–9)? God has special concern that his teachers teach the unadulterated truth.
- When we approach God honestly and rightly, God receives us. God holds us. God remembers us (3:16–18). This is our confidence as we serve God in faith. Continue to cast yourself upon his grace, mercy, provision, and protection.

PART III

EXPLORER'S GUIDE TO THE NEW TESTAMENT

Before transitioning from the Old Testament to the New, let's take a look back and consider the long, arduous, sometimes meandering, sometimes treacherous path we've already taken over the course of several millennia.

In the beginning, God created all things good, but while in the bliss of the garden of Eden, Adam and Eve were tempted by the crafty serpent. They sinned, and this change brought about death and destruction for all humanity. Nevertheless, even in the midst of chaos, God didn't abandon his creation. Years later he called Abraham and promised him that he would be the father of a great *nation*, who would reside in a promised *land*, and who would bring about a *world-wide blessing*.

Although blessed by God, Abraham's descendants eventually found themselves in harsh bondage in Egypt. So, God called Moses to lead them out of Egypt and slavery. Even though God delivered his people, their hard, stubborn, unbelieving hearts got the best of them. They had eagerly entered into a covenant relationship with the Lord, the stipulations of which were expressed in the Ten Commandments and the whole Mosaic law (including the sacrificial system) and in the tabernacle where God dwelt with his people. Yet almost immediately they broke the covenant, turned their backs on their deliverer, and sought their own way. Because of this, instead of immediately entering the land of promise, they wandered in the desert for forty years until most of that original generation had died. But during this time, the only thing as stubborn as the Israelites' hearts was God's unrelenting love.

By and by, a new generation entered the land of promise. However, that generation—and those that followed—increasingly rebelled against God and disobeyed his laws. Many failed to trust that he had their best interests in mind, that he really would see to it that their enemies were vanquished, and that he would bless them in all the ways he said he would, provided they kept the covenant of the law. As God had warned the people of Israel through Moses, they consistently found themselves suffering oppression and hardship in the land, calling out for God to save them by the hands of judges only to return to their old ways after finding relief.

Tired of the cycles of judges, eventually the people of Israel cried out for a king to lead them—a king like the nations around them. The first king to measure up to their worldly standards, Saul, was reckless and didn't follow God faithfully. The next king, David, would never have won first prize in a "king contest" by the world's standards, but he was God's own choice. Far from perfect, David yearned for the heart of God. To David God promised through a covenant not only a permanent line of descendants, but also an eventual eternal King who would have a kingdom that would last forever. This promised Savior would be the ultimate ruler—incorruptible in every sense of that word.

Upon David's death, his son Solomon became king and built a temple for God. While wise in the ways of the world and shrewd in international politics, Solomon was not always wise in the ways of God. When Solomon died, his son Rehoboam became king, taxing the people so much that they rebelled. This marked a turning point in the history of Israel, for the nation split into two kingdoms—one southern (Judah), and one northern (Israel). Most of the kings for both nations were evil and didn't follow God's covenant law.

During this time God sent prophets to call the people to repentance. But lasting repentance never came, so judgment did. The northern kingdom of Israel fell first—in 722 BC to the Assyrians. The southern kingdom of Judah collapsed in 586 BC under the Babylonians. What Moses warned centuries earlier had come to pass in its fullest sense: faithfulness led to blessing, and unfaithfulness led to judgment. The Israelites were now captives in foreign lands, longing for the days of the blessings of God.

Yet that shocking judgment didn't alter God's promises. He would bring his people home. In 538 BC, under the Persian king Cyrus, God's people were released to return to their land and rebuild the city and the sanctuary. The exiles returned in three primary groups under the leadership of Zerubbabel, Ezra, and Nehemiah. Although they were again in the land of promise, all was not well. Israel's enemies were still present, social injustices prevailed, and God's presence, which once filled the temple, was nowhere to be found. They weren't experiencing the time of everlasting peace the prophets said would come. And where was this Davidic King—a Messiah, "anointed one," or "Christ" that had been promised? That King was supposed to reign in justice and power. He would save the people from their own sin and deliver them from their enemies. The final prophets of the Old Testament era anticipated this messianic ruler who would come and make all things right. Their message was one of hope: one day the Messiah will arrive, but first, another prophet in the power of Elijah would prepare the way. This forerunner would call the people to repentance in anticipation of the coming King.

With the last of the post-exile prophets, the Old Testament era comes to a close. The resounding words of the prophets—from Isaiah to Malachi—echo into the future. And what of their harmonious chorus of warning and promise, repentance and restoration, judgment and hope, all centered on the mysterious figure of the coming descendant of David who will reign from Jerusalem over a regathered Israel and Judah . . . and through them around the world? Those deep desires for times of the refreshing and restoration of all things written in the prophets become a steady melody in the hearts and on the lips of generation after generation in the land of promise.

Yet just as the prophet Daniel had foretold, the times of the Gentiles and their dominion over the land continued. Following the return of the Jewish exiles under Persian rule, the empire of Alexander the Great rose up in the West and spread its territory eastward, eventually swallowing up the Promised Land and subjecting its people to the influence of Greek culture and language—Hellenism (see Dan 8). When Alexander died in Babylon in 323 BC, his kingdom was divided among his four generals, with the land of Israel falling under the rule of Ptolemy I (Soter), all in fulfillment of Daniel's vision of the beast that would rise after Persia with "four heads" (Dan 7:6; cf. 8:8, 21–22).[1]

Yet even under this foreign rule, the restored Jewish community in the Promised Land continued to thrive. In fact, under Ptolemy II (Philadelphus), who reigned until 246 BC, a team of about seventy scholars gathered in Alexandria, Egypt, to begin translation of the Hebrew Scriptures into Greek. By the first century, all of the Old Testament as well as several valued writings—known as the Old Testament Apocrypha—had been translated into Greek. This translation is collectively referred to as the Septuagint, a Greek term meaning "seventy" in reference to the story that the project was accomplished by seventy (or seventy-two) scholars in seventy days.[2] The Septuagint (referred to with the abbreviation LXX) became the standard translation of Hellenistic (Greek-speaking) Jews as well as the version used by earliest Christians. In fact, when the New

---

[1] Stephen R. Miller, *Daniel*, vol. 18, The New American Commentary (Nashville: B&H, 1994), 200.

[2] Martin Hengel, *The Septuagint as Christian Scripture: Its Prehistory and the Problem of Its Canon*, trans. Mark E. Biddle (London: T&T Clark, 2002), 25–26.

Testament authors quoted from the Old Testament, they mostly relied on the Septuagint.

Dominion would lead to oppression and a new crisis in the history of Israel. When the fractured Greek kingdoms wrangled with each other for power, the people of God suffered. By the second century BC, the Promised Land fell under the control of the Seleucid king, Antiochus IV Epiphanes. His heavy-handed, brutal rule and zeal for imposing Greek culture and norms upon his conquered territories led Antiochus to plunder and desecrate the temple in Jerusalem, including offering an "abomination of desolation" on the altar of the temple, burning Hebrew Scriptures, and executing Jews who kept the law (1 Macc 1:54–61). In response to this outrage and sacrilege, the faithful among Israel staged the campaign known as the Maccabean Revolt, under the leadership of Judas Maccabeus. The revolt successfully drove out the Greek invaders and reestablished temple worship—an event celebrated every year by the Jewish festival of Hanukkah (1 Macc 4:52–59). The Maccabean kingdom grew in power and influence over much of the original land of Israel.

Yet maintaining this military success also required an alliance with another rising power—the Roman Empire (1 Macc 8). This alliance of necessity, though, would eventually lead to another phase of oppression as the Roman Empire spread its boundaries and control over much of the Mediterranean world, including the province of Judea. By the first century BC, the descendants of the Maccabean rulers—the Hasmoneans—had secured its rule over the kingdom of Israel, but they ultimately served under the overarching authority of Rome.

During the closing decades of the first century, Herod the Great secured the title "King of the Jews" through political maneuvering with Rome, effectively ending the Hasmonean reign and beginning the Herodian dynasty— the line of rulers in place during the birth of Jesus until the destruction of Jerusalem in AD 70.[3]

---

[3] See Everett Ferguson, "The Herodian Dynasty," in *The World of the New Testament: Cultural, Social, and Historical Contexts*, ed. Joel B. Green and Lee

Sects, Parties, and Peoples in Israel by the First Century

The origins of some of the various competing sects and parties within Judaism by the first century are not always clear. By the time we get to the New Testament, certain groups have risen to prominence and play a significant role in the accounts of the Gospels. Two of these—the Pharisees and Sadducees—appear too frequently not to mention. The first-century Jewish historian, Josephus, famously simplifies the situation by describing three sects of Judaism: "The first is that of the Pharisees, the second that of the Sadducees, and the third that of the Essenes" (*Life of Flavius Josephus* 1.2.10).[4] Elsewhere he details some of the theological differences between these three. The Pharisees embraced a kind of middle ground on the issue of determinism and free will, believing some things are subject to one's own choices, other things to God's determination. They also observed traditions not written in Scripture but handed down through their ancestors. In addition, they taught that the soul of a person continues after death, receiving either punishment or reward, and that the righteous will be restored to life again in resurrection. In contrast, the Sadducees embraced a radical view of free will, in which nothing was determined and all people were free to conduct themselves as they pleased. They only embraced what was specifically written in the law, and they denied the continued existence of the soul after death. Finally, the Essenes were the strictest and most sectarian form of Judaism, believing that all things were predestined, that the soul was immortal and could attain eternal rewards, and that the temple system in Jerusalem was corrupt. While the Essenes kept to themselves in strict asceticism, the Sadducees were popular only among the rich, powerful elites; and the Pharisees enjoyed wide popularity among the common people (Josephus, *Antiquities of the Jews* 13.5.9; 13.10.6; 18.1.3–5). It is commonly believed

---

Martin McDonald (Grand Rapids: Baker, 2013), 54–76.

[4] William Whiston, trans., *The Works of Josephus: Complete and Unabridged*, new updated ed. (Peabody: Hendrickson, 1987), 1.

that the Qumran community, which preserved the Dead Sea Scrolls, was part of the Essene sect.[5]

Beyond these religious traditions, first-century Israel also had several political factions, usually defined by their relationship to the Roman occupation. The office of the high priest had developed great political power since the time of the Maccabean Revolt, and even under the occupation of the Romans. Though in the Old Testament the priesthood had no real political power (that was reserved for the king), the interference of occupying powers and their desire to influence the people of Judea resulted in a high priesthood that ultimately served at the will of the oppressing nation. One historian notes that in the intertestamental period "we see foreign political rulers breaking with Jewish tradition by deposing legitimate high priests early in their tenure (they normally served for life) and replacing them with others who would serve the king's interests better."[6] To preserve their position, then, the high priests had to walk a political tightrope.

Another political force was the ever-present Roman soldiers under the appointed governor, among whom Pontius Pilate was the most notable in the narrative of the New Testament (Luke 3:1). However, besides the occupying political presence, the family line of Herod the Great, who had been established as a puppet-king over Judea by the Roman Emperor, looms large. His line of descendants continued throughout the first century, appearing frequently in the biblical narratives: Herod the Great (Matt 2:1, 15), Herod Archelaus (Matt 2:22), Herod Antipas (Luke 3:1; 13:31–33), Philip the Tetrarch (Luke 3:1), Herod Agrippa (Acts 12:20–23), Herod Agrippa II (Acts 25:13; 26:1).[7] Those Hellenistic (Greek-cultured) Jews who were loyal to the Herodian dynasty are called "Herodians" in the New

---

[5] C. D. Elledge, "The Dead Sea Scrolls," in *The World of the New Testament: Cultural, Social, and Historical Contexts*, ed. Joel B. Green and Lee Martin McDonald (Grand Rapids: Baker Academic, 2013), 228–29.

[6] Steve Mason, *Josephus and the New Testament* (Peabody, MA: Hendrickson, 1992), 119.

[7] See F. F. Bruce, *New Testament History*, Doubleday-Galilee ed. (New York: Doubleday, 1980), 20–31.

Testament (Matt 22:16). On the other political extreme were those who despised Roman control and occupation and resented those who cooperated with them—these were often called the "Zealots" (cf. Matt 10:4). These Zealots were primarily responsible for the various local uprisings and ultimately widespread revolts against Rome that occurred in the late first century and early second.

A few prominent people groups appear on the scene in the New Testament period. The phrase *the Jews* refers primarily to those descendants—mostly from the tribe of Judah—who had returned from the exile from the time of Ezra and Nehemiah (Ezra 4:12; Neh 2:16; Matt 2:2). With these, the priesthood from the tribe of Levi was also firmly established (John 1:19). Also, the "Samaritans" appear in the New Testament. By most Jewish people at the time, Samaritans were regarded negatively as "half-breeds"—descendants of the remnants of the northern tribes of Israel who had intermarried with foreign settlers after the Assyrian invasion in 722 BC. Jews regarded Samaritan ethnicity, culture, and religion as impure. The relationship between Jews and Samaritans is best illustrated in the surprising response by the Samaritan woman with whom Jesus interacts at a public well: "'How is it that you, a Jew, ask for a drink from me, a Samaritan woman?' she asked him. For Jews do not associate with Samaritans" (John 4:9). Jews also kept their distance from Gentiles, both Romans and Greeks, though many Jews, known as "Hellenists," were more open to Greek and Roman culture than others.

The apostle Paul wrote that God sent forth his Son to be born as a man in this world "when the time came to completion" (Gal 4:4). That time and place was first-century Judea under Roman oppression, where both Jews and Samaritans longed for the coming Messiah to fulfill the promises and set all things right. Yet they were divided in their expectations, their political loyalties, and their religious beliefs. Into that confusing and sometimes chaotic world, the eternal Son of God—the Word—"became flesh and dwelt among us" (John 1:14).

Exploring the New Testament

Approximate Dates in Which Recorded Events Likely Occurred				
4 BC–AD 33	33–62	63–67	68–90	90–100
Gospel of Matthew (written c. 60?)	Acts (written c. 60?)	1 Timothy 2 Timothy Titus	Jude?	1 John 2 John 3 John
Gospel of Mark (written c. 50?)	Romans 1 Corinthians 2 Corinthians Galatians Ephesians Philippians Colossians Philemon 1 Thessalonians 2 Thessalonians James	Hebrews 1 Peter 2 Peter		Revelation
Gospel of Luke (written c. 60?)				
Gospel of John (written c. 90?)				

KEY

GOSPEL

HISTORY

LETTERS

PROPHECY

GOSPEL OF MATTHEW

SNAPSHOT

Do you long to know how to act as a believer? Not sure your background qualifies you for membership in the new community of Christians? The structure and themes of the book of Matthew work together to invite everyone into a distinctly Christian community to build the confidence needed for telling others the good news about Jesus.

ORIENTATION

Date: After the middle of the 1st century, about AD 60
Author: Matthew
Audience: Originally Jewish and Gentile Christians in Antioch
Outline: 1. Introduction: Genealogy, Birth, and Baptism (1–3)
                2. The People of the Kingdom of Heaven (4–7)
                3. The Kingdom Heals (8–10)
                4. The Kingdom Is for Everyone (11–13)
                5. Now, the Authority of Jesus (14–20)
                6. Then, Prepare for the Authority of Jesus (21–25)
                7. Anointing and Passover (26)

8. Conclusion: Crucifixion, Resurrection, and
   Commission (27–28)

YOU ARE HERE

Episode 7: Dawn of a New Era

Traditionally the first book of the New Testament canon, Matthew is the first of four "Gospels" introducing the person, teachings, and work of Jesus Christ.

EXPLORING MATTHEW

The first book of the New Testament begins with a genealogy. That's right: *a genealogy* (1:1–17). But anybody who's worked their way through the Old Testament will recognize the fittingness of that introduction to the advent of the long-awaited Messiah. Matthew starts with Abraham, then traces his descendants to King David, then follows the lineage of David to the exile in Babylon, then concludes the family line at its climax: "and Jacob fathered Joseph the husband of Mary, who gave birth to Jesus who is called the Messiah" (v. 16). Along the way, the genealogical record goes out of its way to include women—Tamar, Rahab, Ruth, the last two of whom were foreigners—and even reminds the readers that Solomon was the son of David "by Uriah's wife" (v. 6). Like the Old Testament itself, Matthew's genealogy doesn't shy away from the unexpected twists and turns that lead to the birth of the promised "offspring" of Abraham (Gen 12:7; cf. Gal 3:16). The Lord Jesus, the Messiah, entered this world in all its messiness, immersed in its poverty and pain.

The Gospel of Matthew, especially, provides a perfect transition from the expectations of the Old Testament to the realization of the promises in the New. Matthew is rightfully considered the most *Jewish* of the Gospels because of the number of Old Testament quotations. Yet its content also appeals to a broader audience to relay a backstory that invites all people into the kingdom of God—Jews, Greeks, Romans, men, women, children, everybody.

This "origin story" of the Gospel of the person and work of Christ also describes who and how these new Christians should act to represent the kingdom of God in this world. This is especially evident in the "Sermon on the Mount," material unique to Matthew (5–7). Matthew's reference to "the church" in Jesus's affirmation of Peter's important confession and leadership role in chapter 16 continues the kingdom of heaven as a theme and further links it to practical activity on earth. This ethic of responsibility and commitment of a distinctively Christian community models Christian behavior after Jesus's example. Discipleship—following Jesus's teaching, come what may—is to live as a citizen of the coming kingdom.

However, Jesus warns that this new kingdom lifestyle would not be welcome (10:1–42; 11:20–24). Through a structure of description and teaching, Matthew contrasts what it means to do God's will on earth, what acceptance of Jesus's offer of salvation looks like, with the surprising rejection that awaits those who reject the messengers. This is especially seen in some of the parables (13:1–53; 21:28–22:14). Also, we see the increased resistance and hostility of the Pharisees, Sadducees, chief priests, and elders—leaders who knew the Old Testament Scriptures but applied them with favoritism and inconsistency. Such descriptions of their hypocrisy, like in Matthew 23, also reveal their implicit responsibility for killing the messengers of truth.

These condemnations simultaneously highlight the contrasting character of the leaders of the newly formed community: share everyone's burdens, act justly, show mercy—teachings that echo the Old Testament Wisdom literature as well as the constant exhortations of the Major and Minor Prophets. This would be what the values of the kingdom of heaven look like manifested on earth. The same behaviors done partially, like for the wealthier citizens but not the poor as described in Matthew 25, will result in eternal rejection that will surprise the hypocrites.

Jesus's life and works described through the lens of prophecy trace several themes Matthew uses to establish Jesus's identity as the long-awaited Messiah and King. Early chapters emphasize that events in Jesus's life occurred to fulfill what was spoken through the prophets (1:22; 2:15, 17; 2:23; 4:14). These highlights wed the Old Testament expectation to the person and work of Jesus Christ. Jesus's suffering, crucifixion, and resurrection as Messiah, then, are not just required stories for the narrative to be called a "Gospel"; they are intentionally situated to become key events of our redemption from sin and adoption as children of God. Having arrived after centuries of promises and a long, long wait between the last prophet and the proclamation of John the Baptist . . . Jesus accomplished his mission and promises those who believe in him, "I am with you always, to the end of the age" (28:20).

START YOUR JOURNEY

- In what ways does Jesus match the expectations of the Old Testament longing for a Messiah and King? In what ways does he seem to disappoint some of his hearers? Consider how this aligns with people's expectations and estimations today about who Jesus is and why he has come.

- As you work through Matthew, you'll notice a lot of encounters with critics, unbelievers, and opponents. How does Jesus deal with those detractors? How might this help us "live like Jesus" in a world increasingly skeptical and critical of Christianity?

- On the surface, Matthew looks like he was using formulas about how to behave as a Christian, like the various activities and prayers in chapters 5–7. Instead of looking for formulas as you read, outline the various ways people are invited to experience deeper trust in God while engaging in those activities.

GOSPEL OF MARK

SNAPSHOT

What does it take to follow Jesus? Do you ever feel like you might not be able to live up to what Jesus wants? In the Gospel of Mark, Jesus invites disciples to give up everything to follow him. It's a huge request, and life as a disciple is risky. Nonetheless, the gift that Christ gives in exchange of his own life is worth the journey. And, most importantly, he doesn't leave us to do it in our own power. Jesus has gone before us and made the way.

ORIENTATION

Date: Middle of the 1st century, about AD 50
Author: Mark
Audience: Originally Christians in Rome
Outline:
1. Prologue: John the Baptist Introduces Jesus (1:1–13)
2. Jesus's Galilean Ministry Culminates in Conflict (1:14–3:6)
3. Jesus's Galilean Ministry Culminates in Rejection (3:7–6:6)
4. Jesus's Galilean Ministry Culminates in Confession (6:7–8:30)

5. Jesus Travels to Jerusalem to Face His Death (8:31–10:52)
6. Jesus Confronts the Religious Leaders and Condemns Them (11:1–13:37)
7. Jesus Suffers and Is Crucified in Jerusalem (14:1–15:47)
8. Jesus Is Raised from the Dead (16:1–8)

YOU ARE HERE

Episode 7: Dawn of a New Era

As the second book in the section of the Scripture called the "Gospels," and one of the books called the Synoptic Gospels (along with Matthew and Luke), the Gospel of Mark describes Jesus's ministry, his death, and his resurrection.

EXPLORING MARK

In the first part of his Gospel (1:1–8:30), Mark answers the question, Who is Jesus? By the end of chapter 1, Jesus's ministry had received the attention that required an investigation from the religious leaders (1:44). These authorities question Jesus's authority and identity in a series of conflict stories (2:1–3:6) and decide that he should be destroyed (3:6). Jesus concludes that his presence brings something new that the old system can't contain (2:21–23). Meanwhile, the demons know that he's the "Son of God" (1:24, 34; 3:11; 5:7). The disciples see him overcome nature (4:35–41), demons (5:1–20), disease, and death (vv. 21–43). The first half of the Gospel concludes with Peter's climactic confession: "You are the Messiah" (8:29).

In the remainder of the account, Jesus describes his role as the Christ. After Peter's confession, Jesus predicts his rejection, suffering, and death three times (8:31; 9:31; 10:33–34). His final journey to Jerusalem sets the context for these predictions, making these sayings more striking. And while

Jesus states his purpose as not "to be served, but to serve, and to give his life as a ransom for many" (10:45), the disciples show their misunderstanding by arguing who will be the best (9:33–34; 10:35–37). Even after his confession, Peter "rebukes" Jesus for his prediction of suffering (8:32). Jesus responds by calling Peter "Satan" (v. 33). After each prediction, the disciples argue about who is the greatest in the group (9:33–37; 10:35–40). The disciples grasped Jesus's identity but misunderstood what that meant. They wouldn't have considered the Christ coming to die, but rather to be victorious over their enemies.

Jesus looked forward to the kingdom of God, but he framed its arrival as imminent. He called his audience to repent as it drew near (1:15). He used parables to describe the kingdom. It's like a seed, which begins very small, but grows to something large (4:30–32). People respond to it in different ways (vv. 1–20). The disciples are to become like children to come into it (10:14–15). On the other hand, the wealthy come into the kingdom with difficulty (vv. 23–25). Jesus's invitation involves giving up everything—even the entire world—to follow him (8:34–37).

Not only did Jesus proclaim the kingdom, he also saw himself playing a significant role in its inauguration. His miracles demonstrated his authority to bring the kingdom (2:10; 3:20–27). As the Christ, the Messiah, the Son of God, Jesus isn't just a prophet predicting the kingdom, he is the King. This becomes clear in Jesus's last week. When he comes into Jerusalem, the people welcome him as a king (11:8–10). And immediately, he indicts the temple (vv. 12–25) and the religious leadership (vv. 1–12). His condemnation of the high priest (14:61–62) leads to his death. But his identity—and his teachings—are vindicated by his resurrection from the dead.

START YOUR JOURNEY

- Mark is thought by many to be the earliest Gospel. It is certainly the shortest. It tends to be action-packed and to the point. As you compare it to the Gospel of Matthew's long emphasis on Jesus's teachings and the incorporation of many Old Testament allusions, think about the implications for retelling the same message of the gospel for different kinds of people. How do different people in your own life need to hear the gospel in different ways?

- The best Greek manuscripts end the Gospel at Mark 16:8. A number of manuscripts add a longer ending (16:9–20), but the content does not quite fit with the remainder of the Gospel, suggesting that the Gospel ends at Mark 16:8. This shorter ending invites readers to respond to the empty tomb, longing for the rest of the story. How might that ponderous ending have played out among its original readers? Where would they have turned for more?

- Mark uses unusually harsh language to describe the disciples. He calls them hard hearted (6:52; 8:17) and "lacking in understanding" (7:18). On one occasion he calls Peter, the leader of the Twelve, "Satan" (8:33). Reflect on the significance of the fact that these men who walked with Jesus often misunderstood him and how your own struggles lead to greater dependence on God and his promise never to abandon us (Heb 13:5).

GOING DEEPER

"When You Have a Prodigal Son"

— By Stanley D. Toussaint —

Every year, countless teenagers run away from home. Runaways aren't unique to modern society; young people have always become fugitives from home in an attempt to escape from problems or to secure freedom from restraints. Perhaps the most famous runaway of all time is described in Luke 15, where the Lord Jesus recounts the parable of the prodigal son.

While this parable is known for the infamous prodigal, he is not the main character at all. The story actually revolves around the father. It begins with the words, "A man had two sons" (15:11). That "man" is the key figure through the entire parable.

Many believe this narrative is the most beautiful short story in all of human literature. One feature in this unadorned account that strikes the reader as a thing of beauty is the attitude of the father. From him we may learn much regarding the role of fathers in their relationship with runaway children today.

But first, consider the parable as to its setting and interpretation. "All the tax collectors and sinners were approaching to listen to him. And the Pharisees and scribes were complaining, 'This man welcomes sinners and eats with them'" (15:1–2). In response to this criticism, the Lord Jesus proceeds to relate three great parables—the lost sheep, the lost

257

silver, and the lost son. In effect, the Messiah is rebutting his critics. The self-righteous Pharisees and scribes accused him of socializing with the wrong crowd—of welcoming quislings and irreligious people and eating with them. Christ said in parabolic form, "Yes, I do welcome sinners—because God welcomes sinners."

In each of these parables, there are three characteristic words—*lost*, *found*, and *rejoice*. The sheep, silver, and son were all lost, and when each was found, there was rejoicing. By this the Lord is telling his detractors and slanderers that when a sinner is found, there is rejoicing in God's heaven.

The one most debated question concerning the interpretation of the parables involves the identity of the lost sheep, coin, and son. Some feel these portray a child of God who goes astray and then is restored. But a closer look reveals that the prodigal son went astray as an unbeliever. The determining factor is the context. First, the sinners and publicans are looked upon as lost until they come into contact with Christ; they are the lost sheep, silver, and son who have been found. Second, the very word *lost*, which punctuates all three parables, describes the condition of the unbeliever; it's the same word translated as *perish* in John 3:16. Finally, the treatment of the lost son beautifully portrays the reception of a lost man into the community of the redeemed. He's given a robe, a ring, and shoes—pictures of righteousness, authority, and position in God's family. When all is said and done, it may be stated with some confidence that the lost son pictures a lost soul who is saved by contact with Christ.

We see a stark contrast to the lost-but-found son in the final paragraph of the parable (15:28–32). The self-righteous older brother criticizes the father for making merry at the return of his prodigal younger brother. Our Lord uses this as a powerful indictment of the Pharisees and scribes. They are the older brother! It's a poignant picture the Lord draws of the father beseeching the older son to come into the house (of faith) and join in the festivities.

And there the story ends.

Jesus is leaving it to the Pharisees to make their own ending. They have the alternative of remaining outside the house or of coming into the house with the Savior. Every reader of the parable is left with the same decision. We can't leave the parable neutral.

While the main thrust of the story is clearly the portrayal of God as one who delights in forgiving all hues and stripes of sinners, there's also much that can be transferred to the behavior of parents today. Here are a few basic actions that serve as examples for parents.

First, this father *forgave*. He had every right to be resentful—the prodigal had left home to go to a distant land; he wasted his father's hard-earned money on prostitutes and wild living (*prodigal* means extravagantly wasteful); and he defamed the family name. Further, the fact that he left home indicates that the younger son was dissatisfied with the lifestyle of his father. There must have been tensions over this. In spite of all these things, the father joyfully forgave the son.

We see that the forgiveness was genuine in the restoration of the son. The prodigal thought he was coming home to be a hired hand—but the father received him home as a son. Genuine forgiveness not only left all bitterness behind; it also restored the son to his former position.

Humans, fallen as they are, can be restored to wholeness—becoming children of God—through Jesus Christ.

Second, the father *responded with joyful enthusiasm*. When the son came home to bargain, his father enthusiastically welcomed him— without any strings attached. In fact, the father interrupts the son's prepared speech and doesn't even give the prodigal an opportunity to propose his contract.

It's important to observe, however, that the son had a repentant spirit. He took the initiative, and the father responded. Those who work with runaways say this is a crucial principle. If a runaway is forced to return home and doesn't come voluntarily, he or she will be more hostile and will almost certainly leave again. In this parable the father didn't seek out the son; the father took more initiative with the self-righteous older son than he did with the prodigal younger son. He only waited for the son to come to himself, repent, and return home. But this in turn caused the father to be moved with compassion, to run, embrace, and kiss the son. In other words, he responded with enthusiasm and joy.

Third, this father *kept communications open* after the son returned. The killing of the one solitary fatted calf for especially significant occasions, the festive banquet, the music, and the rejoicing were ways of saying, "My son is home, and home is where we can be joyfully communicative." The father and the son were in the house together.

When a person comes to the Father through faith in Christ, communication with God becomes a reality. God hears and answers the prayers of his children. As earthly parents, we must forgive, respond with joyful enthusiasm, and keep communication open. After all, these are simply the outworkings of New Testament love (1 Cor 13:4–7). As parents, we are to model our parenthood on the fatherhood of God, and his example is beautifully set forth in this lovely parable of Luke 15.[1]

---

[1] Adapted from Stanley D. Toussaint, "When You Have a Prodigal Son," *Kindred Spirit* 1, no. 4 (Fall 1977): 19–20. © 1977 Dallas Theological Seminary.

GOSPEL OF LUKE

SNAPSHOT

So, what did our Lord teach anyway? Luke—author of both this Gospel and Acts—wrote more of the New Testament than any author. He also gives us the widest array of teaching from Jesus. Fully half of all the parables we know from Jesus come uniquely from Luke. Jesus's ethical call for how to live is also most prevalent in this Gospel. All of this sets up his sequel in the book of Acts to show how the church grew out of what Jesus taught and preached about God's promised kingdom.

ORIENTATION

Date: Early to mid-60s
Author: Luke
Audience: Theophilus, an otherwise unknown individual
Outline:
  1. Prologue (1:1–4)
  2. Infancy Material (1:5–2:52)
  3. From John the Baptist to Jesus (3:1–4:13)
  4. Jesus's Galilean Ministry (4:14–9:50)
  5. Journey to Jerusalem (9:51–19:44)
  6. Last Week in Jerusalem (19:45–24:53)

YOU ARE HERE

Episode 7: Dawn of a New Era

Luke is the third of four Gospels, and with Matthew and Mark, it's part of what are called the Synoptic ("seen together") Gospels because they share so much content.

EXPLORING LUKE

Luke, an erstwhile companion of Paul in his missionary efforts among Gentiles, is an astute, keen, well-educated, and articulate physician who carefully researched and set forth an accurate account of the birth, life, death, resurrection, and ascension of Christ. And he did this not for mass publication, not for a public reading to a crowded stadium, not for a church family, not even for an emperor. No, he wrote both these books for an individual named Theophilus. The opening lines show the labor he was willing to expend for the sake of instructing a single soul: "Many have undertaken to compile a narrative about the events that have been fulfilled among us, just as the original eyewitnesses and servants of the word handed them down to us. So it also seemed good to me, since I have carefully investigated everything from the very first, to write to you in an orderly sequence, most honorable Theophilus, so that you may know the certainty of the things about which you have been instructed" (1:1–4). Of course, likely from the moment of its composition, this lengthy writing has had an impact far, far beyond its original narrow audience.

The Gospel of Luke sets out to explain how even though Christianity appears to be a new faith, it is rooted in many promises made long ago to Israel on behalf of the world. In the ancient world, it's not what's *new* that's valued, but what's old and time tested. So, Luke presents Jesus as the center of a divine program that brings light and blessing to the world not only for Israel, but also for all people. This is the burden of the praise found in three prophetic hymns of praise in the opening chapters (1:46–55; 1:67–79; 2:29–32). This good news is for all people!

Luke then reveals the thrust of Jesus's ministry in Galilee, which combines word and deed in harmony. He proclaims a release for captives and a care for all sorts of people. His ministry reflects that care. He calls people to love their enemies, not just their friends. In claiming authority over sin and healing on the Sabbath, he begins to experience opposition from some religious leaders (Luke 3–9).

Once his disciples confess him as Messiah, Jesus begins to reveal to them that he will suffer death in Jerusalem, something they're not expecting. As opposition rises, he warns them that they will be treated as the world treats him. He sets forth the challenge and demands of discipleship. He calls them to an ethical compassion and care toward others despite such opposition (Luke 10–19).

The opposition, of course, fears losing their power, prestige, and personal pride. They despise and reject Jesus, just as the prophet Isaiah said would happen (Isa 53). As they plot against him, Jesus warns the nation of coming judgment for rejecting the Messiah that God has sent. He teaches that whatever comes of him now, God will vindicate him, and he will assume his rightful place at God's right hand, sharing in providing the forgiveness and benefit of God's enablement in the Spirit for those who embrace his coming with faith. On the cross, Jesus dies unjustly for people, but God brings the promised vindication in a resurrection that frees him to bring God's enabling Spirit to God's people (Luke 19–24), a story continued in the sequel to Luke's Gospel: the book of Acts.

START YOUR JOURNEY

- Luke 1–3 especially provides important connections to the Old Testament promises and how those are realized in the coming of Jesus. Read through those carefully and highlight the ways in which Jesus demonstrates that God can be trusted to keep his promises.

- As you read, keep your eye on the ethical heartbeat of Jesus as he calls his followers to live in a manner not like the world, especially in how they are to love others.
- Reading a chapter a day will allow you to read this Gospel within a month. It will also allow you to meditate on the person and work of Christ and ponder how his teachings can be followed in your life.
- See how Jesus shows he is at the center of what God is doing. Jesus is not a mere teacher of ethics; he is the Messiah who is Lord at the center of a kingdom God has at work in the world. How does he expect his followers to live in light of those kingdom values and priorities?

GOSPEL OF JOHN

SNAPSHOT

Have you ever wondered what it would be like to go back in time and follow Jesus as his disciple during the years of his earthly ministry? To observe many important miracles and participate with his disciples in the upper room? The Gospel of John allows us to do just that, guided by one of Jesus's closest followers, the "Beloved Disciple," who is best identified with the Apostle John.

ORIENTATION

Date: Late first century, about AD 90
Author: John the Apostle, known in the Gospel of John as the beloved disciple
Audience: Both Christians and non-Christians, both Gentiles and Jews
Outline:
1. Prologue (1:1–18)
2. The Book of the Seven Signs (1:19–12:50)
3. The Book of Glory (13:1–20:31)
4. Epilogue (21:1–25)

YOU ARE HERE

Episode 7: Dawn of a New Era

John is the fourth of the New Testament "Gospels." It differs in many ways from the Synoptic Gospels (Matthew, Mark, and Luke), providing unique elements of Christ's words and works.

EXPLORING THE GOSPEL OF JOHN

John's Gospel is about knowing Jesus personally not just in the future, but in the present (5:24). Eternal life is a present reality, not just a future one (17:3). While no one has ever seen God, we can see God and know what he is like by looking at Jesus, who has fully revealed God (1:18; 14:9).

John's Gospel is full of symbolism, though the symbolism overlays the historical events rather than replacing them (4:19–22; 7:37–39). This allows John's Gospel to be read at different levels, all of which are profitable and edifying for the reader, whether a newcomer to the Christian faith or a seasoned veteran of years of study and devotion.

Unlike the other gospels, which begin with an infancy narrative (Matthew, Luke) or with Jesus's baptism by John the Baptist (Mark), John's Gospel begins in eternity past with the preexistent Christ, the Word (logos), in the presence of God and more than that, just as much God as God the Father is (John 1:1; cf. Gen 1). While the other Gospels present Jesus's earthly life as his disciples gradually realized who he was, John presents Jesus from a heavenly perspective, as the one sent from God to reveal what God is like (3:11–13).

The Gospel of John and 1 John are the only two NT books with a clearly stated purpose statement (John 20:31; 1 John 5:13). John calls on his readers to make a personal faith response (John 3:16; 6:40, 47, 51).

Between the prologue (1:1–18) and the epilogue (21:1–25), John's Gospel divides into two parts. The first, the "Book of the Seven Signs," centers around seven "sign-miracles" that are specifically chosen for what they reveal about Jesus:

1. Water changed into wine (2:1–11)
2. Healing of the nobleman's son (4:46–54)
3. Healing of the paralytic (5:1–18)
4. Feeding of the multitude (6:6–13)
5. Walking on the water (6:16–21)
6. Healing of the man born blind (9:1–7)
7. Resurrection of Lazarus (11:1–45)

The second major part of John's Gospel focuses on the Passion Week, beginning with the triumphal entry into Jerusalem (chapter 12). In John 13:1–17 Jesus washes his disciples' feet, symbolically acting out his sacrificial death on the cross beforehand (cf. Phil 2:5–8). The following three chapters (John 14–16) are Jesus's farewell discourse to his disciples followed by a prayer of dedication (John 17). Jesus's arrest and trials make up chapter 18, followed by the crucifixion (John 19). The resurrection account (John 20) and the restoration of Peter following his denials of Jesus (John 21) conclude John's Gospel.

John's Gospel is about Jesus preparing his disciples to testify (witness) about him after he returns to his Father (15:27). It is about the personal, intimate relationship believers can have with Christ by believing in him. The term John uses for this is *abiding/residing* (6:54, 56; 14:16–17, 20, 23; 15:4–7).

START YOUR JOURNEY

- As you read the Gospel of John, note how the author alternates between the sign miracles (carefully selected) and the dialogues or discourses to bring out the significance of the miracles. Make a list of the sign miracles and their interpretation included by John as you read.
- Note the different names and titles John uses for Jesus as you read: Word, Lamb of God, Messiah, Son of God, King of Israel, Son of Man, rabbi, Teacher, prophet, Savior of the world, etc. Note the passages where these occur. What do these tell us about Jesus?

- Why does John speak so much about "eternal life" but so little about "the kingdom of God"? In what way does this represent an adaptation for non-Jewish readers?
- How does John use the symbol of "living water" in the Gospel of John? (Hint: Read John 7:37–39.)
- What does the purpose statement, John 20:31, tell us about why John wrote the book? Meditate on the elements of that verse and relate them to what you learn about Christ elsewhere in the book and to your own life as a believer.

GOING DEEPER

"Sanctify Them by the Truth"

— Mark L. Bailey —

S kepticism isn't new. We live in a world influenced by human percep-
tions, personal preferences, and manipulation of impressions. We
face a crisis of confidence in governmental institutions, public leaders,
higher education, and news media. People wonder what truth means and
where to find it. As Christians shining the light of the gospel in the world
around us, we know that the biblical model of truth is both propositional
and personal, revelational and relational. Exposure to truth demands a
personal response.

In John's Gospel, the theme of truth is of critical concern. John 3:21
and 18:37–38 form bookends for his Gospel, highlighting the importance of a right response to truth as revealed in Jesus. The first states,
"Anyone who lives by the truth comes to the light," and in the second,
Jesus states, "Everyone who is of the truth listens to my voice."

From John's opening prologue to Jesus's climactic interchange with
Pilate, what is true about Jesus was on trial. The contest between the
world's opinion of truth and God's view of truth is seen clearly in the
exchange between Jesus and Pilate. That short passage in John 18:37–38
includes the affirmation of Jesus's kingship, his claim to be the divine
testimony to truth, and the judgment that people's response to him

indicates their relationship to what is true. The echo of Pilate's reactionary question—"What is truth?"—continues to resound today.

We see the importance of rightly defining truth in Jesus's high priestly prayer, the night before he went to the cross: "Sanctify them by the truth; your word is truth" (17:17). We might initially assume that the immediate referent is the Bible, and sanctification is the result. As conservative evangelicals with a high view of divine inspiration and the resultant quality of inerrancy, we rightly believe the Bible to be God's truth in written form. But a closer look at the term *truth* in the context of John's Gospel may yield a more focused understanding of this specific request.

Of the four Gospel writers, John centralizes the theme of truth in relation to the Trinity, especially in the ministry of Jesus. God is said to be true (3:33; 7:28; 8:26), the only true God (17:3). Jesus reveals the truth he "heard from God" (8:40). As the incarnate Word, Jesus is "full of grace and truth" (1:14). The truth that Jesus taught and embodied can set people free from sin (8:32, 36). Jesus spoke the truth (7:18; 8:14, 16, 45; 16:7), and Jesus himself is the very essence of truth (5:33; 14:6). The Holy Spirit is called "the Spirit of truth" who dwelt with the disciples before the day of Pentecost and now indwells all believers (14:17). The Spirit is identified as a minister of truth because he was sent by Christ from the Father to bear witness to the truth (15:26) and to be a guide into all truth (16:13). He does not speak with his own authority. As John clarifies, what belongs to the Father belongs to Jesus, and the Spirit declares what belongs to Jesus, all to the glory of Jesus Christ (16:14). Therefore, the word of truth in the Gospel of John is centered on the person and work of Christ (14:6).

In John 17, Jesus prayed that the disciples would be prepared to bear witness to Christ in a contrary world. The word *sanctify* means to set apart for a sacred use or service as designated by God. That passage mentions two sanctifications: that of Jesus and that of his followers. In a world hostile to the gospel, Jesus didn't ask that his followers be taken out of the world but that they would be sanctified and protected as they're set apart and sent into the world. To this end, Jesus said he will sanctify himself, that the disciples would be sanctified in truth (17:15–17).

The self-sanctification of Jesus was his willing submission to all that the Father consecrated him to do in his life and death; as the Father sent Christ into the world, so Jesus is sending his disciples into the world (17:18). The mission is always to bear witness to the reality of the truth— the gospel of Jesus Christ in all its fullness. The truth makes it possible for guilty sinners to be declared holy and to be used by God for his sacred purposes. Those who rightly respond to the truth are to worship in the Spirit and truth (4:23) and witness to the truth in the power of the Spirit (15:26, 27). John the Baptist and John the Gospel author exemplify this witness to the truth (5:32, 33; 10:41; 19:35; 21:24).

Jesus modeled this testimony in his confession before Pilate. Pilate's cynical question about the definition of truth is a climactic mirror for John's Gospel. Pilate was speaking to the truth standing right in front of him—and yet he refused to see truth. By contrast, the overarching purpose of John's Gospel is to present the crucified Jesus as the Messiah and the Son of God, affirming that faith in him is not only the means to eternal life but also the right response to the truth (20:31).[1]

---

[1] Adapted from Mark L. Bailey, "Sanctify Them in the Truth; Your Word Is Truth," *DTS Magazine* 8, no. 3 (Fall 2022): 24. © 2022 Dallas Theological Seminary.

ACTS OF THE APOSTLES

SNAPSHOT

What were the first generations after Jesus's resurrection like? How did this minority of people manage to grow despite having no social, political, or cultural power? Above all, how did they manage to bring together two such disparate peoples as Jews and Gentiles into one group so that their testimony to God's work could not be missed? Luke covers all of this in the sequel to his gospel, the book of Acts.

ORIENTATION

Date: After the Gospel of Luke, about AD 60–65

Author: Luke

Audience: Theophilus, an otherwise unknown individual

Outline:
1. Introduction: Jesus Ascends to the Father (1:1–11)
2. The Early Church in Jerusalem (1:12–6:7)
3. Persecution in Jerusalem Pushes the Church to Samaria (6:8–9:31)
4. The Gospel to Gentiles and More Persecution in Jerusalem (9:32–12:25)

5. The Mission from Antioch and Full Incorporation of
   Gentiles (13:1–15:35)
6. Paul's Second and Third Missionary Journeys
   (15:36–21:16)
7. To Rome: Paul's Arrest and Trials (21:17–28:31)

YOU ARE HERE

Episode 7: Dawn of a New Era

The only book of "history" in the New Testament, Acts focuses on key elements in the earliest years of the church.

EXPLORING ACTS

Though called the Acts of the Apostles, the book is really about how God through Jesus and the Spirit led believing Jews and Gentiles to form a church that had impact across the world. In a racially divided world, Jesus not only brings salvation to individuals but also forms a community around the Messiah whose working together shows God's presence in the world. Acts is about the acts of God through this new community; in short, it's a book about missions (1:8).

The sign of the arrival of the long-expected promise is the raised and ascended Messiah giving God's people his Spirit (Acts 2). The provision of the Spirit at Pentecost is both one of the key events in the book and a repeated theme throughout Acts. The Spirit's enablement, shown primarily in Peter's activity, leads to a series of miracles that cause persecution to arise in Jerusalem. A series of speeches shows how faith in Jesus has been God's plan from the ages and brings his followers into a new relationship with God in a new community being formed by him (Acts 1–6).

The martyrdom of Stephen shows the seriousness of the persecution that the church experienced. This persecution causes the church to scatter, leading providentially to her expansion into Samaria and other regions in Israel. At the same time, Jesus calls the persecutor Saul to be a messenger for the Lord to the Gentiles, as he now realizes Jesus really is risen from the dead (Acts 6–9).

God leads Peter to take the gospel to Cornelius, who, as a Gentile, receives the Spirit from God without having to be circumcised, showing that Gentiles are also beneficiaries of God's promise of salvation and enablement. Later, Peter is also miraculously delivered from jail (Acts 10–12).

The Spirit directs Barnabas and Paul to take the gospel to Gentiles. A pattern emerges. They go to the synagogue, some believe, persecution arises, and then they go to the Gentiles until persecution causes them to move on. In the meantime, the way God saved Cornelius helps the church to understand Jews and Gentiles can be one without Gentiles having to become like Jews. They can be one and are to be respectful of their cultural difference (Acts 13–15).

Two more missionary journeys of Paul show the expansion of the gospel as far as Athens, Corinth, and Ephesus. The transformed lives of those who believe impact cities like Ephesus as things like idolatry, divination, and magic begin to decline (Acts 16–21).

Paul falls victim to an arrest on false pretenses but is providentially protected as he ends up in Rome about to testify before Caesar concerning the promise of God. In his defense speeches, he says he is in chains because of his commitment to God's promises and the hope of the resurrection. This hope represents the realization of promises made to Israel on behalf of the world long ago (Acts 21–28).

START YOUR JOURNEY

- Keep an eye on how God is active in the book, whether it be what is said about the Father, Son, or Spirit. The book is also full of examples of faithfulness in figures such as Peter, Barnabas, Stephen, Paul, and many others. Consider what makes them faithful.

- Reading a chapter a day will allow you to complete this book within a month. As you read, reflect upon God's work through a community of people, not simply individuals.

- One of the key themes of Acts is how Jews and Gentiles work to understand and respect one another in the midst of some cultural differences that are not moral in scope. This is central to the church's effectiveness and is evidence of God's work of accomplishing reconciliation in corporate relationships. Mark moments of reconciliation and unity as you read through the book.

- Since Acts is, in part, about how God brings different groups together, this book is well suited to be studied together in groups, especially groups where different backgrounds or ages are represented. Consider joining or establishing such a group at your local church.

- How can the accounts in the book of Acts spur us on to ever-widening missionary endeavors, similar to the first-century church's Jerusalem, Judaea, Samaria, and the ends of the earth (1:8)? What needs do you see in your own neighborhood and hometown (Jerusalem), your local community or region (Judaea/Samaria), and around the world ("ends of the earth")? How can you get involved in that mission more directly?

ROMANS

SNAPSHOT

People usually consider Paul's letter to the Romans a deeply theological book, and it is. But it's so much more than that. The book of Romans addresses a problem that faces every church: the problem of cultural, and even ethnic, division. On what basis can the church find unity? And once that foundation is clear, how does a community of people live out their love for one another?

ORIENTATION

Date: About AD 57

Author: Paul

Audience: Churches at Rome

Outline:
1. Righteousness before God Comes by Faith Alone (1–4)
2. Life before God Requires Faith-Producing Grace (5–8)
3. God's Grace Will Eventually Reach Israel (9–11)
4. Live Sacrificially: Receive One Another as Christ Received You (12:1–15:14)
5. Epistolary Closing (15:15–16:27)

YOU ARE HERE

Episode 7: Dawn of a New Era

As one of Paul's thirteen epistles and the first of twenty-one New Testament "Letters," Romans presents a thorough description of God's redemptive work by grace through faith.

EXPLORING ROMANS

Romans is a treasure for Christians in that it provides crucial information about what Jesus accomplished for humanity and how we may appropriate his great work. Paul begins the book by establishing humanity's need for his grace. Chapters 1–3 show that everyone—Jews and Gentiles—is utterly lost in sin and rebellion.

About halfway through chapter 3, Paul shifts to consider Christ's sacrifice in atonement for human sin. By his work, he paid the penalty for our sin, leaving no room for boasting on our part. Indeed, God justifies human beings (declares us righteous) only through the gift of faith, chapter 4 teaches. And because of Christ's work and our justification, we now live a life reconciled to God (Rom 5).

Many have misunderstood chapters 6 and 7. Commonly, interpreters read those chapters as explaining why human beings are so inured to sin. Paul calls all believers to present yourselves "as slaves to righteousness, which results in sanctification" (6:19). The apostle recognizes, however, that while we may discipline our actions, the reality of sin within human beings runs much deeper than individual actions. More than once in chapter 7, Paul explains that though he wants to do good, evil is present within him. Here, Paul addresses a different understanding of sin than mere action. Though he sets out to do what the law commands, indwelling sin produces the violation of the very law that he was trying to obey, even against his own will. As a result of this sinful condition, the human need for grace is absolute.

Chapter 8 includes great and precious promises. The divine assurances in the passage, especially those after verse 28, provide a measure of comfort and security for the Christian seeking to live faithfully before God. The chapter's primary point is to affirm that no suffering can in any way separate us from God's love: not even the suffering that is caused by personal sin. God is the judge at our court hearing; Jesus is the defense attorney. As a result, there really is "no condemnation for those in Christ Jesus" (8:1).

Chapters 9–11 concern the question of Israel's future. After highlighting the sovereignty of God to save whomever he will, Paul acknowledges the rampant unbelief among his people of origin. Israel needs to hear the message of salvation, and Paul clearly believes that there is a future for his people (11:1).

Having established an expansive theological vision for all people—Jew and Gentile alike—Paul turns in chapters 12–15 to ethical and relational calls that accompany his presentation of God's work on our behalf. The apostle emphasizes the responsibilities that believers have for one another as members of the same body: behaviors such as showing hospitality (12:13), living at peace with all (v. 18), and making no provision for the flesh (13:14). Following this series of exhortations, Paul spends time detailing the relations between weak and strong within the community, ultimately calling every believer to accept one another (15:7).

START YOUR JOURNEY

- Read the book of Romans as one sustained argument, in one sitting, from chapter 1 to chapter 16. Assume that each chapter gives you information that you need to take with you all the way through the book. Write down these insights along the way. Reading only snippets here and there makes it much harder to grasp the meaning of the book.

- Treat the book as a piece of persuasive literature. Paul is arguing for the gospel in the first section (1–11) and then makes practical application for how people changed by the gospel should live. As you read the book, think, "how is my life different because of the hope of the gospel?"

- Allow Paul to define his own terms. Read the book in many different translations to see how they vary in their treatment of each passage. Make a list of key terms, how Paul uses them, and where they appear in the book.
- Use chapters 12–15 to consider what it means to be a "living sacrifice" (12:1) who has been "transformed" (12:2). What kinds of actions does Paul command? How should we relate to one another?

1 CORINTHIANS

SNAPSHOT

In the book of 1 Corinthians, Paul writes to a church very much like many modern-day churches. Worldly influences from outside have seeped inside, causing divisions as well as a toleration of immorality among its members. In answer to these problems, Paul directs the church how to live in Christian community in a countercultural and Christ-honoring way.

ORIENTATION

Date: About AD 54–56
Author: Paul
Audience: The church founded by Paul in Corinth (Acts 18:1–18)
Outline:
1. Greetings and Thanksgiving (1:1–9)
2. Problems in the Church Reported by Chloe's Household (1:10–6:20)
3. Replies to Questions from the Corinthians (7:1–14:40)
4. About the Resurrection (15:1–58)
5. Final Instructions and Greetings (16:1–24)

YOU ARE HERE

Episode 7: Dawn of a New Era

The second item of the section of the New Testament called the "Letters," Paul's letter to the Corinthian church addresses a number of controversies causing division and confusion.

EXPLORING 1 CORINTHIANS

To better appreciate 1 Corinthians, understanding the culture of the city of Corinth is a must. Originally an independent Greek city, Corinth was destroyed by Roman forces in 146 BC but was later reestablished in 44 BC as a Roman colony by settling 3,000 freed slaves and army veterans there. Because of its strategic location controlling both land and sea trade routes on the Greek peninsula (ships and cargo wanting to avoid the stormy journey around the southern tip of Greece were transported four miles across the isthmus), Corinth became a large (the third largest city in the Roman Empire) and wealthy cosmopolitan city which was at the crossroads of Greek, Roman, Asia Minor, and North African cultures, philosophies, and religions.[1]

Corinth was known for its immoral reputation even by pagan standards. The Greek term translated "to corinthianize" literally became synonymous with sexual depravity and debauchery. The Corinthian culture valued smooth-talking celebrities, greed, sex, and power/status at the expense of others. Many of the problems Paul addresses in 1 Corinthians come from the Corinthian Christians' tendency to reflect the values of their city rather than those of the body of Christ.

First Corinthians is a practical and pastoral letter, addressing a wide variety of spiritual and moral issues raised by "members of Chloe's people"

---

[1] See David K. Lowery, "1 Corinthians," in *Bible Knowledge Commentary: New Testament*, ed. John F. Walvoord and Roy B. Zuck (Colorado Springs: David C. Cook, 1983), 505.

(1:11; cf. 5:1; 11:18) and from another letter sent to him (7:1; cf. 7:25; 8:1; 12:1; 16:1). The topics addressed by Paul include arrogant church factions (1:10–4:21), incest in the family of a member of the church (5:1–13), lawsuits between one another (6:1–11), *overall* sexual immorality tied to cultic worship practices (6:12–20), marriage and divorce (7:1–40), whether to eat food sacrificed to idols (8:1–11:1), proper conduct in worship (11:2–34), proper use of spiritual gifts (12:1–14:40), and the resurrection (15:1–58).

These problems can be summarized as conflicts within the church and compromises with the hedonistic values of the Corinthian culture. First Corinthians is about living as followers of the resurrected Christ in a wayward world. Believers are under the authority of the name of our Lord Jesus Christ as his servants (1:2; 1:10; 1:13; 5:4; 6:11). Instead of an upward mobility, "me first" attitude, Paul calls the Corinthian believers to put others first (concern for the weak and the marginalized) and to live a glorifying holy life set apart in community as God's temple (3:16) and the body of Christ (6:15; 12:12–13). To do this, the Holy Spirit indwells and empowers each of these believers (6:19), unifying them under the head of the resurrected Christ (6:14–17; 15:30–34).

Throughout the letter, Paul consistently points the reader back to Jesus Christ and his work. The gospel of the death and resurrection of Jesus Christ is central. Paul's extensive treatment on the resurrection of Jesus in 1 Corinthians 15 is the climax of the letter. We are saved sinners and our only hope is now anchored in our resurrected Lord Jesus Christ. The good news of the gospel is that, through the work of Christ and by the power of the Spirit, we can live transformed lives as God's holy people.

START YOUR JOURNEY

- The Corinthian church has problems, which is why Paul has written to them. As you read the book, make a list of their particular sins, as well as the impact those sins have had upon their community life. Consider the similarities between Corinth and where you live today.

- In many ways, 1 Corinthians is Paul's most communal letter. While the majority of his epistles are written to groups rather than individuals, we often miss the community aspects of these letters. What metaphors does Paul employ in this letter to describe the church?

- Paul uses the recurring phrase "now concerning" (7:1; 7:25; 8:1; 12:1; 16:1; and 16:12, NASB) when changing from one topic to the next. These transitions likely mark his shift to address the various questions that were asked of him. What church-related questions would you ask Paul if you could write him a letter? Spend some time reflecting on how these issues have been addressed in Scripture.

- Paul's teaching on public worship and spiritual gifts (11:2–14:40) is one of the most discussed portions of the letter. Read this entire section in one sitting and then reflect upon how you use (and can use) your spiritual gifts in the context of your local church.

GOING DEEPER

"Bootstraps and Belief"

— Lewis Sperry Chafer —

It's utterly out of the question that any of us could ever save him or herself. Of course, it depends on what we mean by "being saved." If it's merely to make yourself a slightly better citizen in this world, perhaps with a good deal of effort you could bring that to pass. But if it's a matter of writing your name in heaven, of forgiving one's sin forever, of imparting eternal life, or of clothing oneself in the righteousness of God, surely we must declare—if we are honest at all—that this is something we cannot do. And, we are just as ready to admit that all the people in the world put together—should they undertake to do this for us—couldn't approach one of these things. God alone is able to save. The whole plan and thought of saving sinners originated with God. It never originated with humans. They hardly identify it when it's brought to them, and oftentimes they have no response to it at all.

With God, this proposition of saving sinners is the most intrinsic, the most enticing, and the most desirable thing. All his love is expressed in that salvation. It is the outlet of his infinite love toward the sinner. To him that plan of saving the lost is more important than it could be to all of those that are lost put together. It's worthwhile to fix in our mind that the salvation of one's soul means more to God than it means ever to the soul. It means more to God to have us saved than it means to all the saved people put together. It's his great satisfaction in the exercise of his love on behalf of us. And because he loves us, he has devised this. He has taken away the hindrances we could not remove. All this unworthiness, all this intense sinfulness as seen by his holy eye, is removed. He himself did this long, long ago—before we were born. He prepared the situation into which we should come and provided the salvation which would be unhindered by our sins. People are constantly saying, "Oh, I'm not worthy to be a Christian. I'm not worthy." But friend, every unworthy thing in your life that you can name—or that God can name—has been taken by the Son of God to the cross and borne for you. The only other thing that hinders God's infinite love from saving you is your own will.

"For God loved the world in this way: He gave his one and only Son, so that everyone who believes in him will not perish but have eternal life. . . . Anyone who believes in him is not condemned. . . . These are written so that you may believe that Jesus is the Messiah, the Son of God, and that by believing you may have life in his name" (John 3:16, 18; 20:31). These words are only a fraction of what the New Testament declares. Upwards of 150 passages in the New Testament condition our salvation upon one thing: believing. Nothing else. It is ruinous—tragic—to add anything. Just the one thing: "Believe in the Lord Jesus, and you will be saved" (Acts 16:31).

Thirty-five passages use another word, which is of course just a synonym, and that's *faith*. This great principle of turning from confidence in ourselves or anything else and looking directly to the Lord Jesus Christ—the only qualified Savior in all this universe—that principle of looking to him is *faith* or *believing*.

The great Apostle described his attitude when he said, "I know whom I have believed" (2 Tim 1:12). I have believed him, he's my savior. He has told me of his saving grace, and I believe it. It answers all the burdens and the distress of my heart and life forever. I believe on him.

Now there are constantly those who are insisting that there must be something added to this one simple requirement of believing. "You must believe and confess," or "you must believe and repent," or "you must believe and pray," and so on. But dear friend, if that were true, if anything were to be added to the one requirement of believing, then every one of these 150 passages are incomplete. And if that were true, when Christ told Nicodemus, "God loved the world in this way: He gave his one and only Son, so that everyone who believes in him will not perish but have eternal life" (John 3:16), then Christ was only telling Nicodemus part of the truth and left him stranded without knowing it all. And when Paul and Silas said to the Philippian jailor when he had asked what he had to do to be saved, "Believe in the Lord Jesus, and you will be saved" (Acts 16:31), were they giving him only a partial statement? Are they to be reprimanded for having misguided this poor man and leaving something so important out?

My dear friend, the greatest passages of the New Testament that have to do with the human responsibility in this question of being saved never confuse the issue. It's just one and only one thing. Believe. Why? Because the other things add nothing at all. Shall I have to soften God with my tears? Must I persuade him with my pleading? Have I got to make a public display in order to prove that I am genuine in what I think? All of this is utter folly when we are dealing with God in a matter of this kind.

Look at the great elements that make up our salvation: our name is written in heaven, our eternal life is bestowed, our sins are forgiven, and we are clothed in the righteousness of God. Who is going to do this? God said he will do it through Jesus Christ. It's made possible on the grounds of what Christ did for us on the cross. Therefore, I can't add anything. There's nothing for me to cooperate in. There's not some teamwork here in which I do my part and he does his. I fall helplessly and hopelessly at his feet and into his hands and his arms. I simply commit myself to the saving grace of God as it is through Jesus Christ our Lord. He never refused one who came like that. Therefore, once more I leave the word definitely upon you today: "Believe in the Lord Jesus, and you will be saved" (Acts 16:31).[1]

---

[1] Adapted from Lewis Sperry Chafer, "Bootstraps and Belief," *Kindred Spirit* 1, no. 4 (Fall 1977): 22–23. © 1977 Dallas Theological Seminary.

2 CORINTHIANS

SNAPSHOT

What happens when relationships are broken within the church community? Is it ever appropriate to turn away from the apostles who have delivered the message of the gospel? Some of the Corinthian Christians had struggled with Paul's authority in the wake of his previous communications. In 2 Corinthians, the apostle seeks to promote reconciliation within the local church and with himself.

ORIENTATION

Date: AD 53–57
Author: Paul
Audience: The Church at Corinth, along with all the saints in Achaia
Outline: 1. The Need for Reconciliation (1:1–2:17)
               2. Paul's New Covenant Ministry Models Reconciliation
                  (3:1–5:19)
               3. Paul Exhorts the Corinthians to Reconcile (5:20–7:16)
               4. An Evidence of Reconciled Relationship: Giving from
                  the Heart (8:1–9:15)
               5. Finding Strength in Our Weakness (10:1–13:13)

YOU ARE HERE

Episode 7: Dawn of a New Era

The third of Paul's "Letters" in the New Testament and the second to the Corinthian church, this epistle details continued problems in Corinth, emphasizing the need for reconciliation.

EXPLORING 2 CORINTHIANS

The Apostle Paul founded the church at Corinth where he spent two and a half years as their spiritual father and pastor (Acts 18:9–11). Paul's preaching in synagogues led to many conversions among both Jews and Gentiles, but also resulted in severe persecution (2 Cor 1:8–9). Despite this persecution, Paul sought to minister comfort to the Corinthians on the basis of their shared sufferings (vv. 3–15).

Rather than comfort, Paul's hardships emboldened some in the church to oppose him, even to the point of questioning his apostleship. This left Paul feeling the need to commend himself to them as a true apostle of the Lord (3:1; 12:11). In so doing, Paul writes one of his most moving letters as he shows his love for this church.

Second Corinthians could almost be called an autobiography of the apostle himself as he unveils his love for the churches through the many persecutions he experienced on their behalf. Instead of giving them a formal letter of (re)commendation, he offers them the analogy of a letter written on their heart: the new covenant. They are his letter of (re)commendation written on his heart (3:1–3). Since Paul is a minister of this new covenant, he works to see Christ reconciled to his people, calling the Corinthians to join him in this ministry of reconciliation. This new covenant ministry is not like the old covenant, where Moses used to cover his face because of the fading glory, but rather the Lord uses this ministry to transform believers into a greater glory: reflecting Christ's image (v. 18). Paul, in his desire to become more like Christ, identified deeply with the suffering of Jesus (4:10–12). He illustrates this by visualizing believers as earthen cracked pots that hold an incredible treasure inside (v. 7). It is not the pot that matters, but what the pot holds: the gospel message in the new covenant ministry of Christ. This ministry brings persecution, but Paul remains committed to the work, focusing on eternal impact rather than temporary trials.

Paul encourages the Corinthians toward reconciliation with God and with him in chapters 5–7. The apostle implores these Christians to be reconciled to God, in order that they might turn from sin and toward righteousness (5:20). Later, he asks them to make room in their hearts for him (7:2), before again emphasizing the deep affection and pride he feels toward the Corinthian believers.

In chapter 10, Paul addresses an especially fierce group of opponents within the church.[1] He strategically gives in to them, giving them his version of a letter of (re)commendation, but it is not what they expected. Instead of giving them a letter of all his qualifications or recommendations from others, he gives them a list of all his persecutions and sufferings for Christ (11:22–33). Paul even humbly refuses to name himself as one who has gone to the third heaven (the throne room of God, 12:1–5).

Finally, the last section deals with opponents who may not even be believers as he sternly warns them to see if they are even in the faith (11:13–15; 13:5). Through all these warnings, Paul takes the opportunity to admonish them to do their part in the offering for the believers in Israel who are suffering a drought and intense persecution (8:1–9:15).

START YOUR JOURNEY

- Paul's principle for success in the Christian life is to become weak in our flesh, then we can become strong in Christ (12:9–10). In what ways does Paul illustrate his own weakness in this letter?

---

[1] Scott J. Hafemann, *2 Corinthians, The NIV Application Commentary*, ed. Terry Muck et al. (Grand Rapids: Zondervan, 2000), 390.

- Persecution and suffering are not evidence of a failed Christian life, but rather they are often evidence of sacrificial ministry and dying daily so others might live in Christ's example of his death on the cross. In what ways does Paul sacrifice on behalf of the Corinthian believers? What kinds of sacrifices do you make on behalf of the gospel?
- Consider Paul's role as an ambassador of Christ (5:20–21). What kinds of work do ambassadors do, and how might those things correspond to Paul's gospel ministry in the world?
- The book concludes with several excellent exhortations toward proper communal living (13:11–13). Memorize this final passage of the book as an encouragement to orient yourself toward the same kind of attitude in your own local church.

GALATIANS

SNAPSHOT

If salvation is through no merit of our own, then what's the role of obedience? If we're not saved by works, how do good works fit into the Christian life? Do they? In this book Paul lays out for us the fact that works neither save nor keep us. We're saved and walk with God in his mercies by grace alone! The love of God motivates us through our profound appreciation for so great a gift. This the false teachers denied, so the apostle in this letter writes to explain what makes the apostolic message "good news."

ORIENTATION

Date: About AD 48–50

Author: Paul

Audience: Churches in the region of Galatia (modern-day Turkey)

Outline:
1. Introduction (1:1–10)
2. Paul's Gospel Defended (What God Has Done: Revelation) (1:11–2:21)
3. Paul's Gospel Defined (What God Wants Us to Know: Instruction) (3:1–4:31)

   4. Paul's Gospel Practiced (What God Calls Us to Do:
      Ethics) (5:1–6:16)
   5. Conclusion (6:17–18)

YOU ARE HERE

Episode 7: Dawn of a New Era

The fourth book in the New Testament section known as the "Letters,"
Galatians is among the earliest books—if not *the* earliest book—of the New
Testament canon.

EXPLORING GALATIANS

Paul's letter to the Galatians is a prime candidate for the earliest letter that
we have from the apostle Paul, written after the establishment of churches
in Galatia during the first missionary journey (Acts 13–14). The churches
were threatened by erroneous teaching claiming that Gentiles had to be circumcised and keep the Mosaic law to be saved. These were the teachings of
a diverse group of opponents of the gospel known as the "Judaizers." There
is some debate whether the letter was written before or after the Jerusalem
Council (Acts 15). The basic meaning of the book fits either scenario.

   In chapters 1–2, Paul defends the message that he preached to the
Galatians, that it was not of human conception (Gal 1:11–24), his pre-
Christian life bearing stark witness. The radical change came through direct
revelation from Jesus and only much later did he have contact with the
apostles. Further, the message (2:10) he preached to the Galatians was confirmed through Paul's clash with Peter in Antioch (vv. 11–21). The intruders
into the churches—the Judaizers—simply taught a false "gospel" of works
salvation.

   From his personal experience, the apostle moves to the foundation of
his message (Gal 3–4). He begins by appealing to their own personal experience in coming to Christ (3:1–5); supernatural realities cannot be the

result of finite causes—whether it be their initial conversion (justification) or their spiritual growth (sanctification). This he illustrates in Gal 3:6–9, appealing to Abraham and making the point that just as Abraham was saved by faith, so now—and always—God's children are redeemed only through faith in the promise of God. In fact, the law, which came centuries after the promise to Abraham, can neither save nor keep us (3:10–4:7). The law was meant to reveal our need for Christ ("the seed," 3:16), not the means to Christ.

Following a personal, strident entreaty (4:8–20), Paul uses the lives of Sarah and Hagar to illustrate the vast difference between two covenants, between the fruit of law keeping and the bounty of grace (vv. 21–31). In the illustration, Hagar was cast out, just as the ineffectual role of works is rejected as a means of salvation.

Rule keeping doesn't commend us to God; grace commends God to us. The Galatians had begun the walk of faith well, but they stumbled badly (5:1–12). Freedom is not the ability merely to make choices; it's the ability to make godly choices. Godly choices are expressions of the character of God. The root of Christian motivation is love, never the thought of advantage (vv. 13–15). The internal work of the Holy Spirit in the lives of the truly saved results in fruits of righteousness (vv. 16–26)—and in service to others (6:1–16).

START YOUR JOURNEY

- Paul's message was a simple one: we come to Christ through the free, unmerited gift of divine grace, and the resultant lifestyle seeks to please him by grace through faith. We don't come to Christ through grace and walk in Christ by works. And we certainly don't earn a place in God's family by any good works or rituals, however pious or well-intentioned. Do you seek to be pleasing to God by offering your obedience? Or do you seek to please him because you have received his grace? There's a difference. The good news of the cross and the empty tomb cannot be improved by adding your good works.

- The Judaizers thought of obedience as a cause of favor with God rather than an effect of God's favor. Obedience doesn't and can't cause God to love us. However, obedience is a Spirit-enabled response to God's love. How easy it is for us to forget this foundational truth of the gospel!

- There's a tendency toward such Christian legalism in all of us. A Christian "legalist" is somebody who believes that their choices, those not defined and regulated by the Bible, are necessary for others to obey. They believe they are more pleasing to God than others who don't adopt their non-required morals. As you read through Galatians, note the ways in which Judaizers/legalists tried to force their human standards on others. How do people try to do this today?

EPHESIANS

SNAPSHOT

In today's age, Christians and nonbelievers alike struggle with purpose, calling, and identity. The letter to the Ephesians dives deep to provide answers to these questions by reminding believers they have been chosen and adopted as children into the family of God through the redemptive, reconciling work of Christ. This book may be regarded as a practical "guidebook" for navigating everyday Christian life by highlighting the importance of godly relationships and ecclesial unity.

ORIENTATION

Date: About AD 60–62
Author: Paul
Audience: The church in Ephesus and the surrounding region
Outline: 1. The Introduction, Prayer, and Thanksgiving (1:1–23)
                2. Salvation by Grace through Faith (2:1–10)
                3. Unity of the Body and the Peace of Christ (2:11–22)
                4. The Mystery of God's Plan and Paul's Prayer (3:1–21)
                5. Unity and Gifts of the Church (4:1–16)
                6. Paul's Testimony (4:17–24)

7. Encouragement for Holy Living (4:25–32)
8. Living as Children in Love (5:1–20)
9. Holy Relationships and Submission (5:21–6:9)
10. The Armor of God and Conclusion (6:10–24)

YOU ARE HERE

Episode 7: Dawn of a New Era

The fourth of the New Testament "Letters," Ephesians is one of Paul's "Prison Epistles," likely written while he was in prison in Rome.

EXPLORING EPHESIANS

As soon as we step into the book of Ephesians, two themes quickly emerge as Paul reminds Ephesian believers to 1) find their identities in Christ, who has provided reconciliation with God, and 2) remain united—both Jews and Gentiles—as the body of Christ.

Like many other New Testament epistles, Ephesians seeks to solidify Christ-centered doctrines and early church teachings (chapters 1–3). In chapter 1, Paul reminds the Ephesians of the many spiritual blessings God has given us through Christ: being chosen as holy (v. 4), predestined (v. 5), adopted (v. 5), accepted (v. 6), redeemed and forgiven (v. 7), granted wisdom and understanding (vv. 8–9), and sealed by the Holy Spirit with an eternal inheritance (vv. 11–14). These profound truths remind us that God the Father has chosen us, Christ the Son has redeemed us, and the Holy Spirit seals us.

In chapter 2, Paul describes how these blessings of salvation are gifts of God. Paul says, "For you are saved by grace through faith, and this is not from yourselves; it is God's gift—not from works, so that no one can boast" (vv. 8–9). But the true beauty of this letter emerges in verses 11–22. Paul describes how both Jews and Gentiles are welcome in the kingdom of God, describing how Christ tore down the "dividing wall of hostility" by his death and resurrection (v. 14). Spoiler alert: God's plan is about ethnic and cultural reconciliation between Jews and Gentiles; that is, God's plan isn't just about Israel's long-sought-after reconciliation with God. In a world still fraught with strong racial divides today, spiritual submission to the will of God by building loving relationships with "the other" feels more relevant and necessary than ever. This theme continues in Ephesians 3, which centers on the "mysterious" revelation of Christ. The first three chapters not only present what God has done for the world, but also evoke powerful transformation and healing for a world rooted in oppression, cultural divides, unrighteousness, and injustice.

The middle of the letter indicates a shift in Paul's ideas as it moves from doctrine in the first three chapters toward development of practical exhortations for everyday Christian living and encouragement in the face of persecution (Eph 4–6). Chapter 4 highlights the blueprints of what makes a godly, unified church. Many different leadership gifts function in the church, and these roles are for the purpose of shared faith, growing maturity, and demonstration of love to the world. Some of our most oft-quoted verses come from this section, where Paul encourages the Ephesians to "take off your former way of life, the old self" (4:22), "be renewed" (v. 23), and "put on the new self" (v. 24). He calls believers to newness of life in Christ! This theme continues in chapters 5 and 6, which highlight how believers are to live within the light of the gospel and to grow in wisdom as they embrace and share the message with others.

The entire letter rounds out with an exhortation to godly relationships and biblical submission—along with a powerful reminder that sin and evil are rampant in the world. Thus, we must take up arms and prepare for the battle, remembering that God is the one who fights for us, defends us, and gives us the spiritual victory over the forces of evil in this world (Eph 6).

START YOUR JOURNEY

- It's easy to consider these "old" letters as relics of the past. However, consider reading this letter as if it were written to your church specifically. What strikes you as important in the words Paul writes? What might Paul be encouraging you and your ministry to think or do in light of our culture and context today?

- Paul includes two prayers (1:15–22; 3:14–21) and one request for prayer (6:18–20). Notice how these prayers center on a main theme: revelation of the "mystery" of the gospel of Jesus Christ. Consider how you have heard and seen the gospel revealed in your own life—whether through Scripture, prayer, or fellow believers.

- Ephesians 2:8–9 is a foundational passage for understanding that we are saved by grace through faith, not by works. However, sometimes we forget that Paul's thought continues and concludes in verse 10, which reveals the relationship between salvation and good works in the Christian life. Memorize Eph 2:8–10 and meditate on its significance for your personally.

- If teaching this book to children, you may find it fun (and interesting!) to have them act out the "armor of God" in chapter 6. Using props and visuals will help bring the text to life. Do a little research on the various elements of armor in the ancient world but don't lose sight of the spiritual significance of Paul's image. What things do you need to "put on" to be strengthened by God's armor every day?

GOING DEEPER

"Empowered Walking: Giving Legs to God's Love"

— Harold W. Hoehner —

The love chapter of the New Testament is 1 Corinthians 13, but the love *book* of the New Testament is Ephesians. The word *love*, found twenty times in this book (in its verb and noun forms), occurs more than twice as many times per thousand words of text in Ephesians than in all the other Pauline letters.

After the prologue (1:1–2), Paul gives praise for God's planned spiritual benefits (vv. 3–14) and points out that God provides all the blessings necessary for the spiritual well-being of believers. The three persons of the Trinity are involved. First is the selection by the Father that we might be holy and blameless before him in love, having been adopted into God's family (vv. 4–6). Second is the sacrifice of the Son providing redemption and wisdom to understand the mystery of God's will to head up all things in Christ (vv. 7–12). Third is the sealing of the promised Holy Spirit, which indicates the security of God's ownership of believers (vv. 13–14).

This magnificent eulogy is followed by Paul's prayer for those who have everything, namely, all the spiritual blessings mentioned in verses 3–14. He prays that the believers might know God more intimately, in order to know (1) the hope of his calling, which looks to the past; (2) the wealth of his glorious inheritance in the saints, which looks to the future when this inheritance will be fully realized in Christ's coming for his saints; and (3) the greatness of God's power demonstrated by raising Christ and seating him in heaven, which looks at the present (vv. 15–23).

Having described God's eternal plan, Paul then demonstrates the execution of that plan. First, God's love is demonstrated by grace, saving sinners who deserved God's wrath and seating them in the heavens (2:1–10). Second, God's love is shown by uniting individual redeemed Jews and Gentiles into one corporate body, the church, Christ's body (vv. 11–22). Christ is the cornerstone of the foundation, and the Holy Spirit resides in this corporate body of believers.

Paul then begins to pray for these believers (3:1) but pauses, abruptly digressing to the mystery of Christ (vv. 2–13) with two emphases. First, he states his responsibility to explain the mystery, unknown in previous generations but now revealed to New Testament apostles and prophets by the Spirit, that is, both believing Jews and Gentiles are fellow heirs of Christ (vv. 2–6). This is a revolutionary concept. Although the Old Testament reveals that Gentiles may be saved, it never reveals that believing Jews and Gentiles would become one entity in Christ. Second, Paul states his responsibility to proclaim this mystery to the Gentiles, thus demonstrating through the church God's multifaceted wisdom to rulers and authorities in the heavenly realms (vv. 7–13).

After his digression (vv. 2–13), Paul continues the prayer begun in verse 1 by praying that believing Jews and Gentiles might comprehend and experience Christ's love, which surpasses knowledge (vv. 14–21), thus maintaining their unity.

In chapters 4 through 6 Paul applies the doctrine he has related in the first three chapters. The major divisions revolve around the *walk* in 4:1, 17; 5:2, 8, 15. The only exception is 6:10–20, where believers are to "stand" against evil, after which he gave his conclusion and a benediction (6:21–24).

First, *believers are to walk in unity* (4:1–16). They are to maintain a lifestyle worthy of their call to salvation and union with other believers

by demonstrating humility and gentleness, making every effort to preserve the unity that comes from the Holy Spirit (vv. 1–3). In fact, the
three persons of the Trinity are an example of such unity (vv. 4–6),
the preservation of which is maintained by the bestowal of spiritual
gifts to all believers, thereby equipping them for the work of ministry.
Consequently, the believing body will grow up in Christ as each member
lovingly contributes to that growth (vv. 7–16).

Second, *believers are to walk in holiness* (4:17–32), not in futility like
the Gentiles (vv. 17–19) but as new persons in Christ (vv. 20–32). The
truth in Jesus is that they have laid aside the former old person, having
been renewed by the spirit of their minds, and having put on the new
person created after God's likeness (vv. 20–24). Therefore, they are not
to lie but are to speak the truth to one another, not to steal to satisfy personal needs but work with their hands to share with those in need, and
not to use unwholesome words but to use beneficial words to build each
other up. They are to be kind and compassionate to one another, exhib-
iting the same graciousness that God had already demonstrated toward
them in Christ (vv. 25–32).

Third, *believers are to walk in love* (5:1–6). Positively, they are to imitate God and to love as Christ did (vv. 1–2). Negatively, they are to abstain
from the evil works of unbelievers who will face God's wrath (vv. 3–6).

Fourth, *believers are to walk in light* (5:7–14). They are not to become
involved with evildoers (vv. 7–10) nor with their works (vv. 11–13) but
are to seek to have the approval of Christ (v. 14).

Fifth, *believers are to walk in wisdom* (5:15–6:9). They are to walk
wisely by understanding the Lord's will through the filling of the Holy
Spirit (vv. 15–21). This walk in wisdom, enabled by the Spirit, is applied
to the domestic realm (5:22–6:9): the relationship of wives and husbands
(vv. 22–32), the relationship of children and parents (6:1–4), and the
relationship of servants and masters (vv. 5–9).

Sixth, *believers are to put on the full armor of God in order to be able
to stand against the schemes of evil spiritual forces in the heavens* (6:10–20).

Offensive advance against the devil is not commanded. Instead, believers are to take a defensive stand in order to hold the territory that Christ and his body, the church, have claimed. Such spiritual warfare demands alertness and persistence in prayer for all saints.

The theme of love, dominant throughout the letter, shows God's love in saving sinners by his grace and shows that this love is to prevail in all relationships between believing Jews and Gentiles in the body of Christ, the church. Believers today are responsible for carrying forth this mandate in their relationships with fellow believers.[1]

---

[1] Adapted from Harold W. Hoehner, "Empowered Walking: Giving Legs to God's Love," *Kindred Spirit* 28, no. 2 (Summer 2004): 4–6. © 2004 Dallas Theological Seminary.

PHILIPPIANS

SNAPSHOT

Do you ever feel like the Christian life is difficult? Does it feel futile? Or worse—are you rejected by those you love because of your faith? The book of Philippians describes the life we have in Christ as far better than what we can have from this world. Even though it can be tempting to satisfy our own desires, such a choice leads to death. Rather, Paul calls us to walk as citizens of heaven, in joy.

ORIENTATION

Date: About AD 60–62
Author: Paul
Audience: The Philippian church
Outline: 1. Introduction (1:1–11)
2. The Advancement of the Gospel (1:12–26)
3. Live Worthy of the Gospel (1:27–2:30)
4. Watch Out for False Teachers (3:1–4:1)
5. Final Greetings (4:2–23)

YOU ARE HERE

Episode 7: Dawn of a New Era

As the sixth book in the section of Scripture called the "Letters," and one of the four letters known as Paul's "Prison Epistles," Philippians calls for Christ-centered humility and unity.

EXPLORING PHILIPPIANS

On the surface, Paul's letter to the Philippians provides an update on his own circumstances, thanking them for partnership in his gospel ministry (1:5, 7). It also expresses his deep appreciation for their financial gift (4:10–20). However, a deeper reading shows how believers can handle adversity in their Christian walk. By all appearances, Paul's situation was bleak. He was in prison facing trial before Caesar, and several ministry partners had abandoned him along with their own faith (3:2, 18–19). The outcome would be his death, a fact that he acknowledged (1:21–23). Yet in the face of this adversity, joy continues to be a key theme (1:18–19; 2:2, 17–18; 3:1; 4:4, 10).

How can believers suffering such trials and challenges continue to embrace joy? Paul says they can rejoice in the face of adversity because they are citizens of heaven (1:27; 3:20). Even though they live in a crooked and dark world (2:15), God remains in control and will take care of their needs. Paul assures the readers that God, the one who began a good work in them, will continue it until Christ's return (1:6; 2:13).

Paul exemplifies this in his own life and ministry. He accepts the possibility of dying for the gospel, content that Christ would be glorified in his martyr's death (1:20). On the other hand, Paul remains confident that if Rome releases him from prison (v. 19), it would mean more fruitful ministry for him (1:22, 24–26). Regardless of the outcome, the cause of the gospel would be advanced (vv. 12–17).

At the end of the letter, Paul reiterates this point when he says, "I am able to do all things through him who strengthens me" (4:13). The context of the passage suggests that Paul doesn't mean that he can do anything—climb a mountain, win a ballgame, ace a Greek test, or get a promotion at work. Rather, he can find contentment in any circumstance, either having plenty or being in need (vv. 11–12). Because of his heavenly citizenship, the things of this world should have no control over him.

Paul calls believers to imitate his own approach to ministry (3:17; 4:9). He mentions Timothy (2:19–24) and Epaphroditus—who risked his own life for the sake of the gospel (vv. 25–30)—as examples to follow. In contrast, those who abandoned him rejected Christ and pursued their own appetites (3:19). He calls the Philippians to follow his example by putting aside their own interests to seek the interests of others (2:4, 21). By doing this, Paul calls the Philippians to "work out" the inner working of the Spirit through obedience (2:12; cf. 3:12–15).

In all this, Christ is the ultimate example for believers to follow. In Phil 2:6–11, Paul uses an early Christian hymn or confession to exemplify this Christ-like humility. Even though he is God (v. 6), the Son became human and died for us (vv. 7–8). Christ humbled himself and reduced himself to the lowest part of humanity—the form of a slave—and died on a cross for our salvation. Because of this God exalted Christ, the God-man, through resurrection and ascension to the highest position of heaven.

Finally, Paul discusses the righteousness that belongs to the believer, a righteousness that comes through faith (3:9) and ultimately leads to resurrection (3:10–11, 20–21). He contrasts this with a righteousness that comes from the law. Paul himself had several significant achievements (vv. 4–6). He even claimed to be "blameless" under the law (v. 6); yet he considered it all garbage in comparison to the righteousness that comes through his relationship with Christ (vv. 8–10).

START YOUR JOURNEY

- Philippians 2:6–11 is an early Christian hymn known as the "Kenosis," referring to the Greek word *kenoō* in verse 7, which means "to empty." Since it was probably written before Paul wrote the letter, it indicates that the earliest believers understood Jesus as God. A number of elements of that early hymn demonstrate this truth. First, Paul says that while the Son was "existing in the form of God," he assumed "the form of a servant" (vv. 6–7), indicating that his original nature was preexistent and divine. God the Son didn't exchange his divine nature, but added ("assumed," "took on") a human nature to his divine nature at the incarnation. At the end of the hymn, Paul describes Jesus as one who receives worship, an act reserved only for God. In fact, Paul alludes to Isa 45:22–23 to describe this worship of Jesus. The original context of Isaiah describes worship of God himself, placing Jesus in the same position as YHWH—the name reserved only for the one true God!

- Even though he is in prison, Paul stresses joy as a part of the Christian life (1:18, 25; 2:18, 29; 3:1; 4:4, 10). Luke describes Paul with the same attitude while he was in the Philippian jail (Acts 16:25). We all face difficult times, particularly in our Christian lives, but since difficulty pales in comparison to what we have received from God in Christ, we can still rejoice.

COLOSSIANS

SNAPSHOT

Do you sometimes feel the pull of things in this world competing with Christ for your attention and affections? Amidst confusing conundrums and competing claims, the book of Colossians sets Christ above any and all that might seek to displace him. Christ alone—not empty philosophies or rigorous rules—is sufficient to raise us out of our sinful existence. He directs us to walk in wisdom under his rule.

ORIENTATION

Date: About AD 60–62
Author: Paul
Audience: The churches at Colossae (1:2) and Laodicea (4:16)
Outline: 1. Introduction (1:1–14)
                2. Christ Our Lord (1:15–29)
                3. Resist False Teaching (2:1–23)
                4. Putting on the New Self (3:1–4:6)
                5. Final Greetings (4:7–18)

YOU ARE HERE

Episode 7: Dawn of a New Era

As the seventh book in the section of Scripture called the "Letters," and one of four letters known as Paul's "Prison Epistles," Colossians counters false teaching threatening the church.

EXPLORING COLOSSIANS

In the book of Colossians, the apostle Paul portrays two distinct ways of *seeing* in the world: 1) life under the authority of empty philosophies, angels, or human regulations; or 2) life under Christ, who rules over all things. These lead to a unique way of *being* in the world.

Even in a letter as short as Colossians, Paul repeatedly warns his readers of the dangers that threaten to derail them from following Christ both in belief and in practice. After some general warnings (1:28; 2:4), Paul cautions against the false worship of angels, of elevating these created beings to a level comparable to that of Christ (2:18). He also warns the Colossians away from elevating certain practices—circumcision and ascetic self-denial—as requirements for knowing and following Christ (2:11, 13, 20–23).

Paul lays out the alternative to these false teachings in some of the loftiest Christological language in the New Testament. Having been delivered from the domain of darkness, Christians confess Christ as divine ruler, creator, and authority before all others. He describes Jesus as God's very image (1:15), in whom the fullness of deity dwells bodily (1:19–20; 2:9). Jesus is also the creator—all things, visible and invisible, were created by him (1:16). And finally, Jesus carries a powerful authority, for all things hold together in him as he serves as the head of the church. Paul pictures Christ as before all others so that "he might come to have first place in everything" (v. 18).

The apostle Paul's two ways of seeing the world also extend to *being* in the world. The Colossians' ways before Christ were hostile to God in their minds, and evil deeds marked their lives (v. 21). Paul describes this way as the old self and exhorts the Colossians to commit themselves to truly following Jesus in the world—what Paul calls putting on the new self (3:9–10).

The ways of the old self and the ways of the new self each speak to the rulers of our lives. The book of Colossians makes clear that wicked ways are idolatry (v. 5), while the way of righteousness and renewal comes as a result of the rule of Christ in our hearts (v. 15). What we believe matters, for our beliefs inform our lives. In a similar way, our lives point back to our beliefs. As one writer puts it: "When you wake up in the morning, called by God to be a self again, if you want to know who you are, watch your feet. Because where your feet take you, that is who you are."[1]

Ultimately, as we seek to live under the rule of Christ (1:16–18; 2:10), walk in the ways of Christ (2:6), and work as servants of Christ (3:23), we witness to the world the transformative work of God who makes the dead live (2:13; 3:1–4).

START YOUR JOURNEY

- Because Colossians is such a short book, take some time to read through it in one sitting. After you finish, spend a bit of time writing down impressions and questions for further reflection.
- Create a chart of "Warnings and Wisdom." Under "Warnings," create a list of the false teachings Paul wants the believers to reject. Under "Wisdom," list the truths Paul wants the believers to embrace that directly contrast with the false teachings.
- Much of Colossians is focused on a response to false teaching—both in belief and in action. Think about the book in your own context. What are some false teachings you know of swirling around today? In what ways do those false teachings contradict Christian teaching

---

[1] Frederick Buechner, *The Alphabet of Grace* (New York: HarperOne, 1970), 25.

and/or living? How might the truths of Colossians speak to these current circumstances?

- Colossians has a number of "chunks" that serve as great sections to commit to memory. Consider memorizing Paul's opening prayer (1:9–14), his song of the preeminence of Christ (vv. 15–20), or his description of the new self (3:12–17).

1 THESSALONIANS

SNAPSHOT

Are you curious about God's plans for the future? Ever wonder what's next for you as a believer in Christ? The book of 1 Thessalonians provides hope for the future—especially for those living in a world hostile to our walk with Christ. It also pulls back the curtain to reveal powerful truths about the return of Christ, our resurrection, and our rescue from the coming wrath.

ORIENTATION

Date:	About AD 50–51
Authors:	Paul with Silvanus and Timothy
Audience:	The Church of Thessalonica
Outline:	1. Introduction (1:1–3)
	2. Paul's Commendation of the Thessalonians (1:4–10)
	3. Paul's Description of His Ministry in Thessalonica (2:1–16)
	4. Timothy's Report Regarding the Church (2:17–3:13)
	5. Paul's Instructions for the Church (4:1–5:24)
	6. Conclusion (5:25–28)

YOU ARE HERE

Episode 7: Dawn of a New Era

The eighth of the New Testament "Letters," 1 Thessalonians is one of the earliest New Testament books, written from Corinth shortly after Paul's departure from Thessalonica.

EXPLORING 1 THESSALONIANS

Paul visited Thessalonica on his second missionary journey. He was there at least three Sabbaths (Acts 17:2), and possibly longer—long enough to establish a church. However, Paul's departure from Thessalonica was earlier than he had anticipated. Paul was "forced to leave" them (1 Thess 2:17) due to a riot led by Jewish unbelievers who were hostile to Paul's message and ministry (Acts 17:5–9). Paul believed it was better for the Thessalonian believers if he and his colleagues departed, because he was the primary object of the mob's anger (Acts 17:10).

Even after his departure, the Thessalonians would endure significant persecution (1 Thess 1:6; 2:14–16). Paul writes to encourage the church for their exemplary reputation, to exhort them to continue on this path, and to give the church instruction concerning sexual purity and Christian living. Paul gives special time and attention to the doctrines of the hope of resurrection and warnings about the coming day of the Lord.

Paul commends these first-generation Christians for their wonderful and widespread reputation (1:7–8). They had endured severe suffering for their faith (1:6; 2:14–16). However, there was some confusion in their assembly regarding the coming day of the Lord. Paul writes to clear up the confusion and provide apostolic teaching on these subjects.

It appears that some in the assembly were concerned that their dead loved ones (believers in Christ) would miss out on the gathering of believers to the Lord and thus participation in the expected kingdom of Christ

(4:13). Paul informs them that their dead loved ones who had trusted in Christ would not miss out. In fact, he explains that believers who have died will rise first (v. 16), and then those believers who are still alive when the Lord returns will be caught up "together with them" to meet the Lord in the air (v. 17). From that point forward, believers would be with Christ—and with one another—forever. These are encouraging words (v. 18).

In the final chapter, the Apostle turns his attention to the Day of the Lord (5:1–11). Paul draws a stark contrast between the wicked unbelievers subject to judgment and the righteous believers looking to Christ for rescue (1:9–10)—a contrast as different as night and day. How encouraging must it have been to learn that God's wrath and judgment are not appointed for the righteous but for the wicked (5:9). Paul further explains that for those unprepared (unbelievers), this event will come unexpectedly, just as a thief arrives at night and is unexpected. The language used by Paul was intentionally chosen to harken back to the Old Testament language and imagery of the day of the Lord (see special feature on the "Day of the Lord" in the Old Testament, page 198–99).

START YOUR JOURNEY

- Keep in mind that this is one of the earliest books of the New Testament, so at the time this letter was written, very little apostolic teaching had been written down and disseminated to the early church. Take note of how well-developed the teachings of the person and work of Christ were already in this very early stage of Christian teaching.

- Paul mentions the return of Christ in every chapter of 1 Thessalonians. As you read through, find these passages— sometimes just a verse or two, sometimes whole paragraphs. Take note of the promises for believers and the warnings for unbelievers associated with Christ's return.

- Paul's letter to the Thessalonians has a lot to say about how believers are to live in light of the coming of Christ. As you read, answer the question, What should I be doing (or not doing) as I await the return of Christ? Then consider one or two very specific things you can start doing (or cease doing) to align your actions with that expectation.

2 THESSALONIANS

SNAPSHOT

Have you ever believed a lie that seemed very convincing at the time? This is what appears to have happened to some of the Thessalonian believers—twice. Some appear to have believed a lie that a message sent to them was from the Apostle Paul. Additionally, some believed the lie recorded in this message that the period of the day of the Lord had overtaken them. When faced with "fake news" that contradicts apostolic teaching, fact-checking is urgently needed.

ORIENTATION

Date: About AD 51–52
Authors: Paul, Silvanus, and Timothy
Audience: The church of Thessalonica
Outline: 1. Introduction (1:1–2)
               2. Thankfulness and Prayers for the Church (1:3–12)
               3. Teaching concerning the Day of the Lord (2:1–17)
               4. Prayer for Evangelism and Protection (3:1–5)
               5. Rebukes to the Idle (3:6–15)
               6. Conclusion (3:16–18)

YOU ARE HERE

Episode 7: Dawn of a New Era

The ninth of the New Testament "Letters," 2 Thessalonians is one of the earliest New Testament books, a sequel and supplement to the previous letter sent to Thessalonica.

EXPLORING 2 THESSALONIANS

To understand what was going on in Thessalonica that prompted the writing of this letter, we have to do a little "reading between the lines." It appears that whoever delivered Paul's first letter to the Thessalonians brought back a disturbing report to the Apostle. Someone had convinced many of the Christians in Thessalonica that Paul's teachings about the coming day of the Lord were wrong. Whether by letter, message, or spirit, some in Thessalonica had been thrown into a panic, believing that the period of the day of the Lord had already begun (2 Thess 2:2).

This teaching would have been shocking and disturbing to the church. Hadn't Paul told the Thessalonians that the day of the Lord was a time of judgment and wrath on the wicked (1 Thess 5)? Weren't the believers in Christ the children of light, not appointed to wrath? Coupled with the fact that the Thessalonians were experiencing significant persecution (2 Thess 1:4–7), this report that the dreaded day of the Lord had come upon them seemed believable.

Once Paul learns of this false report, he writes his second letter to the Thessalonian believers to dispel the fears of the church and to combat the false teaching. Two issues had to be resolved: first, the intrusive false teaching misled the Thessalonians regarding end-times expectations; second, the Thessalonians had chosen to believe the competing authority rather than Paul. The question had become, Who are you going to believe and trust? In 2 Thessalonians, Paul appeals to Old Testament language and imagery of the day of the Lord, drawing especially from the book of Daniel, to prove that what the Thessalonians were experiencing may be severe persecution, but it didn't hold a candle to the fires of judgment that were expected when Christ comes as judge (2:3–5).

In this passage, Paul runs through a rapid, bullet-point description of end-times elements like the apostasy or rebellion and the rise of the "man of lawlessness" doomed to destruction (v. 3). His description of that man is vivid: "He opposes and exalts himself above every so-called god or object of worship, so that he sits in God's temple, proclaiming that he himself is God. . . . The coming of the lawless one is based on Satan's working, with every kind of miracle, both signs and wonders serving the lie, and with every wicked deception among those who are perishing" (2:4, 9–10). Readers familiar with the Old Testament prophets would have recognized language and imagery reminiscent of Dan 7:24–25; 9:27; 11:35–37, and Jesus's teaching in Matt 24:15.

By pointing out the biblical (Old Testament) descriptions of the ultimate day of the Lord and reminding them of things he himself taught them when he was with them (2 Thess 2:5–7), Paul shows the Thessalonians that what they were experiencing was not the dreaded day of the Lord judgment. Therefore, the false teaching that had upset them was wrong. Yes, Christ would one day come to judge the world. Yes, the Old Testament prophecies about that period of the day of the Lord would be fulfilled. But no, the persecutions the Thessalonians were experiencing—however severe—were not the fulfillment of those end-times prophecies.

Having cleared the air of the putrid odor of false teachings, Paul fills the final section with clear teaching about how they are to be living in the present (2:13–3:18). Rather than believing every wind of doctrine without discernment, they are to stay true to Paul's teaching. He writes, "Stand firm and hold to the traditions you were taught, whether by what we said or what we wrote" (2:15). That includes clinging to the hope and comfort that comes through a right understanding of the future (vv. 16–17). It also means praying and laboring for the advancement of the gospel of salvation (3:1–18).

START YOUR JOURNEY

- As you read this epistle, remember that Paul is writing for a specific occasion. That occasion is to combat the claims of the false report that the day of the Lord had begun. In other words, Paul had to challenge aberrant and misleading views of the end times. How similar to our own day! People who calculate the date of Christ's return, alarmists who push conspiracy theories, authors and preachers who point to current events as fulfillments of prophecy—these things cause the same kind of confusion among Christians today as they did to the Thessalonians. In light of this, it's important to have a firm understanding of the big picture of biblical prophecy.

- Paul is building upon the theology handed down to him by Christ himself (Matt 24) and the prophecy of Daniel (Dan 9:27). These verses should also be studied for a fuller understanding. Also, the earliest readers of 2 Thessalonians connected these things to the prophecies of the book of Revelation (especially Rev 13). Together, what kind of picture of the end times do these passages project?

- Don't be like the Thessalonians! Don't exchange the teachings of Paul and the apostles and prophets for some other source of information—whether a book that seems convincing, a teacher who feels compelling, or a new "revelation" by a spirit that seems supernatural. Hold firm to the teachings of the Old and New Testaments. They are a sure and firm foundation.

GOING DEEPER

"The New Testament Canon"

— John Adair and Michael J. Svigel —

The term *canon* comes from a Greek word meaning "standard" or "rule." Canonical books of the Bible are those regarded by Christians as the "standard" or "rule" of the faith—the final written authority in all matters of faith and practice. A book of the Bible is not deemed "canonical" because it measures up to some outside standard or rule set by a council, pope, emperor, or scholar. Rather, a book of the Bible is reckoned as canonical because *it is itself the standard and rule for the church*.

The development of the Old Testament canon spans almost two thousand years, from the time of Moses and the Pentateuch (c. 1500 BC) to the beginning of the medieval period (c. AD 500). We have very little direct testimony concerning how, why, and when the books of the Hebrew Scriptures came to be accepted by Israel's prophets and teachers. We do, however, have the final result of that process: the collection of books known as the Old Testament, which continued as the holy Scriptures of the church from the moment of its birth (2 Tim 3:16).

Regarding the New Testament, we have a much clearer picture. Because the first-century apostles and prophets were teaching and writing from their God-given authority as the foundations of the church

(Eph 2:20; 4:11), their official writings carried absolute authority among their recipients. Books like Matthew, Romans, or 1 Thessalonians were written, sent to churches, and received by Christians as apostolic and prophetic. Those first recipients immediately treated those writings as authoritative—as *canonical*. No decision-making process, no hesitancy, no questioning whether those writings should be treated as the standard and rule of faith and practice.

During the apostolic period, a growing number of churches began copying, passing around, and collecting the apostolic writings as the standards of doctrine and practice alongside the Old Testament books. Already around the year AD 65, the apostle Peter was aware of a collection of Paul's writings which he equated with "the Scriptures" (2 Pet 3:16). Then, just a few decades later, around the year 96, a disciple of the apostles named Clement of Rome, wrote to the church in Corinth, "Take up the epistle of the blessed Paul the apostle. . . . Truly he wrote to you in the Spirit."[1]

About a decade after that, Ignatius of Antioch (c. 110) alluded to or quoted from several New Testament writings: Matthew, possibly Luke, John, Romans, 1 Corinthians, Galatians, Ephesians, Philippians, 1 Timothy, 2 Timothy.[2] His contemporary Polycarp of Smyrna (c. 110), who was himself a disciple of the apostle John, wrote a short letter to the church in Philippi and mentioned Paul's book of Philippians (Polycarp, *Philippians* 3.2). He also quotes from Eph 4:26, calling it "holy Scripture" (Polycarp, *Philippians* 12.1). In fact, Polycarp's letter—written just a decade or so after the end of the apostolic era—contains quotations from or allusions to numerous New Testament books: Matthew, Luke, Romans, 1 Corinthians, Galatians, Ephesians, Philippians, 1 and

---

[1] *1 Clement* 47.1, 3. Translation from *The Apostolic Fathers: Greek Texts and English Translations,* ed. and trans. Michael W. Holmes, 3rd ed. (Grand Rapids: Baker Academic, 2007), 109.

[2] Michael J. Kruger, *Canon Revisited: Establishing the Origins and Authority of the New Testament Books* (Wheaton: Crossway, 2012), 214–16.

2 Timothy, 1 Peter, and 1 John, and possibly 2 Corinthians, 1 and 2 Thessalonians, and the Gospel of John.[3]

By the end of the second century, just 100 years after the close of the apostolic period, a disciple of Polycarp, Irenaeus of Lyons (c. 180), wrote a series of books against the heresies threatening the church of his day. Throughout those books, he quotes from or alludes to all the writings of the New Testament with the exception of James, Jude, 3 John, Philemon, and perhaps 2 Peter and Hebrews. Ignatius, Polycarp, and Irenaeus are just a few examples of the many second-century writers who evidence the New Testament books' authority among the churches.[4]

As far as we can tell from the historical evidence, during that first 100 years after the apostles, the pastors and teachers of local churches faithfully received the writings of the Old and New Testaments, then copied, distributed, and passed them down to the next generation of leadership. Those who did the copying and collecting were either original disciples of the apostles or the successors of those disciples. They had a unique perspective to know which writings had come from the authoritative apostles and prophets themselves. As long as they knew the writings had come from the apostles and prophets, those books functioned canonically in all the churches.

During the first two centuries, however, false teachers began to forge their own "scriptures" to compete with the authentic writings of the apostles and prophets. They also began to produce edited versions of canonical writings and eventually produced their own collections of authoritative books to lead people astray. This prompted true Christians to clarify which writings had been received as authoritative and used in the churches since the time of the apostles. So, around the year 180, the church in Rome produced a document describing the New Testament writings officially used in their teaching and preaching. This document

---

[3] See discussion in Kruger, *Canon Revisited*, 216–19.

[4] See Michael J. Kruger, *The Question of Canon* (Downers Grove: IVP Academic, 2013), 155–203.

gives us some indication that the churches of the second century officially accepted the great majority of New Testament writings found in our own Bibles and rightly rejected heretical books.[5]

While the church of the second and third centuries enjoyed strong unity over most New Testament books, a handful of books that are part of the canon were doubted by some people, in some places, at some times. These include Hebrews, James, 2 Peter, 2 and 3 John, Jude, and—later in the third century—Revelation. At the same time, a small group of early Christian writings that are not apostolic and prophetic were wrongly regarded as Scripture by some people, in some places, at some times. These included the *Didache, Epistle of Barnabas, Shepherd of Hermas, Apocalypse of Peter*, and *Wisdom of Solomon*. However, doubts about the inclusion or exclusion of these books were never universal, while Christians appear to have had no doubts about all the other books of the New Testament.

By the end of the period of the early church (about AD 400), all Christians throughout the world shared the same canon of twenty-seven New Testament books we have today. By the time several local churches and regional councils published their official lists describing (not prescribing) the books of the Bible in the fourth century, even the doubted books had been settled through an organic process of corporate discernment, not through an official affirmation or denunciation.[6]

---

[5] This dating of the Muratorian fragment and its role in establishing a second-century canon have not gone unchallenged. See Geoffrey Mark Hahneman, *The Muratorian Fragment and the Development of the Canon*, Oxford Theological Monographs (Oxford: Clarendon, 1992). However, the certainty of a second-century canon is based on more than this fragment, particularly the authoritative use of writings by church leaders throughout the second century. See a positive appraisal of the Muratorian fragment in Charles E. Hill, "The Debate over the Muratorian Fragment and the Development of the Canon," *Westminster Theological Journal* 57 (1995): 437–52.

[6] This essay was adapted, by permission, from John Adair and Michael J. Svigel, *Urban Legends of Church History: 40 Common Misconceptions* (Nashville: B&H Academic, 2020), 39–45.

1 TIMOTHY

SNAPSHOT

Ever felt inadequate for the task ahead? Unprepared to lead others? Unqualified to deal with those who were antagonistic to the gospel? Welcome to Timothy's world as he was called to lead the church at Ephesus. But Timothy wasn't alone. Through admonition and encouragement, Paul—Timothy's mentor in the faith—provided guidelines for directing the church to truth and strengthening relationships for Christian service.

ORIENTATION

Date:	About AD 63–65
Author:	Paul
Audience:	Timothy
Outline:	1. Salutation and Warnings against False Teachers (1:1–20)
	2. Instructions for Church Order—Functions (2:1–3:13)
	3. Addressing False Teachers and False Doctrine (3:14–4:16)
	4. Instructions for Church Order—Relationships (5:1–6:2)

5. Timothy's Challenge: Live in Godliness and Combat False Teaching (6:3–21)

YOU ARE HERE

Episode 8: The End and New Beginning

The tenth of the "Letters" of the New Testament and the first of Paul's "Pastoral Epistles," 1 Timothy gives instructions to the young shepherd, Timothy, entrusted with church leadership.

EXPLORING 1 TIMOTHY

In 1 Timothy, Paul wrote to his young disciple with instructions on how to lead the church at Ephesus. The letter is highly organized (see outline above). Following a brief salutation (1:1–2), Paul states the purpose of the book and the charge to Timothy: stay in Ephesus and combat false teachers. Thus, this letter functions like a handy leadership manual for Timothy. He counsels and instructs the younger man on the problems of deceitful and inaccurate instructors, appropriate public prayer, the responsibilities of believers in worship, the requirements for elders and deacons, and miscellaneous duties regarding relational obligations. In short, 1 Timothy is a book that starts with a basic charge to Timothy to combat false teachers, followed by directives for the church and its leadership, and concludes with a challenge to Timothy to guard the sacred trust of the gospel and to live a life of godliness in anticipation of the return of the Lord Jesus Christ.

The five primary sections of the letter involve a message that alternates between instructions concerning Timothy and false teachers (1:1–20; 3:14–4:16; 6:3–21) and church order for various groups (2:1–3:13; 5:1–6:2). The structure focuses on the central point (3:14–4:16), which leads off with what is likely the pinnacle of the book: 3:14–16. In this passage, and in particular v. 16, Paul emphasizes that God's household—the church—is to emulate the godliness of Christ in which

He was manifested in the flesh,
vindicated in the Spirit,
seen by angels,
preached among the nations,
believed on in the world,
taken up in glory.

This hymnic confession of faith reminds Timothy of the pillar of the foundation of truth: Jesus Christ's person and work. This climactic section (3:14–4:16) also parallels the opening and closing sections. Supporting sections 2 (2:1–3:13) and 4 (5:1–6:2) include material that directly relates to the conflict created by false teachers. This conflict generates the purpose of the letter as the author addresses it in the opening section.

First Timothy contributes greatly to the New Testament. Much more than a letter for pastors (one of the "Pastoral Epistles"), it reminds all believers that truth matters. God's truth must be taught in the church, and truth teachers—God's leaders—must remember that Jesus himself is the way, the truth, and the life (John 14:6). Anchored in him, the church will withstand all the storms the wayward world can throw our way.

START YOUR JOURNEY

- First Timothy is a short book and can easily be read in one sitting. Read through the letter and note the emphasis on "godliness." In doing so, identify how many times "godliness" is positioned as the life trait for believers.
- False teachers and teachings abound. In Timothy's day there were men devoted to "myths and endless genealogies" (1 Tim 1:4). While that false teaching may not be commonplace today, what "false teachings" are abundant and contrary to "sound doctrine"?
- The audience of 1 Timothy was Timothy—Paul's "true son in the faith" (1:2). However, like all New Testament letters, it was to be read to the church at large (Col 4:16). If the false teachers were

EXPLORING CHRISTIAN SCRIPTURE

defective leaders (elders and deacons), how would such a letter possibly impact their thoughts and actions?

- The Pastoral Letters—and in particular, 1 Timothy—have many statements dropped into the flow of the text to grab the reader's attention. For example, 1 Tim 4:9–10 is identified as a "trustworthy" saying. How is that trustworthy statement applicable to the life of a believer in a world without hope?

- Consider memorizing the early hymn/confession in 1 Tim 3:16, knowing that you will be committing to memory one of the earliest Christian hymns ever written and a great reminder of the powerful person and work of Christ.

2 TIMOTHY

SNAPSHOT

Second Timothy has been called Paul's "last will and testament"—the Apostle's final inspired writing before his execution. Christians throughout history have clung to the words of this letter, knowing they represent Paul's final thoughts before meeting Jesus in glory. When it seems like the world is against you because of your faith, take courage in knowing that in the end—*the* end—obedience to Christ brings strength to endure the hardships of life.

ORIENTATION

Date: About AD 67
Author: Paul
Audience: Timothy
Outline:
1. Salutation (1:1–2)
2. Encouraging Timothy (1:3–18)
3. Exhortation to Serve Unashamedly (2:1–26)
4. Expectation of Resistance to the Gospel (3:1–15)
5. Charge to Church Leadership (3:16–4:8)
6. Personal Instructions (4:9–22)

YOU ARE HERE

Episode 8: The End and New Beginning

This eleventh "Letter" of the New Testament is the second of Paul's "Pastoral Epistles" and likely the last words he wrote.

EXPLORING 2 TIMOTHY

The conditions of Paul's final imprisonment are very different from the first "house arrest" in Rome recorded in Acts 28, from which he was freed after a couple years. This time, Paul is in a dark dungeon with no creaturely comforts. Onesiphorus evidently provided some relief for him (2 Tim 1:16–18), for which Paul was extremely grateful. But only Luke was willing to stay with him (4:11). In that context, Paul reaches out to Timothy, his child in the faith.

Paul issues several charges to Timothy that all believers should heed. First, he encourages Timothy to live a life unashamed of the gospel and its ministers (1:8, 12, 16; 2:15). In the midst of major persecution in Rome under the crazed emperor Nero, Paul wanted to make sure Timothy didn't shrink away as others had done.

Second, Paul calls Timothy to accept suffering as part of his "calling" to a life of service to the Lord (1:8–9). Just as Paul had suffered greatly in so many different experiences in his ministry (3:11), Timothy should anticipate persecution for living a godly life (v. 12).

Third, Paul commands Timothy to "guard the good deposit" that had been entrusted to him—all that Paul had taught him (1:13–14). One of the clearest statements about the inspiration of Scripture is found in 2 Tim 3:16–17: "All Scripture is inspired by God"—literally "God-breathed"—and thus authoritative for doctrine and practice. The centrality of God's Word is highlighted throughout the letter. Paul himself had "kept the faith" (4:7) throughout his ministry, an example for those who receive the faith to pass on to the next generation (2:2).

Fourth, Paul warns Timothy to "flee from youthful passions" (2:22). Many times the best strategy to fight temptation is to simply run away—often literally! Conversely, we are to run toward and pursue righteousness, faith, love, and peace.

Fifth, Paul tells Timothy to own his faith by nurturing the seeds planted from his family and from Paul (1:5; 3:14–15). There is a progression of spiritual development hinted at in these verses. We generally believe what we are told by our parents and families because we trust them to tell us the truth. However, each one of us must "continue in what you have learned and firmly believed" (3:14). He encourages Timothy to trust his teachers, because "you know those who taught you" (v. 14). We must transition from our childhood faith to spiritual "adulting," growing through what we've been taught and was modeled for us.

Sixth, Paul instructs Timothy to "preach the word" (4:2) without undue influence from the cultural pressures that might exist. There is no bad time to tell others about the saving knowledge of Christ and to teach them from Scripture how to live a life of righteousness.

Paul's letter ends in a very personal way. Because he is suffering in the dungeon, he pleads for Timothy to come soon (v. 9), before winter, if possible (v. 21), and to bring his cloak for warmth (v. 13). Paul also asks Timothy to bring the "scrolls, especially the parchments" (v. 13), probably a reference to the Old Testament. He also asks to see Mark (2 Tim 4:11; cf. Acts 15:35–41). Even with the prospect of execution looming, he still wanted to study the Scriptures. He anticipates his conviction and execution, even though his first hearing gave him the opportunity to defend himself and proclaim the gospel once again to the Gentiles (2 Tim 4:16–17).

START YOUR JOURNEY

- Paul warns Timothy of those who will behave very badly, "holding to the form of godliness but denying its power" (3:5). Christians are regularly accused of hypocrisy. What will it take for you to embrace the power of the gospel message and live an unashamed life?

- One of God's purposes of the family is to pass the faith from generation to generation (Psalm 78). Lois, Timothy's grandmother, passed her faith to Eunice, his mother, who in turn passed it to him (2 Tim 1:5). Timothy grew up on a steady diet of Scripture (3:15) that led him to salvation in Christ Jesus. Who are your own "Lois" and "Eunice" who passed the faith down to you? How can you be a strong link in that chain, passing the faith to the next generation?

- Paul provides the formula for a winning discipleship strategy in 2 Tim 2:2. If you disciple faithful believers who then disciple others who can disciple still others, the growth of the body of Christ is exponential. Are you being discipled by someone? Are you discipling others? Find a place to get involved in the multiplication of disciples.

GOING DEEPER

"Seven Essential Truths for Reading Scripture Faithfully"

— Michael J. Svigel and Glenn R. Kreider —

As Christians open God's Word, we do so as those who have embraced the foundational truths of the Christian faith. We recall that the Bible was written *by* people of faith *to* people of faith. To read Scripture *faithfully*, then, we do so with our feet firmly planted on fundamental truths. These seven essential doctrines are found in Scripture, as demonstrated by the biblical texts. They are also truths upon which Scripture is founded, as they reflect facts about God, his works, and his ways—who he is and what he has done, is doing, and will do for us in the outworking of his plan of redemption.

As we seek to read Scripture faithfully, we must keep these seven essential truths in mind. They are the foundation of our faith, providing stability to reading Scripture and applying it to our lives. They are also truths that have united Christians for centuries, despite differences of opinion on various issues that have divided us.

1. The authority and inerrancy of Scripture

The Bible is inspired in the sense that the authors were moved by the Holy Spirit to write the words of Scripture. Divine inspiration extends equally and fully to all parts of the writings as they appeared in the original manuscripts. The whole Bible in the originals is therefore without error in everything it affirms and is authoritative in all matters it touches (2 Tim 3:16; 2 Pet 1:21).

2. The Triune God

God is the all-powerful creator and sustainer of all things, who eternally exists in three persons—the Father, the Son, and the Holy Spirit. These three are one God, having the same nature, attributes, and perfections, and worthy of precisely the same homage, confidence, and obedience (Matt 28:18–19; John 1:14; Acts 5:3–4; 2 Cor 13:13; Heb 1:1–3).

3. The full deity and humanity of Christ

The eternal Son of God was born of the virgin Mary, uniting in his person true and proper deity with perfect, sinless humanity. In his incarnation, the Son retains all the attributes of deity, the distinction between the two natures in no way annulled by the union (John 1:1–2, 14, 18; Phil 2:5–8).

4. The spiritual lostness of the human race

Human beings were originally created in the image of God and fell through sin. As a consequence of their sin, they lost their spiritual life, becoming dead in trespasses and sins. This spiritual death has been transmitted to the entire human race, the man Christ Jesus alone being excepted (Gen 1:26–27; Rom 3:10–19; Eph 2:1–3).

5. The substitutionary atonement and bodily resurrection of Christ

Christ voluntarily became God's sacrificial Lamb and took away the sin of the world. Christ's death was substitutionary—the just for the unjust. He arose from the dead in the same body, though glorified, in which he had lived and died (Isa 53:4–6; 2 Cor 5:21; 1 Pet 3:18).

6. Salvation by grace alone through faith alone in Christ alone

Redemption was accomplished solely by the blood of Jesus Christ, and nothing can add to the merit of the finished work accomplished by him. The new birth comes by grace alone through faith alone in Christ alone. No other acts may be added to believing as a condition of salvation (John 3:16; Rom 3:28; Eph 2:8–10).

7. The physical return of Christ

On departing from earth, Christ became head over all things, and in this ministry, he intercedes and advocates for the saved. He will return to the earth with power and great glory to lift the curse which now rests upon the creation and to bring the whole world to the knowledge of God (Acts 1:10–11; Rom 8:19–23; Heb 9:28; Rev 20–22).

Having read through these seven essential truths, explore the citations that support the doctrines. Consider how they relate to the statements and why they are so crucial for right belief and right living.

TITUS

SNAPSHOT

Is it more important for the Christian to embrace right belief or right practice? The letter to Titus reveals this to be a false choice, focusing on the integration of truth and godliness. Paul encourages young Titus to organize the young churches on the island of Crete and offers practical advice on godly living applicable to all. Everyone has a role to play in the church. Godly character matters as we display the grace of Jesus to the world around us.

ORIENTATION

Date: About AD 62–66
Author: Paul
Audience: Titus
Outline: 1. Greeting (1:1–4)
                2. Titus's Instructions for Leadership (1:5–16)
                3. Teach Sound Doctrine (2:1–15)
                4. Importance of Christian Living (3:1–11)
                5. Final Instructions and Greetings (3:12–15)

YOU ARE HERE

Episode 8: The End and New Beginning

This twelfth "Letter" of the New Testament is the third and final of Paul's "Pastoral Epistles," detailing the apostle's directions to Titus for bolstering church leadership on the island of Crete.

EXPLORING TITUS

Titus, a Gentile by birth (Gal 2:1–3), first believed in Jesus under Paul's ministry (Titus 1:4) before the Apostle's first missionary journey. While not mentioned in the book of Acts, Titus serves as a valuable coworker during Paul's missionary journeys, including in Jerusalem and Corinth (2 Cor 2:12–13; 7:5–15; 8:6–14; 12:18; Gal 2:1–3; 2 Tim 4:10).

Paul left Titus on Crete "to set right what was left undone" and "to appoint elders in every town" (Titus 1:5–9). Paul most likely wrote this letter from either Macedonia or Achaia during his fourth missionary journey to encourage Titus in his pastoral work in Crete, appointing godly mature leaders (elders/overseers) to deal with legalistic false teachers affecting the church (1:10–16; 3:9–11).

Was Titus part of the original establishment of churches on Crete? Possibly. Sometime prior to this letter being written (Acts 27:7–13), Paul and Titus may have done missionary work on the island of Crete (located 100 miles south of Greece in the Mediterranean Sea). Another possibility is that Jewish believers from Pentecost (Acts 2:11) may have brought the gospel to Crete.

While not explicitly spelled out in the letter, the false teachers in the Cretan churches came from "the circumcision party" (Titus 1:10). These teachers were advocating "Jewish myths" (v. 14), ritualistic purity (v. 15), and "foolish debates, genealogies, quarrels, and disputes about the law" (3:9). Paul warned Titus to have nothing to do with these false teachers (v. 10).

In contrast to false teachers, Paul described what qualities to look for in elders (1:5–9), men of character in their homes and public life. Paul also gives Titus instructions to various subgroups in the church (older men, older women, younger men, younger women, and bondservants [2:1–15]) on how to live out their Christian faith among one another as well as among unbelievers and even government officials (3:1–8).

The theme of Titus is the fullness of true faith, which includes both orthodoxy (1:1, 4, 13; 2:2; 3:8, 14) and practice/orthopraxy (2:2–14; 3:1–6). This stands in sharp contrast to the false teachers and the religious culture on Crete (1:10–16). Because "the grace of God has appeared, bringing salvation for all people," believers are "to deny godlessness and worldly lusts and to live in a sensible, righteous, and godly way in the present age" as we wait for "the blessed hope" of the return of Jesus (2:11–14).

The grace found in the person and work of Jesus is central in this letter (2:11–14; 3:4–7). The deity of Jesus as Savior (1:3–4; 2:10–13; 3:4–6), his substitutionary atonement (2:14), his justification of us by grace (3:5–7), our regeneration and renewal through the Holy Spirit (vv. 5–6), and Jesus's second coming (2:13) are all highlighted here.

After Artemas or Tychicus arrived in Crete to take over the ministry from Titus, he would join Paul in Nicopolis, in Achaia (3:12), and winter there. Later Paul would send Titus to Dalmatia (along the eastern shore of the Adriatic Sea) to minister there (2 Tim 4:10).

START YOUR JOURNEY

- Paul writes in a very direct way in this letter with a sense of urgency to the task of both teaching and practicing the faith. Make a list of teachings and practices in Titus.
- The terms *elder* (1:5) and *overseer* (1:7) refer to one office, not two separate ones (Acts 20:17, 28). How do you see these qualifications on display in your church leaders?

- Titus 2:11–14 summarizes both the provision of our salvation in the divine Christ as well as our call to live uprightly in light of his work. Consider committing this passage to memory.
- The "blessed hope" of the Christian is "the appearing of the glory of our great God and Savior, Jesus Christ" (2:13). What an amazing promise; our Savior is returning to the earth for us!

PHILEMON

SNAPSHOT

God cares for the humblest and most vulnerable among us. And his people should be willing to intervene on behalf of them. So it was in Paul's day. So it should be in ours. In this brief letter to an individual in the church of the Colossians—Philemon—the apostle Paul steps out of his role as a foundational apostolic leader of the church and steps into the role of an advocate for a runaway slave, making a personal appeal for mercy and freedom.

ORIENTATION

Date: About AD 60–62
Author: Paul
Audience: Philemon
Outline: 1. Introduction: Thanksgiving and Prayer (vv. 1–7)
                2. Appeal for the Release of Onesimus (vv. 8–20)
                3. Greetings and Benediction (vv. 21–25)

YOU ARE HERE

Episode 7: Dawn of a New Era

Philemon is the thirteenth of the New Testament "Letters" and the final Pauline letter. It's also one of four "Prison Epistles" Paul wrote from his cell in Rome.

EXPLORING PHILEMON

Philemon is a unique letter within the New Testament. It doesn't describe new doctrine or address universal moral issues. Rather, Paul addresses an individual, Philemon, with a specific request. In this small but weighty note, Paul urges a slave owner to free his slave in order that the man, Onesimus, might more effectively serve alongside Paul in ministry. Along with 1 Timothy, 2 Timothy, and Titus, Philemon is one of four letters written not to a church body but to an individual.

A little background will help to understand the letter. Paul had come in contact with Onesimus, Philemon's slave. It's uncertain whether Onesimus had been sent by his master or if he ran away. What is certain is that the meeting resulted in the salvation of Onesimus, and the slave had become helpful to Paul (vv. 10–11). In order to appreciate this letter, it's important to recognize that ancient slavery, like every other form, was a horrible institution. Attempts to cleanse Roman slavery by suggesting that it was somehow innocuous are misguided and have ultimately failed. Slavery is the ownership of one human being by another. When one owns something, it's theirs to do with as they please. A master had absolute power over his or her possession in all things.

A surface reading of this letter suggests that it's a rather straightforward request by Paul to Philemon to release his slave (vv. 9–14). However, in a context where honor is valued, it may be better understood as a command. Paul begins the letter with high praise for Philemon (vv. 5–7). Before Paul formally asks for Onesimus's freedom, he suggests that he could order

Philemon to free his slave but rather is confident that Philemon will "do what is right" (v. 8). Further, Paul reminds Philemon that he owes him everything (v. 19). In freeing Onesimus, Philemon will be doing Paul a favor (or paying back a portion of his debt). When one considers the rhetorical effect of this letter, Paul is giving his friend an opportunity to free Onesimus and obtain the honor of doing so. What if Philemon refuses? Paul concludes his letter by informing Philemon that he will be coming soon (v. 22). I wonder what their conversation would be about?

Paul's rejection of slavery and acknowledgement of Onesimus's humanity and equality is evident in a number of ways. First, since Onesimus was Philemon's slave, Paul could have simply asked Philemon to borrow Onesimus. Likely, that would have been acceptable to Philemon. Also, for Paul, this may have been simpler than to send Onesimus back to his master with a risky appeal for his freedom. Second, in Onesimus's role as a slave, he was "useless" but now is "useful" to Paul, Philemon, and the church (v. 11). Paul's appeal for Onesimus's freedom suggests that his usefulness will be enhanced by his freedom. Third, Paul describes sending Onesimus as "my very own heart" (v. 12). The slave was loved by Paul. Fourth, Onesimus is called a "dearly loved brother," a label not only of affection but of recognized status within a family (v. 16).

START YOUR JOURNEY

- All forms of slavery and human trafficking are horrendous and do violence to God's creation. All people are created in the image of God (Gen 1:26–27). Consider how evil sin must be to produce such an institution. Though Paul couldn't overthrow the entire Roman system, he could effect change within his realm of influence. Similarly, even if we can't undo sin that has been woven into the fabric of society, we can still do what we can on an individual, case-by-case basis.

- Given the personal nature of the letter to Philemon, consider why it was preserved as part of the New Testament canon? What does this teach us about the Christian faith that no other book does?
- Note the way Paul deals with Philemon. Rather than a straight-forward order, Paul tactfully appeals to his friend in a manner that will allow him to participate in this good deed. Consider how you can do likewise in your dealings with others.

GOING DEEPER

"Restoration Hardware"

— Roy B. Zuck —

Two unmarried sisters refused to talk to each other. They drew a chalk line on the floor between their beds, and each resolved not to invade the other's domain. Cupboards, the refrigerator, the stove burners, the kitchen table—each sister had her own "territory." They lived that way in silence for years, refusing to be reconciled.

How do you get two people like that to talk, to overlook their differences, to resolve their conflicts? Many husbands and wives are locked in a war of silence, spurning each other because of hurtful words or inappropriate actions. Some people hate going to work because of a mean-spirited boss or a cantankerous coworker. Even some Christians spurn each other at church because of a difference of opinion on music or ministry.

How do you bring together two people who are at odds? How do you help an offended person and the offender resolve their conflict? How can you help them put down their weapons and agree to work together?

The Epistle to Philemon, a short, little-known New Testament book, tells us how the apostle Paul brought about reconciliation between a slave owner and the owner's runaway slave, Onesimus. Regarded as the most compelling letter of reconciliation in ancient history, this epistle is a masterpiece of Christian tact.

345

Running away from Philemon in Colossae, Onesimus traveled to Rome, about a thousand miles away. Somehow, he met Paul, who led him to the Lord. Then Paul sent him back to Philemon with a letter urging the slave owner to take back his slave.

Imagine Philemon's emotions when he saw Onesimus at his door. Philemon was a believer; he even opened his home to a congregation for Sunday worship. But having been offended by the slave's crime, Philemon may have been smoldering with anger ever since the slave left. Philemon could have been thinking, "If I ever get my hands on him, I'll wring his neck." Or, "If he ever shows up, I'll make him pay back everything he stole, and then some." Or Philemon could have said, "He's a criminal. I'll turn him over to the authorities to execute him." Or on a milder note, "What a surprise, Onesimus. I've been hoping you would return. We have been shorthanded ever since you left."

Think of Onesimus. Here Paul was sending him back to face the very person he had offended. Filled with apprehension, he may have reflected, "Philemon will probably punish me severely or maybe even have me put to death. How can I possibly face him after I ran away? And yet Paul insisted that I go back."

To be sure that the slave returned, Paul sent with him a fellow worker, Tychicus. As they arrived, Tychicus handed Philemon Paul's letter. Did Paul order Philemon to take back his slave? Did Paul use his authority as an apostle to demand that the two be reconciled? No. Instead Paul was diplomatic, using a number of tactics that eased the tense situation and helped restore rapport.

First, *Paul commended Philemon; he didn't clobber him.* The apostle wrote of his friend's "faith . . . in the Lord Jesus," his "love for all the saints" (v. 5), and how he had "refreshed" the saints (v. 7). And he added, "I appeal to you . . . on the basis of love" (v. 9). With such a verbal pat on the back, how could Philemon refuse Paul's request?

Second, *Paul built up Onesimus; he didn't blast him.* Onesimus was now a believer in Jesus Christ and thus a spiritual "son" of Paul (v. 10) and a "dearly loved brother" (v. 16). That meant that he and Philemon—slave and slave owner—were now equal spiritually. Onesimus was now a brother of Paul, and he was also a brother in the Lord to Philemon (v. 16). Surely then the two could be rejoined now that they were both in the family of God. Also, Paul wrote that Onesimus, a changed man, would now be "useful" to Philemon (v. 11). The slave, whose name means "useful," would now be living up to his name. What a clever play on words!

Third, *Paul called on Philemon to decide; he didn't coerce him.* Gently the apostle wrote that he "didn't want to do anything without [Philemon's] consent." He wanted his friend's response to be of his "own free will" (v. 14). Reconciliation between two people can't be forced. But it can be encouraged and prompted.

Fourth, *Paul expressed confidence in Philemon; he didn't doubt the slave owner's positive response.* By being optimistic, Paul knew that the slave owner would act favorably and would "do even more" than Paul asked (v. 21). Confidence goes a long way toward encouraging others to take the right steps.

Fifth, *Paul appealed to his own relationship with Philemon; he didn't look down on him.* Philemon, he said, was his "dear friend and coworker" (v. 1), his "partner" (v. 17), and his spiritual "brother" (v. 20). How could Philemon not fulfill Paul's proposal?

Sixth, *Paul used shrewd reasoning, not gruff arguments.* He reminded Philemon that the apostle was "an elderly man" (v. 9) and a prisoner in chains (vv. 1, 9–10, 13). And anticipating his release, Paul asked Philemon to prepare a guest room for him (v. 22). How then could Philemon possibly reject Onesimus? When Paul arrived in Philemon's home in Colossae, he would readily know whether Philemon had complied with his appeal. And by receiving the slave who was now a Christian, Philemon would be refreshing Paul's heart (v. 20). Since the slave owner had already refreshed the hearts of other believers (v. 7), how could he not refresh Paul's heart? Bringing together two people who are at odds calls for careful persuasion, not harsh disputes.

Seventh, *Paul appealed to the power of the Spirit-filled life, not to sinful practices.* The Colossian church met in Philemon's home (v. 2), so that Philemon would have been struck by reading these words in the Epistle to the Colossians: "[Bear] with one another and forgiving one another if anyone has a grievance against another. Just as the Lord has forgiven you, so you are also to forgive" (Col 3:13). Imagine this wonderful reunion of a slave owner embracing his slave, a Christian leader accepting a lower-social-class worker who was now his equal in Christ.

Paul's tactful strategy shows how believers today can help people in emotional tugs-of-war to unleash their strangleholds on each other. As Paul wrote, Philemon's welcome should be the same as if he were reuniting with the apostle himself.

Want to help bring about reconciliation between a squabbling husband and wife, a disputing boss and worker, or two locked-in-conflict Christian workers? Then follow Paul's superb example of spiritual diplomacy. Don't clobber, coerce, doubt, or belittle. Instead, commend, encourage, express confidence, and challenge with Christlike standards.[1]

---

[1] Adapted from Roy B. Zuck, "Restoration Hardware," *Kindred Spirit* 28, no. 4 (Winter 2004): 19. © 2004 Dallas Theological Seminary.

HEBREWS

SNAPSHOT

As time goes by and the initial excitement of the Christian life begins to transition into a more settled daily routine with all its challenges, temptations, and hardships, our old pre-Christian lives may begin to look attractive again. In light of this, the author of Hebrews encourages his readers to stand firm in their faith. On the one hand, he demonstrates that Jesus is superior to everything that our old lives had to offer. On the other hand, he warns his readers of the consequences of turning away from Christ.

ORIENTATION

Date: About AD 60–70
Author(s): Unknown, traditionally Paul or one of his associates
Audience: Jewish Christians likely living in Rome
Outline: 1. Introduction (1:1–3)
                2. The Superiority of Jesus over Angels (1:4–2:18)
                3. The Superiority of Jesus over Moses (3:1–4:13)
                4. The Superiority of Jesus's Priesthood (4:14–7:28)
                5. The Superiority of the New Covenant over the Old (8:1–13)

6. The Superiority of Jesus's Sacrifice (9:1–10:18)
7. Exhortation to Enduring Faith (10:19–12:29)
8. Exhortation to Faithful Living (13:1–19)
9. Greeting and Benediction (13:20–25)

YOU ARE HERE

Episode 8: The End and New Beginning

Hebrews is the fourteenth New Testament "Letter" and first book following the collection of Paul's letters. Because its author is unknown, it transitions us from Pauline to non-Pauline letters.

EXPLORING HEBREWS

Hebrews holds a unique place in the New Testament. It's likely a homily ("sermon") and as such both teaches and encourages its readers to embrace Jesus by faith and continue to live likewise. The author consistently refers to the Old Testament and demonstrates the value of this earlier revelation to help reveal Jesus and his ministry.

Put simply, the book of Hebrews is about Jesus. As the outline makes clear, the author compares Jesus and his ministry with angels, Moses, other priesthoods, Old Testament sacrifices, and the old covenant. In every case, Jesus comes out on top. Who he is, what he did, is doing, and will do—these things are superior to everything else. By his absolutely unique person and work he accomplishes everything necessary for our eternal salvation. In fact, Jesus is explicitly called God (1:8).

Nowhere in the New Testament do we see the explanation of Jesus's work on the cross so vividly explained. The old covenant as recorded in the Torah had provisions that could only temporarily cleanse from breaches of the covenant (10:1–8). However, Jesus, the perfect sacrifice, dealt sin the decisive blow. Nothing further is needed (vv. 9–18). Jesus died once and for all for the sins of the world.

Hebrews reveals Jesus's present ministry as High Priest. He ministers in heaven (3:1; 4:14–16; 7:1–8:13). Jesus can relate to our weakness, because he himself both suffered and was tempted (2:18). Further, Hebrews encourages its readers to gather together as a community to encourage one another (10:24–25). Such gathering was likely dangerous to the author's original audience. Nevertheless, the encouragement of others is essential for a successful Christian experience (3:13).

Finally, Hebrews not only instructs and encourages believers; it also aims to motivate us. God's gracious gifts (e.g., 2:15; 6:4–5; 9:24, 28) should result in proper response to God (e.g., 4:1; 6:12; 10:22; 12:15). Many faithful men and women have come before us, and this should motivate us to press on (12:1). Hebrews contains sobering warnings for those who don't take seriously what Jesus has done for them (2:1–4; 3:7–4:13; 5:11–6:12; 10:19–39; 12:14–29). His sacrifice is a reason not to embrace the very sin from which he came to deliver us. Rather, we must live our lives by faith in God. We won't live perfect, faultless lives, as is evident by imperfect examples mentioned by the author (11:4–40). But we are encouraged to live lives of faith. The key is to focus on Jesus (12:2). Hebrews and its message about the superiority of Christ and his remarkable work provides us with an excellent way of focusing on Jesus.

START YOUR JOURNEY

- Because Hebrews was originally a sermon rather than a letter, read it out loud slowly in your best preacher's voice (or listen to it as audio Bible) and consider the big-picture argument of the book.
- Consider the people praised in chapter 11 in light of their stories in the Old Testament. They are flawed individuals, some more so than others (such as Samson: Heb 11:32). They are not remembered for their imperfections but for their faith. We also fall short of God's standards—sometimes miserably. Yet, in the end, it is our faith that pleases God. Believe in our Lord. We have a trustworthy God.

- Believers are secure in their relationship with God (John 10:28; Rom 5:1; 8:1; Eph 1:13–14; Heb 7:25; 1 John 5:13). The five warning passages (Heb 2:1–4; 3:7–4:13; 5:11–6:12; 10:19–39; 12:14–29) are not intended to put this relationship in doubt but rather to emphasize the seriousness of this relationship.
- Hebrews uses many Old Testament themes and passages. This should help us recognize the continued relevance of the Old Testament. We don't discard it or disregard it.
- Hebrews 1:8 is an explicit reference to Christ's deity. Consider other ways that Jesus is identified as God throughout the book in both his person and work.
- The Old Testament describes access to God as extremely restricted. However, because of Jesus's work, we have access to God. In light of the Old Testament, read Heb 4:16 and 10:19–22 with thankfulness. Let us draw near to God with confidence.

JAMES

SNAPSHOT

How difficult it is to live wisely in a world of folly! James, the brother of the Lord Jesus Christ, penned this heartfelt letter to those believing Jews dispersed among the Gentile nations promoting wisdom living in the community of the Messiah. His profound compassion, proverbial wisdom, and practical advice enrich his exhortation. James longs to see his readers stand firm in the faith through the daily and daunting trials of life. He reminds his readers that every trial is God's opportunity to strengthen their faith and forge their character toward godly living for cultivating a flourishing church and community.

ORIENTATION

Date:	About AD 45–50
Author:	James, brother of Jesus
Audience:	Jewish-Christian diaspora among the Roman Empire
Outline:	1. Greetings to the Believing Jews among the Nations (1:1)
	2. Find Joy in All Trials (1:2–18)
	3. Listen and Obey the Word (1:19–27)
	4. Love Others without Prejudice (2:1–13)

5. Exercise Faith with Action (2:14–26)

6. Watch What You Say (3:1–12)

7. Seek Wisdom from Above (3:13–18)

8. Replace Pride with Humility (4:1–17)

9. Move from Self-Indulgence to Generosity (5:1–6)

10. Be Patiently Prayerful in Suffering (5:7–20)

YOU ARE HERE

Episode 7: Dawn of a New Era

The fifteenth of the New Testament Letters and first of the General Epistles, James is one of the earliest and—with Matthew and Hebrews—one of the most "Jewish" New Testament books.

EXPLORING JAMES

James is a powerful book filled with practical wisdom to help us develop a triumphant faith that leads to right living in the face of a broken and sinful world. Though it's written in the form of a letter, it also fits comfortably in the genre of wisdom literature with similarities in thought and content with the book of Proverbs.

Readers will first be encouraged by James's teaching that every burden can give way to a tremendous blessing (1:2–4, 12). As we encounter much hardship and suffering in life as followers of Christ, we learn that the Lord gives wisdom freely to those who ask (vv. 5–8). Applying his divine wisdom helps us then respond well to every kind of trial.

Second, James challenges us to consider the character of God in a new way. James recognizes the importance of knowing the goodness of God and its contribution to a resilient faith. Unlike the gods of the pagans, the true God of the Old and New Testaments is good and doesn't tempt or provoke anyone to sin (vv. 13–15). He doesn't toy with us or lead us into harm. Rather, God gives only perfect gifts from above (vv. 16–17). He is faithful and doesn't change (v. 17). God is the giver of life and salvation by grace through faith (v. 18). He resists the proud but lavishes grace on the humble (4:6). God keeps his word to come near to us as we draw near to him in humility and contrition (v. 8), lifts us up in our time of deep need (v. 10), and will fulfill his promises at the return of Christ (5:7–8). God is so good, and meditating on his character is essential for navigating life's troubles.

Third, James motivates us to reflect on these and other formative questions of the heart. For example: Do I listen *and* obey the Word of God with integrity (1:22)? Do I love others with consistency *and* without prejudice (2:8–9)? Do I practice my faith *in* action (v. 26)? Do I speak words that intentionally build others up (3:9–10)? Do I put on Christlike humility over self-centered pride (4:6–10)? Do I seek heavenly wisdom from above—yielding to the Spirit (3:17)? Do I manage my wealth wisely, considering the needs of others in a spirit of generosity (5:5)? James yearns for his readers to mature in their faith through a growing congruency between their internal beliefs, spoken words, and external actions.

Fourth, we should be amazed by how this colorful epistle, written originally for a Jewish audience, points us to the heroes of the faith in the Old Testament, where James illustrates his teaching through the example of Abraham, Isaac, Rahab, the Prophets, Job, and Elijah. He also highlights themes from the teaching of Wisdom incarnate, the Lord Jesus Christ.

Finally, James encourages us to keep doing what our good God has called us to do in our personal walk with the Lord, our interpersonal relationships, financial matters, and gospel service in the church and community. James reminds us that every single trial is an opportunity to deepen our faith in him and to forge our character toward godly living for the benefit of others, our good, and the glory of God.

START YOUR JOURNEY

- Read James as a collection of wise insights for right living. Notice how similar it is to the book of Proverbs.

- Commit to reading this five-chapter book in one sitting, thinking about a present challenge or obstacle in your life. Read through the passages with that in mind, asking the Lord to speak into your situation. Mark any sections that are particularly applicable to your life.
- Don't misunderstand Jas 2:24, "You see that a person is justified by works and not by faith alone." It sounds like James is contradicting the apostle Paul's teaching on justification by faith alone. However, James's emphasis is that faith that saves is never alone. Faith's presence is evidenced by works, since, "In the same way faith, if it does not have works, is dead by itself" (2:17). The word *justified* can mean "declared righteous" (as in Paul) or it can mean "demonstrated to be righteous" or "vindicated" (as in James). As believers, we must embrace both these truths.

1 PETER

SNAPSHOT

Do you feel alienated and alone? Are you experiencing some form of suffering or persecution? Peter understands. First Peter encourages those who are suffering and alone by reminding them that Jesus, too, experienced these things. Yet these trials are only temporary. Christ overcame them, and Peter reminds us that we will also share in Jesus's exaltation.

ORIENTATION

Date:	About AD 62–64
Author:	Peter
Audience:	Scattered believers in Asia Minor
Outline:	1. Introduction (1:1–12)
	2. Living as God's Chosen People (1:13–2:10)
	3. Living in a Foreign Land (2:11–4:11)
	4. Suffering for the Lord (4:12–5:11)
	5. Greetings (5:12–14)

YOU ARE HERE

Episode 8: The End and New Beginning

First Peter is the first of two letters written by the apostle Peter. This is one of the so-called "General Epistles" because it doesn't address a specific church or person. It is also the sixteenth of the collection of New Testament writings known as "Letters."

EXPLORING 1 PETER

First Peter was written to those who were in a hostile culture, likely facing difficulties or persecution, and in need of encouragement. Peter addresses his readers' needs immediately. He tells them that they are chosen by God—saved through the death of Christ, born again into a new hope in the resurrection, with an assured inheritance and protection from God (1:1–5). Such reminders serve to encourage the readers to live out their faith in the midst of a hostile world. Difficult circumstances are temporary, but salvation is forever (vv. 13–25).

In light of their new life in Christ, Peter instructs his readers how they are to relate to one another. Followers of Jesus must carefully live their lives honorably, avoiding damaging activities resulting from envy, slander, and other such harmful thoughts and behaviors (2:1–2, 11–12). Instead, as recipients of God's mercy and now members of God's holy people, we should live in ways that avoid those sinful actions that damage our souls (2:3, 9–10).

Despite their hostile environment, those who follow Christ are to live a life of honor and submission. They are instructed to honor the ruling authorities (2:13–14, 17), to be submissive to one another, to be understanding of one another, and to be loving toward one another (2:13–14, 18; 3:1–9; 4:8; 5:5). Believers must do good even in thankless and difficult situations because they have been blessed by God. In this way, their lives will impact those around them (2:15, 19–20).

If the readers need an example of Peter's description of selfless living, he provides one by describing Christ (2:21). For Peter, the earthly life of Jesus is central. This may be because he witnessed Jesus's life first-hand and marveled at what he saw. Being entirely blameless, Jesus suffered pain and humiliation. He didn't retaliate or even complain. Rather, he trusted himself to God and paid for our sins with his life (1:19; 2:21–24). In fact, although the New Testament mentions many things about Christ, Peter emphasizes Christ's sufferings (2:21–24; 3:18; 4:1; 5:1). This is likely the most relevant aspect of Christ's life and ministry for the original readers of this letter. Suffering in this life was pretty much guaranteed for everyone—and for some more than others. However, Christ persevered through inestimable physical, emotional, and spiritual suffering and accomplished great things for God. As such, Peter instructs his readers to humble themselves before one another and before God (5:5–6). God cares for them and invites them to lay their anxiety upon him (v. 7). The readers' faithful suffering and intentional humility will also result in great things—including their own exaltation (4:12–19; 5:6).

For those in the midst of suffering, Peter knew what to say. He watched Jesus suffer and overcome. Those who are similarly facing suffering because of their steadfast faith can confidently put their trust in him. Then they, too, will share in Christ's victory.

START YOUR JOURNEY

- First Peter was written to those who felt like displaced aliens or foreigners, separated from their homeland. Many around the world today are in the same situation—literally. First Peter is especially meaningful for such people. For those of us not transplanted from our homes, consider how we can help those in our midst who are not presently experiencing such comfort and security.
- Peter acknowledges that his readers have not personally seen Jesus but love him nonetheless (1:8). This describes all of us since the first

century. Peter says our faith will result in salvation (v. 9). Reflect on this wonderful gift.

- Peter encourages Christians to be prepared to explain why they have hope in their lives despite their suffering (3:15). Are you ready to clearly articulate what Christ has done for you? Prepare a brief outline of your faith and practice it with a close friend.

- Remember that suffering is not a sign that you are doing anything wrong; rather, it's to be expected in this life between Genesis 3 and Revelation 21. Christ suffered, though he did nothing wrong. And we will suffer, even when we do what's right. First Peter is written for those who suffer to be able to draw comfort in the midst of their uncomfortable circumstances, encouragement in the midst of discouragement, and joy in the midst of distress. Lay your concerns before God because he cares for you (5:7).

Q&A

The Bible and Apologetics

With Dr. Timothy Yoder

Dr. Timothy Yoder (MDiv, Trinity Evangelical Divinity School, MA/PhD Marquette University) is author of *A Logical First Step: A DIY Primer on Logical Reasoning*, and, in a teaching career that has spanned thirty years, he has taught a wide variety of theology, philosophy, and apologetics courses at Marquette University, Cairn University, and Dallas Theological Seminary.

Q: First things first—what is "apologetics," and what does it have to do with the Bible?

A: The simplest definition of *apologetics* is "the defense of the faith." It doesn't have anything to do with apologizing, but it comes from the Greek word *apologia*, which means to defend oneself, as in a trial. The word *apologetics* doesn't appear in the Bible, but the Greek word used in a similar sense is found in 1 Pet 3:15, where Peter tells his readers that they should always be prepared to offer a defense (or a reason) for the hope that they have. The best example of apologetics in action in the New Testament is Paul's speech to the Epicurean and Stoic philosophers in Athens in Acts 17:22–34. He uses philosophical categories, logic, and even their own secular poets to make a case for Christian belief.

Q: Some people say we should defend the Bible like we would defend a lion—just let it out of its cage. Is there truth to this? Or would you say there's a place for defending Scripture against critics?

A: There is a sense in which we don't need to defend the Bible, just read it. The Bible says the Word of God is like a sword that cuts deep (Heb 4:12); that it, the truth of God's Word, pierces deep into a person's being—into their most strongly held convictions and beliefs. Another analogy for the Word of God is light (Ps 119:105; 2 Pet 1:19). It's the true light that leads us to the truth. The Bible is God speaking, so we just need to listen to it.

However, there is also a place for defending it. The Bible can be taken out of context, and thus its message is twisted (2 Pet 3:16). People also make false claims about the Bible, saying it's just like any other human book with errors and mistakes. In these cases, it's necessary to defend the Bible by knowing better what it is and how to interpret it. An important apologetic task is to understand and defend the doctrines of inspiration and inerrancy. The Bible is God's Word, given by the Holy Spirit through the prophets and apostles who wrote it down. If the Bible is God's Word, superintended by the Holy Spirit, and if God is perfect and true, then God's word is also perfect and true.

Q: How does the Bible compare with other books that claim to be divine revelation, like the Qur'an or the Book of Mormon?

A: The sacred books of other religions also claim to have the answers to life, and sometimes they claim to contain God's words. Some of these sacred texts include Hindu books like the Bhagavad Gita or Confucius's *Analects*. But the two that are probably closest to the Bible in claiming to be God's Word are the Qur'an of Islam and the Book of Mormon. One of the key distinctives that separates the Bible from these books is its historicity; that is, the stories of the Bible are rooted in divine encounters with genuine people in real places at established times. These claims of historicity are supported by archaeology, fulfilled prophecy, and the corroboration of non-biblical resources. Neither the Qur'an nor the Book of Mormon displays the historicity in the same way and to the same degree as the Old and New

Testaments. Having read and studied the other sacred texts, I'm firmly convinced that if in fact there is a God who chose to reveal his truth in a book, by far the best candidate for that revelation is the Bible.

Q: What, in your experience, are some of the most common objections to the Bible's truthfulness and authority today?

A: One frequent objection is that the historical details in parallel accounts don't always line up. For instance, in each of the four Gospels, there are different lists of the women who came to Jesus's tomb. What's required is a credible harmonization. In this case, we shouldn't expect that each author names all the women that came. For various reasons, each Gospel mentions different people.[1] Another common charge is that there are scientific mistakes, like the claim that the earth stands still (Ps 93:1). This is a matter of misinterpretation. Scripture uses a lot of figurative and poetic language (especially in the Psalms!). In that passage the immovability of the earth as God's throne is meant in a spiritual sense—not that it doesn't move physically, which is obviously false. More recent objections often focus on the character of God as presented in the Bible. Some skeptics and atheists say that Scripture presents God as violent or misogynistic or homophobic. These challenges actually present a great opportunity for apologists. People are questioning the way that God is characterized, so let's look at the Bible together to see what God is really like.

Q: I know you can't possibly answer every objection people have toward Scripture. But if you could recommend a few resources—books or websites—that do a good job addressing some of these things, what would they be?

A: We live in a golden age of apologetics, when we have access to a great bounty of resources for equipping people to defend the faith. Apologists

---

[1] See a helpful harmonization of the resurrection narrative in Charles R. Swindoll, *Matthew 16–28*, *Swindoll's Living Insights New Testament Commentary*, vol. 1b (Carol Stream, IL: Tyndale House, 2020), 303, 311, 319.

like William Lane Craig, Lee Strobel, Nabeel Qureshi, and Alister McGrath have done great work. I think Tim Keller's *The Reason for God* is the best work of apologetics since C. S. Lewis's *Mere Christianity*. Two books that are especially helpful with questions about the Bible are Rebecca McLaughlin's *Confronting Christianity* and Amy Orr-Ewing's *Why Trust the Bible?*.

2 PETER

SNAPSHOT

During dangerous times, some may be discouraged and tempted to give up hope for the second coming of Jesus Christ. Second Peter encourages us to be prepared, to look forward to the rewards of the future kingdom, and to avoid false teachers in the meantime. In light of rampant deceptions and doubts, Peter teaches the certainty that Jesus will return to usher in his eternal kingdom and a perfect world that will never pass away.

ORIENTATION

Date: About AD 65–67

Author: Peter

Audience: A general letter written to Christians of Asia Minor

Outline:
1. Introduction: The Knowledge of Christ as the Basis for Godliness (1:1–11)
2. The Coming Kingdom of Christ Is Sure (1:12–21)
3. False Teachers Condemned, but the Godly Saved (2:1–22).
4. Repent before the End to Experience the Future Kingdom (3:1–13).

    5. Conclusion: Patiently Await the Return of Christ (3:14–18).

YOU ARE HERE

Episode 8: The End and New Beginning

Second Peter is the seventeenth "Letter" of the New Testament and the third of the "General Epistles." It is also the second letter from Peter, the disciple of Jesus, written toward the end of his life.

EXPLORING 2 PETER

Peter writes to Christians who have received the same faith as his own to encourage them to increase in their experiential knowledge of Jesus Christ (1:1; 3:18). By the power of God, they have all the necessary resources for their spiritual lives (1:3), and they have precious and magnificent promises (v. 4). The specific promises that motivate godly living are the return of Jesus Christ (v. 16) and the new heavens and earth (3:4, 13).

The experiential knowledge of Jesus Christ is developed by means of a practical Christian piety (1:5–8). The Apostle reminds them of their Christian duties (1:12–15; 3:1–2) in light of the soon return of the Lord Jesus Christ (1:16; 3:14). Godliness confirms the true faith of a Christian, reveals that they are called and chosen by God, guards them from stumbling into the sinful practices of the false teachers (2:20–22; 3:17), and assures them that they will be rewarded in the future kingdom (1:11).

In contrast to the godly believers, the mockers of 3:3–4 deny the coming of Christ. But Peter, an eyewitness of Christ's life and resurrection, knows that his Lord will truly return and establish his kingdom. In fact, he saw Christ transfigured before his very eyes, giving him a glimpse of the future kingdom (2 Pet 1:16–18; Mark 9:1; Matt 16:28; Luke 9:27). Peter also reminds his readers to pay diligent attention to the Scriptures

(2 Pet 1:19–21; 3:2), which includes even an early collection of Paul's letters (3:15–16). The prophetic Scriptures carry absolute authority, because the prophets didn't speak on their own authority but spoke for God as they were "carried along by the Holy Spirit" (1:19–21). As an eyewitness to Christ's majesty, Peter links his and the apostles' writings to the prophets in the Old Testament.

Despite all these proofs of the soundness of the apostles' teachings, false teachers will come who deserve condemnation (2:1–22; 3:3–5, 16). They will deny the Lord, engage in sensual practices, and exhibit greed, rebellion, licentiousness, and deception. Such false teachers are clearly unbelievers, who were "bought" (2:1) by Christ's infinitely valuable atonement, but not "redeemed" (1:18) by the application of that atonement by grace alone through faith alone in Christ alone. Christ paid the debt of sin of all humanity, but only believers are actually forgiven. Peter claims that the false teachers will come to destruction (2:3–10). Weak Christians are in danger of being deceived by these false teachers and entangled in their sinfulness (vv. 20–22). Peter describes the sad condition of true Christians seduced by false doctrine with the same words of condemnation that describe the fate of the seducers. Christians must stay on their guard to avoid such deception (3:17).

Peter assures his readers that despite the doubts of many, the time of the Lord's judgment will come unexpectedly upon the unbelieving world in which the present universe will be judged (vv. 10–12). In powerful language drawn from Old Testament imagery of a refining fire, Peter affirms that all wickedness in this creation will be burned away. Neither the deeds themselves nor the systems and structures of this present dark world will endure the coming judgment. In light of the destruction of this world, Peter exhorts his readers to live holy and godly lives while they eagerly await the future coming of their Lord. The present world system of wickedness will be replaced with the promise of a new heaven and earth where Christians will dwell in righteousness (vv. 12–13).

Peter desires nothing more than that Christians grow in their experiential knowledge of Christ through personal godliness by God's grace resulting in God's glory both now and forever (1:2; 3:18).

START YOUR JOURNEY

- Second Peter 2 and Jude have similar illustrations from the Old Testament and Jewish literature. The Lord's brother, Jude, may have copied 2 Peter 2; or it may be that the two authors reflect the same teachings that were common in the early church. What is clear, however, is that Peter and Jude share the same expectation of the coming of Christ and the same warning about false teachers in the present age of waiting.

- The future hopes in 2 Peter reflect beliefs about Jesus Christ's future earthly kingdom and rewards for faithful Christians. It also anticipates a final purification and judgment of creation before the period referred to as "new heavens and a new earth" (2 Pet 3:13; cf. Isa 65:17; 66:20; Rev 21:1). Rather than explain all the details, Peter teaches how people should be prepared.

- In Old Testament prophecy, the Messiah will not only die for sin (Isa 53) but also rule over all creation. These prophecies did not arise from an act of human will but were inspired by the Holy Spirit. The prophecies of the Old Testament were not written as private explanations of the prophets themselves, but they all have a divine origin. Both the Old Testament and Paul's letters are equally inspired (2 Pet 1:19–21; 3:15–16). Therefore, we can trust what they teach about the past, the present, and the future.

1 JOHN

SNAPSHOT

An influential group has challenged the eyewitness testimony about who Jesus is, fashioning a different "Jesus" with a different set of moral principles to suit their purposes. Sound familiar? False Christians trying to turn the truth of the faith upside down is nothing new. This powerful epistle from the apostle John alternates between comforting and reassuring the faithful Christians who have remained true to his original eyewitness testimony and refuting and condemning the opponents who have departed from the true Jesus and his authentic teaching.

ORIENTATION

Date: Late 1st century
Author: John the apostle
Audience: A church or group of churches in Asia Minor whose primary influencer/leader is the apostle John and who have access to the Gospel of John
Outline: 1. Prologue (1:1–4)
               2. God Is Light, so Walk in the Light (1:5–3:10)
               3. God Is Love, so Love One Another (3:11–5:12)

    4. Conclusion: Purpose of the Letter (5:13)

    5. Epilogue: Implications for Assurance of Eternal Life (5:14–21)

YOU ARE HERE

Episode 8: The End and New Beginning

First John is the eighteenth "Letter," fourth "General Epistle," and first letter of the apostle John, placed toward the end of the New Testament after the letters of James and 1–2 Peter and before the letters of 2–3 John and Jude. This placement among the General Epistles reflects the absence of a specified destination in 1 John itself.

EXPLORING 1 JOHN

First John is difficult to read as a letter, because it doesn't follow any of the conventions of first-century letters. Outlining it in any detail proves particularly challenging because it doesn't seem to present a linear argument. It's often referred to with terms like *repetitive, circular, wandering,* or *random* or is seen as more like narrative literature than a letter. These descriptions are true as far as they go, but when we compare 1 John to the Gospel of John, a pattern of similarity begins to emerge.

    First John, like the Gospel of John, has both a prologue and an epilogue. Also like the Gospel of John, 1 John has two major sections, centered around "God is light" and "God is love" (see outline). These and other similarities have suggested to many interpreters an intentional relationship between the Gospel of John and 1 John. First John (written after the Gospel of John) deals with the nonorthodox view of the opponents regarding Jesus. The opponents were likely proponents of a form of the heresy known as "adoptionism"—that Jesus was adopted by the descending Spirit of Christ at his baptism by John the Baptist (John 1:32) but abandoned by the Spirit before dying on the cross (John 19:30). Thus, the Word did not really fully take on humanity in a real sense, but only appeared to do so (John 1:14).

First John shows how, consistent with the apostolic eyewitness testimony, the Gospel of John can be read and understood in a completely orthodox (that is, not adoptionistic) way. First John also focuses its second half on three means of assurance for the believer: (1) possessing the Holy Spirit (3:24; 4:13); (2) confessing Jesus as Christ come in flesh (4:2) and as Son of God (4:15; 5:5); and (3) obeying the commandments, especially to love one another (4:7, 12). When believers saw those signs of the true regenerating grace of the Spirit in their lives, they would see the sharp contrast with the bad teaching and wicked living of the false teachers.

First John offers both a solid refutation of the opponents' aberrant beliefs about Jesus and a strong affirmation of personal assurance of salvation for those faithful to the apostolic eyewitness testimony. The false teachers, whom John calls "antichrists" (2:18) had not only departed from the truth and lifestyle of believers (2:22; 4:3); they had physically departed from the loving fellowship of the family of God (2:19). The true believers, however, not only continued to walk in the light and confess the real incarnation of God the Son; they remained in the community of the church established by the apostles to continue on as disciples of the true Jesus.

START YOUR JOURNEY

- As you read 1 John, pay attention to the pronouns *we, you,* and *they.* This helps keep track of who is being addressed by the author. *We* typically refers to the author and the other apostolic eyewitnesses (especially in 1 John 1:1–4) and sometimes includes the faithful Christians to whom the author is writing. *You* refers to the faithful Christians who were originally reading the letter—and those of us who believe in Jesus today. *They*, however, refers to the separatist opponents—the "antichrists" (2:18–19).

- Note the stress on "eternal life" (as in the Gospel of John) and the ways in which the Christians being addressed can have assurance that they possess it. Note that these signs of life are not things Christians do to earn or to keep eternal life; they are the normal fruit produced by those who are truly saved. John's purpose is not to produce doubt in real believers, but to give them assurance of their genuineness.

- Note that John declares that he was one who had seen and touched the Word of life; he was an eyewitness to who Jesus was and is (1:1–3). He defines an antichrist as one who rejects the truth that Jesus came in the flesh (4:2–3). Consider some of the implications that Jesus remains fully human as well as fully divine.

GOING DEEPER

"How Does the Bible Command
Us to Love One Another?"

— J. Dwight Pentecost —

John writes, "For this is the message you have heard from the beginning: We should love one another" (1 John 3:11). "Love one another" is not an exhortation, but a commandment. And the one who does not love as God has loved him is a lawbreaker and a violator of the commandment of God. No violator of God's commandment can enjoy fellowship with the Father and the Son.

In Matt 22:35–40, we read of one of the lawyers of the Pharisees coming to Jesus to ask him a question. He was not asking him a question for information, but to embarrass him. You see, Jesus had said he came to fulfill the law.

So the lawyer asked Christ, "Teacher, which command in the law is the greatest?" And without hesitancy, our Lord answered, "'Love the Lord your God with all your heart, with all your soul, and with all your mind. This is the greatest and most important command. The second is like it: Love your neighbor as yourself. All the Law and the Prophets depend on these two commands.'"

Love for a neighbor or for a brother is the outflow of your love for God. Love for God takes precedence over all else, and love for God produces a love in the family of God for those whom God loves. And so our

373

Lord was able to meet this challenge by showing that from the beginning love for God—and the consequent love for members of the family and for those nearest to you—was that which God required of man. That which was commanded in the Old Testament was also commanded by the Lord Jesus. For to the disciples gathered in the upper room on the eve of his crucifixion, our Lord said, "This is my command: Love one another as I have loved you. No one has greater love than this: to lay down his life for his friends. You are my friends if you do what I command you" (John 15:12–14).

Our Lord is emphasizing the connection between love and obedience. Obedience does not bring forth love for God, but love for God produces obedience. And the way to please God is to have a heart that is settled upon him. And so our Lord issued a commandment to love one another. He said, "By this everyone will know that you are my disciples, if you love one another" (13:35).

Now, the concept in John's mind as he writes in 1 John 3:15 is that a person who knows the command of God and does not obey it is viewed by God as a lawbreaker, and no lawbreaker can have fellowship with a holy God. John, in the verses that immediately preceded, has defined sin as any violation of the law of God. The consequent teaching is that the only way we can enjoy fellowship with the Father is to obey his commandments. And the greatest commandment that tests someone's obedience is that they love the members of the family.

So John says, I want to remind you of God's commandment—love one another. If you do not love, you're violating God's commandment. And the one who is violating God's commandment cannot enter into the joyous experience of an intimate fellowship with the Father and the Son. "This is my commandment, that you love one another" (John 15:12, NKJV).

Christ's joy in the Father came from the love he had for the Father, which produced perfect obedience. John says we know that we have passed from death to life because we love the brethren, and if there is love in the heart for a brother in Christ, it is evident that we have been born into God's family.

John emphasizes to his spiritual children that his aim in this book is to introduce them to the joy of intimate fellowship with the Father and the Son. He wants the same radiant joy that characterized the Lord Jesus Christ during his earthly life to characterize them. So he points out that the Lord Jesus, when he was on earth, loved the Father through perfect obedience. If they are to enter into that fullness of joy that Christ had, they must love the Father, manifest that love to the Father, and keep his commandments. His first command is that we love the family of God. John made it very clear that division, anger, strife, maliciousness, gossip, and backbiting among believers put us out of the will of God and under the judgment of lawbreakers. We have violated the command of God to love one another.

Love is not simply the absence of hate, so that we don't go around doing evil things to somebody else. *Love is a careful concern for the needs of those whom we love, and love necessitates expression.* The expression will be both in words and acts.

"*This is my commandment, that ye love one another, as I have loved you*" (John 15:12, KJV).[1]

---

[1] Adapted from Bryant Black, "Your Questions for the Dallas Seminary Faculty: How Does the Bible Command Us to Love One Another?, Question Answered by J. Dwight Pentecost," *Kindred Spirit* 16, no. 1 (Winter 1991–1992): 2–3. © 1992 Dallas Theological Seminary.

2 JOHN

SNAPSHOT

False teachers disguising themselves as Christians is nothing new. It endangered the believers in the first century as it does believers today. John's small but powerful note of warning and exhortation helps to refocus a church on the one who is truth incarnate.

ORIENTATION

Date: Late 1st century
Author: The apostle John
Audience: Though some take "elect lady" (2 John 1) as literal, it's more likely a term of endearment for a local church or churches in Asia Minor.
Outline: 1. Greetings in the Fellowship of Truth (vv. 1–3)
                2. Commendation for Loving Obedience (v. 4)
                3. Exhortation to Continue in Loving Fellowship (vv. 5–6)
                4. Warning about False Teachers (vv. 7–11)
                5. John's Desire for Personal Fellowship (vv. 12–13)

YOU ARE HERE

Episode 8: The End and New Beginning

Second John is the nineteenth "Letter," fifth "General Epistle," and second letter of the apostle John.

EXPLORING 2 JOHN

John wrote as "the elder" of churches in Asia Minor, his area of apostolic ministry. The "elect lady" was likely a beloved church (or churches), whom John loved because they faithfully walked in the truth (2 John 1–3). "Love" was sacrificial service in the family of God, which was a gift from the Father to the Son (John 17:6) in the Spirit (John 14:15–21). Fellowship was characterized by obedience to Christ, who exemplified loving obedience among his followers.

John was "very glad" to hear that the church's "children" were "walking" in the truth in accord with the Father's command to love one another (2 John 4–6; 1 John 2:7–8). This encouraged the apostle, because deceiving antichrists were spreading false teaching that Jesus Christ did not come in the flesh (cf. John 1:14; 1 John 2:22–23). There were several cults in the first century, such as the Docetists, who taught that Jesus's humanity was not real. He only appeared to be human. The problem clearly was a denial of the incarnation, which led to a lawless lifestyle (1 John 1:5–2:7). On the other hand, believers were not to show hospitality to the heretics to avoid any appearance of sharing their false teaching about the Lord. Believers in a sister church, who were chosen by the Father, sent their greetings to the "elect sister" (2 John 13). Contrary to the heretics, true believers should affirm one another in their mutual love of the Savior and thus experience true fellowship in the family of God.

START YOUR JOURNEY

- As you read through this brief letter, what do you recognize as the marks of true disciples of Jesus and false Christians? How does fellowship in Christ, the truth (John 14:6), promote unity and love in his churches?
- Consider why the person of Christ—who he is—is so important for true believers, not just his saving work and content of his teachings?

3 JOHN

SNAPSHOT

Bullies in the church are nothing new. The apostle John dealt with them in the late first century just as we deal with them today. His words are as relevant now as they were then.

ORIENTATION

Date: Late 1st century

Author: The apostle John

Audience: Likely churches in Asia Minor

Outline:
1. Greeting and Commendation of Gaius (vv. 1–8)
2. Condemnation of Diotrephes (vv. 9–11)
3. Commendation of Demetrius (v. 12)
4. John's Desire for Personal Fellowship (vv. 13–14)

YOU ARE HERE

Episode 8: The End and New Beginning

Third John is the twentieth "Letter," sixth "General Epistle," and third letter of the apostle John.

EXPLORING 3 JOHN

John, "the elder," needed to write his "dear friend" Gaius (cf. 2 John 1; 1 John 2:7) about an arrogant leader in Asia Minor who was spreading "malicious words" about John's circle of faithful believers (3 John 10). John greeted Gaius warmly with a wish for his physical and spiritual health (v. 2). His source of joy was that fellow believers reported Gaius's faithfulness in Christ despite difficult circumstances (3 John 4; cf. 2 John 4–6). This abiding was expressed in hospitality toward other believers. Hospitality was vital in the early church, because it provided lodging, supplies, news, correction, and encouragement to itinerant brothers and sisters, whom he lovingly sent on their journey (3 John 6; cf. 1 John 2:12–14; 3:16). These members of God's family would receive no help from unbelievers, but hospitality bonded them in ministry for the truth (3 John 8).

The commendable Gaius stands in sharp contrast to the scoundrel Diotrephes, who refused to welcome his fellow believers (cf. 2 John 10). He spread false gossip about them, forbade other believers from hospitality, and put them out of his church (3 John 10). We may infer that he was an anti-christian heretic, but the letter merely accused him of hostility toward truth because he loved to hold the "first place," that is, he had a desire for selfish gain rather than for serving the family of God (cf. John 13). The goodness of hospitality reflected godly character; evil opposition to hospitable behavior indicated unbelief (3 John 11; cf. 1 John 3:6).

Ending on a good note, Demetrius—the bearer of the letter—exemplified loving service and came with John's commendation. The apostle had much to share, but, as in 2 John, he wanted to talk with their mutual friends face to face (3 John 13).

START YOUR JOURNEY

- If you had to cast the characters of Gaius and Diotrephes with modern examples in your own circle, who would fit the bill? Who "loves to be first" rather than the servant of others? Is it possible that others might have you on their list? Spend some time in self-reflection.
- Consider how you can better reflect the warmth of hospitality and fellowship expected of God's faithful followers. How could you build community in the body of Christ?

JUDE

SNAPSHOT

The number of false teachers, false churches, and false doctrines passing themselves off as "Christian" may feel overwhelming today. But the book of Jude gives us a playbook for responding to the schemes of those who oppose the truth of God's Word. And the best part? We don't have to undertake this task in our own strength. Our efforts are supported by the lovingkindness of God and his promise of eternal protection for us.

ORIENTATION

Date:	Latter half of 1st century
Author:	Jude, the brother of Jesus
Audience:	Originally Jewish Christians
Outline:	1. Greeting (vv. 1–2)
	2. Contend for the Faith (vv. 3–4)
	3. God's Judgment on False Teachers (vv. 5–16)
	4. Christians' Response to False Teachers (vv. 17–23)
	5. Doxology (vv. 24–25)

YOU ARE HERE

Episode 8: The End and New Beginning

As the twenty-first of the "Letters" and the seventh of the "General Epistles,"
Jude's warning against false teachers shares a lot in common with 2 Peter.

EXPLORING JUDE

In his letter, Jude implores his readers to defend vigorously the Christian
faith against the false teachers who had infiltrated their community. He
begins by reminding his readers that they are loved by the Father and kept
secure in their salvation (v. 1). Although it seems he initially planned to
focus his letter on that theme (v. 3), ultimately he feels compelled to warn
his readers about the dangerous false teachers operating—sometimes quite
stealthily—in their midst (v. 4). His memorable charge is worth committing to memory: "Contend for the faith that was delivered to the saints once
for all" (v. 3). Jude then uses a variety of examples from the Old Testament
to illustrate the severity of the judgment coming on these false teachers
(vv. 5–7). This judgment, though harsh, is appropriate because of their bla-
tantly sinful lifestyles (vv. 14–16).

It would have been natural for Jude's readers to panic, especially since
the false teachers posed such a clear and present danger to their community
(vv. 12–13). But Jude reminds them that these enemies have not taken God
by surprise (vv. 17–18). Their presence should not be a cause for despair.
By growing in their faith and remaining focused on their future hope of
eternal life (vv. 20–21), Jude's readers would be well positioned to stand
strong against the false teachers and to protect others from believing their
lies (vv. 22–23).

Jude closes his letter by praising God with some of the most beautiful,
moving language in the New Testament: "Now to him who is able to protect you from stumbling and to make you stand in the presence of his glory,
without blemish and with great joy, to the only God our Savior, through
Jesus Christ our Lord, be glory, majesty, power, and authority before all

time, now and forever. Amen" (vv. 24–25). What a grand description of God's ability to preserve his readers' salvation until they obtain their promised eternal life!

Modern believers still face myriad attacks on the historic Christian faith, but we need not lose hope. The same God who loves us deeply has promised to sustain us no matter what we encounter. Through what Jesus accomplished on the cross and resurrection, we can give our lives to him with full confidence in the Father's ability to safeguard our salvation for all eternity. As one writer has said: "Christians have many reasons to be anxious. But one thing we do not need to worry about: God's faithfulness in maintaining us in our faith."[1]

START YOUR JOURNEY

- Because Jude is such a short book, consider committing to read through it once a day for a month. When you've finished, you may be surprised at how much of the book you're able to remember, even if you weren't trying to memorize it.

- Much of Jude is devoted to exposing the dangers of false teaching, primarily related to the false teachers' denial of Christ through their sinful lifestyles. In our modern culture, consider some of the dangerous teachings that have gained traction within the church. What does Jude have to say about the importance of resisting these teachings?

- The importance of community as a means of defense against false teaching is a subtle yet critical theme in Jude. Consider discussing the book with fellow Christians in order to encourage one another in your faith and strengthen your resolve to contend for the faith.

- Despite his brevity, Jude still well describes the role of the triune God in our spiritual lives. As a means of worship, list and reflect on what he says about the Father, Son, and Holy Spirit.

---

[1] Douglas J. Moo, *2 Peter and Jude*, ed. Terry Muck, The NIV Application Commentary Series (Grand Rapids: Zondervan, 1996), 226.

REVELATION

SNAPSHOT

The capstone of biblical prophecy, Revelation is a profound book that evokes intense reactions. Its dramatic but elusive visions, seen while John was "in the Spirit" (1:10; 4:2; 17:3; 21:10), disclose heavenly realities and the future destiny of the earth and its inhabitants ("what must soon take place," 1:1). This inevitably provokes fascination but also controversy. But Revelation explicitly promises blessing to all who read and obey its message (1:3; 22:7).

ORIENTATION

Date:	Late 1st century
Author:	Though some tried to identify the author as a different "John," the earliest evidence of authorship assigns it to the apostle John, author of the Gospel and epistles (1:1, 4, 9; 22:8)
Audience:	Originally, seven churches in Asia Minor (1:4, 11), but through them to all Christians everywhere (2:7).
Outline:	1. Introduction (1:1–8)

2. Christ Exalted and His Messages to the Churches
   (1:9–3:22)
3. Heavenly Throne Room and Three Judgment Cycles
   (4:1–16:21)
4. Destruction of Babylon the Great (17:1–19:10)
5. From Babylon to the New Jerusalem (19:11–21:8)
6. The New Jerusalem (21:9–22:9)
7. Conclusion (22:10–21)

YOU ARE HERE

Episode 8: The End and New Beginning

As the only whole book of "Prophecy" in the New Testament, Revelation supplies the fitting conclusion to the entire narrative of Scripture.

EXPLORING REVELATION

Though the book promises "blessing" to those who heed its message (1:3), many Christians throughout history have tended to avoid the book of Revelation. And modern sermon series on Revelation often focus heavily on the first several chapters that seem more directly applicable to churches and believers—the glorious vision of Christ in chapter 1, the messages to churches in chapters 2–3, and the awe-inspiring picture of the heavenly throne room in chapters 4–5.

After those chapters, the reader is ushered into a parade of images that have been interpreted in countless ways. Revelation's middle sections (Rev 6–18) trace three cycles of future judgment in broad chronological sequence. Various interludes give heavenly previews of events about to occur. These unprecedented end-time woes immediately precede Christ's coming as conquering King (Rev 19–21) to consummate God's acts of judgment and redemption.

John's visions of God's coming redemption are anchored in Old Testament prophecies about the sure fulfillment of divine promises through

Abraham and his descendants to blessing all the nations (Gen 12; Exod 19). The protection of the 144,000 "every tribe of the Israelites" (Rev 7:4–8; also 14:1–5) reminds us that God has not forgotten his Old Testament promises to his people. He will regather a full complement of the nation through their faith in the Messiah, the promised seed of Abraham and King in the line of David (5:5; 22:16), and ultimately fulfill the promises to Abraham, Isaac, and Jacob.

The climactic visions of Rev 19–22 reveal Christ's long-awaited return as victorious "King of kings and Lord of lords" to reign with his saints over the whole earth. These events were predicted in both testaments (e.g., Dan 7; Isa 11; 24–27; 65; Jer 31; Zech 14; Rom 8; 1 Cor 15)—and prayed for through the ages (Matt 6:10). According to the earliest interpretations of the book of Revelation, Christ's earthly rule is seen in two phases: his thousand-year reign over the existing world (Rev 20:1–10), which transitions into God's eternal rule over his restored creation in the new heaven and new earth (21:1–22:9). Though others have interpreted the "millennium" in different ways—as a spiritual kingdom between Christ's first and second advents or as a golden age on the earth prior to Christ's return—all anticipate a glorious future in which Christ rules forever over a creation free from suffering and death, sin and evil (21:4). The fulfillment of the Bible's prophecies brings more than purely spiritual, heavenly, or individual victories (i.e., my personal salvation from sin and eternal life with God); it also brings earthly, geographic, and cosmic renewal—in keeping with the Old Testament promises and prophecies.

The book of Revelation certainly contains some confusing images, many of which Christians have long struggled to understand. Yet it also contains profound passages to ponder. Regardless of how we understand the details, we can all rest on certain truths revealed in these pages: the opening vision of the glorious, resurrected Christ standing among his churches and commissioning John to write down his visions and what they mean (1:9–20); Christ's messages to the churches calling for costly devotion and service amid a society opposed to God and his ways (2:1–3:22);

the worship of God on his heavenly throne and of Jesus as the Lamb who was slain to redeem individuals from every tribe, language, people, and nation (4:1–5:14; 7:9–17); the announcement from heaven's perspective of God's rule established on earth, overcoming the existing evil empires, "the kingdom of the world has become the kingdom of our Lord and of his Christ" (11:15), as Handel's *Messiah* celebrates so magnificently in the "Hallelujah Chorus." This is a preview of Christ's return to reign over the earth (Rev 19–22), those words of surpassing comfort and hope for all who long for a better day: "Look, God's dwelling is with humanity, and he will live with them. They will be his peoples, and God himself will be with them and will be their God. He will wipe away every tear from their eyes. Death will be no more; grief, crying, and pain will be no more, because the previous things have passed away" (21:3–4).

START YOUR JOURNEY

- In approaching Revelation, avoid two extremes: 1) shying away from Revelation because it's too puzzling or foreboding and 2) becoming obsessed with it or argumentative about it. Respond to Revelation with godly fidelity and hope, not curiosity or controversy about what will happen next.

- Discern the basic meaning of the book and don't get lost in the details. Note how John uses symbols and patterns from the Old Testament in a heightened way (plagues on Egypt, Daniel's bizarre beasts, day of the Lord imagery from Isaiah, Joel, Amos) as well as Jesus's teaching about his second coming (Matt 24).

- Avoid "reading between the lines" in search of tomorrow's head-lines. Remember that the symbols refer to earthly and spiritual realities; "symbolic" does not mean purely imaginary or abstract. For example, "the Lamb" in Revelation symbolizes Jesus as our sacrifice for sins.

GOING DEEPER

"Answering Deception with the Truth"

— Mark M. Yarbrough —

In John 18, hours before our Lord's crucifixion, we find an interesting exchange between Jesus and Pilate. After Pilate questions Jesus about his kingship, we find the following dialogue in verse 37: "'You are a king then?' Pilate asked. 'You say that I'm a king,' Jesus replied. 'I was born for this, and I have come into the world for this: to testify to the truth. Everyone who is of the truth listens to my voice.'"

And Pilate, echoing humanity's scorn heard through the ages, retorts, "What is truth?"

Devotion to the truth is foundational for walking with God. But Scripture is full of examples of people who were lost to the lies that blinded them to the knowledge of God. The opening chapters of Genesis illustrate this first deviation from God's clear path. The setting is the paradise of Eden, and the repeated phrase throughout the creation narrative reminds readers that God's creation was *good*. Yet, after the serpent enters, it doesn't take long for the beautiful scenes of God's relationship with Adam and Eve to fracture.

Deception characterizes the first interaction recorded between the serpent and humanity. In John 8:44, Jesus describes the harsh reality of the serpent's identity: "He was a murderer from the beginning and does not stand in the truth, because there is no truth in him. When he tells a lie, he speaks from his own nature, because he is a liar and the father of lies." Jesus identifies Satan as a murderer: he murdered Adam and Eve when he enticed them to eat the forbidden fruit, an action that doomed them and their descendants to death, painful toil, and suffering. But how exactly did he murder? Through clever and cunning *deception*, he twisted and perverted the truth.

Rewinding to the serpent's entrance in Genesis 3, we see his deceptive plan on display as he converses with an innocent Eve. He begins by raising a simple question in Gen 3:1: "Did God really say, 'You can't eat from any tree in the garden'?" The adversary's initial ploy plants untruth from the first sentence and presents God as the one who withholds good and desirable things. Attentive readers can see from the surrounding text that God abundantly provided *every other tree* in the garden for their eating enjoyment and nourishment. But the serpent exploits the weakness in Eve's timid response and boldly lies, "You will certainly not die" (v. 4).

Of course, this was a lie, and the rest of the story is a downward spiral. Cain refuses the truth offered him when God confronts his jealousy of Abel, leading Cain to murder him. Soon after, we see humanity caught in the cycle of death throughout the generations that increasingly embrace murder and violence.

Satan still slaughters with clever and cunning *deception*. The world has remained blinded to God's vision since the fall of humanity, and we now live in a time of a skyrocketing assault on truth. Lies circle the world at the speed of light. Misleading ideas travel faster and more easily than ever. Truths once widely accepted face redefinition and replacement by lies that infect and destroy people not prepared to mount a defense.

The fall reminds us that seeking and loving truth is at the heart of a relationship with God. "Teach truth. Love well" has been the Dallas Theological Seminary slogan for several years. Its foundation is the nearly century-old mission of the seminary: "to glorify God by equipping godly servant-leaders for the proclamation of His Word and the building up of the body of Christ worldwide." All people still ask, "What is truth?" So our slogan and mission remain relevant. Thus, we must allow God's truth and love to strengthen us to obey.

What is truth? It is the crucified and risen Son of God. Dallas Theological Seminary has the privilege of carrying the timeless truth of Jesus Christ into the world to answer the burning question of truth with compassion and boldness. We bring light and hope to those in darkness and bondage. In a world that, with Pilate, scoffs at the authority of truth, let us lift high the torch of Jesus's words in John 14:6: "I am the way, the truth, and the life."[1]

---

[1] Adapted from Mark M. Yarbough, "Answering Deception with the Truth," *DTS Magazine* 8, no. 3 (Fall 2022): 4. © 2022 Dallas Theological Seminary.

PART IV

WHERE DO YOU GO FROM HERE?

"Please exit through the gift shop."

By the time most of us have spent a couple hours in a museum looking at artifacts, the last thing we want to do is spend another second browsing souvenirs, books, postcards, and—let's be honest—overpriced trinkets in a gift shop. But for others, the walk through the exhibits not only sparked curiosity; it ignited a passion for more. The slender program they handed you at the ticket counter, the self-guided audio tour, or the handy app on your phone—those were helpful, but you want more.

Hence, *the gift shop*.

Now, don't get worried. We have nothing to sell you. You already have a Bible. In fact, if you have an internet connection, you have access to most Bibles out there. But we would be remiss if we didn't share with you some additional opportunities to go even deeper.

Exploring Christian Scripture Online

First, we want to invite you to use the link below or the QR code that will lead you to an ocean of resources for *Exploring Christian Scripture*: essays, videos, sermons, podcasts . . . even free online courses. You'll find a large and ever-growing collection of materials to explore—from academic to practical. If you haven't already done so, visit the site now and dig in.

https://www.dts.edu/exploringchristianscripture

Accordance Bible Software (www.accordancebible.com)

Regarded by many scholars as both powerful and easy-to-use, Accordance Bible Software includes cutting-edge original language tools and other resources for deep Bible study.

Best Commentaries (www.bestcommentaries.com)

Billed as the "Rotten Tomatoes" for biblical studies, bestcommentaries.com collects expert reviews and ratings along with those of site users with the goal of enabling Bible students at all levels to make good, informed decisions about which commentaries they should purchase.

Bible.org (www.bible.org)

A nondenominational, Bible-centered website offering free access to thousands of articles and Bible study materials from pastors and scholars around the world. Its sister site, www.netbible.org, provides access to the

New English Translation (NET) Bible, with over 58,000 study and translation notes.

BibleGateway (www.biblegateway.com)

Bible Gateway is a searchable online Bible tool hosting more than 200 versions of the Bible in over seventy languages that you can freely read, research, and reference anywhere.

BibleProject (www.bibleproject.com)

With a mission to help people experience the Bible as a unified story that leads to Jesus, BibleProject produces free videos, podcasts, blogs, classes, and educational resources to make the story of the Bible accessible to everyone.

BiblicalStory (www.thebiblicalstory.org)

The purpose of thebiblicalstory.org is to reveal the power of the Word of the triune God of Israel through the careful understanding of the narrative of the biblical story.

"Constable's Notes" (www.planobiblechapel.org/soniclight)

Colloquially known as "Constable's Notes," this priceless collection of free Bible study notes by Dr. Thomas Constable covers every book of the Bible in commentary-level detail . . . for free!

Logos Bible Software (www.logos.com)

With a range of packages available for every level of biblical studies, Logos Bible Software provides access to a vast library of resources for students, pastors, and scholars.

The Museum of the Bible (www.museumofthebible.org)

Opened in 2017, the Museum of the Bible in Washington, D.C., is an innovative educational institution whose purpose is to invite all people to engage with the transformative power of the Bible.

Our Daily Bread (www.odb.org)

The mission of Our Daily Bread is to make the life-changing wisdom of the Bible understandable and accessible to all. Resources include online and print devotionals, articles, podcasts, and more.

Shelf Space: Recommendations for your library

Besides the online and electronic resources above, we also recommend the following books for your library. Most are available in both hardcopy and e-book format. For your convenience, we've rated each book as "beginner," "intermediate," or "advanced."

Books on Bibliology/Authority/Canonicity

Blomberg, Craig L. *The Historical Reliability of the New Testament*. B&H Studies in Christian Apologetics. Nashville: B&H Academic, 2016. [INTERMEDIATE]

Bruce, F. F. *The Canon of Scripture*. Downers Grove: InterVarsity Academic, 1988. [INTERMEDIATE]

Cowan, Steven B., and Terry L. Wilder, eds. *In Defense of the Bible: A Comprehensive Apologetic for the Authority of Scripture*. Nashville: B&H Academic, 2013. [INTERMEDIATE]

Feinberg, John S. *Light in a Dark Place: The Doctrine of Scripture*. Foundations of Christian Theology. Wheaton: Crossway, 2018. [INTERMEDIATE]

Geisler, Norman L., and William E. Nix. *A General Introduction to the Bible*. Rev. and exp. ed. Chicago: Moody, 1986. [BEGINNER]

Geisler, Norman L., ed. *Inerrancy*. Grand Rapids: Zondervan, 1979. [BEGINNER]

Kruger, Michael J. *The Question of Canon*. Downers Grove: IVP Academic, 2013. [INTERMEDIATE]

Kruger, Michael J. *Canon Revisited: Establishing the Origins and Authority of the New Testament Books*. Wheaton: Crossway, 2012. [INTERMEDIATE]

McDonald, Lee M. *The Biblical Canon: Its Origin, Transmission, and Authority.* Peabody, MA: Hendrickson, 2007. [ADVANCED]

Meade, John D., and Peter J. Gurry. *Scribes and Scripture: The Amazing Story of How We Got the Bible.* Wheaton, IL: Crossway, 2022. [BEGINNER]

Metzger, Bruce M. *The Canon of the New Testament: Its Origin, Development, and Significance.* Oxford: Clarendon, 1987. [ADVANCED]

Nichols, Stephen J., and Eric T. Brandt. *Ancient Words, Changing Worlds: The Doctrine of Scripture in a Modern Age.* Wheaton: Crossway, 2009. [BEGINNER]

Ryrie, Charles C. *What You Should Know About Inerrancy.* Chicago: Moody, 1981. [BEGINNER]

Warfield, B. B. *The Inspiration and Authority of the Bible.* Phillipsburg, NJ: Presbyterian and Reformed, 1948. [INTERMEDIATE]

Wegner, Paul D. *The Journey from Texts to Translations: The Origin and Development of the Bible.* Grand Rapids: Baker, 1999. [INTERMEDIATE]

Single-Volume Commentaries/Study Bibles

Adeyemo, Tokunboh, ed. *Africa Bible Commentary: A One-Volume Commentary Written by Seventy African Scholars.* Grand Rapids: Zondervan, 2010. [INTERMEDIATE]

Carson, D. A., ed. *NIV Biblical Theology Study Bible: Follow God's Redemptive Plan as It Unfolds throughout Scripture.* Grand Rapids: Zondervan, 2018. [INTERMEDIATE]

Duvall, J. Scott, and J. Daniel Hays, eds. *The Baker Illustrated Bible Background Commentary.* Grand Rapids: Baker, 2020. [BEGINNER]

Evans, Tony. *The Tony Evans Bible Commentary: Advancing God's Kingdom Agenda.* Nashville: Holman Bible Publishers, 2019. [BEGINNER]

Hanna, Kenneth G. *From Moses to Malachi: Exploring the Old Testament.* Reprint edition. Bloomington, IN: WestBow, 2015. [BEGINNER]

Hanna, Kenneth G. *From Gospels to Glory: Exploring the New Testament.* Bloomington, IN: Westbow, 2015. [BEGINNER]

Hindson, Ed, and Elmer L. Towns. *Illustrated Bible Survey: An Introduction.* Rev. ed. Nashville: B&H Academic, 2017. [BEGINNER]

Kaiser, Walter C. Jr., and Duane Garrett, eds. *Archaeological Study Bible: An Illustrated Walk through Biblical History and Culture.* Grand Rapids: Zondervan, 2006. [BEGINNER]

Radmacher, Earl, Ronald B. Allen, and H. Wayne House, eds. *The Nelson's New Illustrated Bible Commentary: Spreading the Light of God's Word into Your Life.* Nashville: Thomas Nelson, 1999. [BEGINNER]

Rydelnik, Michael, and Michael Vanlaningham, eds. *Moody Bible Commentary: A One-Volume Commentary on the Whole Bible by the Faculty of Moody Bible Institute.* Chicago: Moody, 2014. [BEGINNER]

Walvoord, John F., and Roy B. Zuck, eds. *The Bible Knowledge Commentary: New Testament.* Colorado Springs: David C. Cook, 2002. [BEGINNER]

Walvoord, John F., and Roy B. Zuck, eds. *The Bible Knowledge Commentary: Old Testament.* Colorado Springs: David C. Cook, 2002. [BEGINNER]

Helpful Commentary Series

Ancient Christian Commentaries. Downers Grove: InterVarsity, 1998–2010. [ADVANCED]

Asia Bible Commentary. Carlisle, Cumbria, UK: Langham Global Library, 2007–2019. [INTERMEDIATE]

Baker Exegetical Commentary on the New Testament. Grand Rapids: Baker Academic, 1992–2022. [ADVANCED]

Christian Standard Commentary. Nashville: Holman Reference, 2020–. [INTERMEDIATE]

Evangelical Exegetical Commentary. Bellingham, WA: Lexham, 2011–2020. [INTERMEDIATE]

Expositor's Bible Commentary. Grand Rapids: Zondervan, 1976–1992. Rev. ed., 2012. [INTERMEDIATE]

Kregel Exegetical Commentaries. Grand Rapids: Kregel, 2013–2022. [ADVANCED]

New American Commentaries. Nashville: Holman Reference, 1991–2019. [INTERMEDIATE]

New International Commentaries on the Old and New Testaments. Grand Rapids: Eerdmans, 1974–2020. [ADVANCED]

New International Greek Testament Commentaries. Grand Rapids: Eerdmans, 1978–2016. [ADVANCED]

NIV Application Commentaries. Grand Rapids: Zondervan, 1994–2004. [BEGINNER]

Pillar New Testament Commentaries. Grand Rapids: Eerdmans, 1988–2015. [INTERMEDIATE]

Swindoll's Living Insights New Testament Commentary. Carol Stream, IL: Tyndale, 2014–2020. [BEGINNER]

Tyndale Old/New Testament Commentaries. Downers Grove: InterVarsity, 1968–2020. [INTERMEDIATE]

Zondervan Exegetical Commentary on the Old Testament/New Testament. Grand Rapids: Zondervan Academic, 2009–. [ADVANCED]

Biblical Theology

DeRouchie, Jason S., Oren R. Martin, and Andrew David Naselli. *40 Questions about Biblical Theology*. Edited by Benjamin L. Merkle. 40 Questions Series. Grand Rapids: Kregel, 2020. [BEGINNER]

Goldsworthy, Graeme. *According to Plan: The Unfolding Revelation of God in the Bible*. 2nd ed. Downers Grove: InterVarsity, 2002. [BEGINNER]

Hamilton, James M. Jr. *What Is Biblical Theology? A Guide to the Bible's Story, Symbolism, and Patterns*. Wheaton: Crossway, 2013. [BEGINNER]

Kaiser, Walter C. Jr. *The Promise–Plan of God: A Biblical Theology of the Old and New Testaments*. Grand Rapids: Zondervan, 1978. [INTERMEDIATE]

Köstenberger, Andreas J., and Gregory Goswell. *Biblical Theology: A Canonical, Thematic, and Ethical Approach*. Wheaton: Crossway, 2023. [ADVANCED]

Rosner, Brian S., T. Desmond Alexander, Graeme Goldsworthy, and D. A. Carson, eds. *New Dictionary of Biblical Theology: Exploring the Unity & Diversity of Scripture*. IVP Reference Collection. Downers Grove: InterVarsity, 2000. [INTERMEDIATE]

Scobie, Charles H. H. *The Ways of Our God: An Approach to Biblical Theology*. Grand Rapids: Eerdmans, 2003. [ADVANCED]

VanGemeren, Willem. *The Progress of Redemption: The Story of Salvation from Creation to the New Jerusalem*. Grand Rapids: Baker Academic, 1988. [INTERMEDIATE]

Vos, Geerhardus. *Biblical Theology: Old and New Testaments*. Grand Rapids: Eerdmans, 1948; reprint ed., 1971. [ADVANCED]

Old Testament History and Theology

Arnold, Bill T., and Bryan E. Beyer. *Encountering the Old Testament: A Christian Survey*. 3rd ed. Encountering Biblical Studies. Grand Rapids: Baker Academic, 2015. [BEGINNER]

Bullock, C. Hassell. *An Introduction to the Old Testament Prophetic Books*. Chicago: Moody, 2007. [BEGINNER]

Bullock, C. Hassell. *An Introduction to the Old Testament Poetic Books*. Chicago: Moody, 2007. [BEGINNER]

Garrett, Duane A. *The Problem of the Old Testament: Hermeneutical, Schematic, and Theological Approaches*. Downers Grove: InterVarsity, 2020. [ADVANCED]

Goldingay, John. *An Introduction to the Old Testament: Exploring Text, Approaches, and Issues*. Downers Grove: InterVarsity, 2015. [ADVANCED]

Hasel, Gerhard F. *Old Testament Theology: Basic Issues in the Current Debate*. 4th ed. Grand Rapids: Eerdmans, 1982. [ADVANCED]

Hess, Richard S. *The Old Testament: A Historical, Theological, and Critical Introduction*. Grand Rapids: Baker Academic, 2016. [INTERMEDIATE]

House, Paul R., and Eric Mitchell. *Old Testament Survey*. 3rd ed. Nashville: B&H Academic, 2023. [BEGINNER]

House, Paul R. *Old Testament Theology*. Downers Grove: InterVarsity, 2018. [INTERMEDIATE]

Howard, David M. Jr. *An Introduction to the Old Testament Historical Books*. Chicago: Moody, 2007. [BEGINNER]

Kaiser, Walter C. Jr., and Paul D. Wegner. *A History of Israel: From the Bronze Age through the Jewish Wars*. Rev. ed. Nashville: B&H Academic, 2017. [INTERMEDIATE]

Longman, Tremper III, and Raymond B. Dillard. *An Introduction to the Old Testament*. 2nd ed. Grand Rapids: Zondervan, 2006. [INTERMEDIATE]

Merrill, Eugene H., Mark F. Rooker, and Michael A. Grisanti. *The World and the Word: An Introduction to the Old Testament*. Nashville: B&H, 2011. [BEGINNER]

Merrill, Eugene H. *Kingdom of Priests: A History of Old Testament Israel*. 2nd ed. Grand Rapids: Baker Academic, 2008. [BEGINNER]

Provan, Iain, V. Philips Long, and Tremper Longman III. *A Biblical History of Israel*. 2nd ed. Louisville: Westminster John Knox, 2015. [ADVANCED]

Waltke, Bruce K. *An Old Testament Theology: An Exegetical, Canonical, and Thematic Approach*. Grand Rapids: Zondervan Academic, 2007. [ADVANCED]

Walton, John H. *Chronological and Background Charts of the Old Testament*. Grand Rapids: Zondervan, 1994. [BEGINNER]

Zuck, Roy B., ed. *A Biblical Theology of the Old Testament*. Chicago: Moody, 1991. [BEGINNER]

New Testament History and Theology

Beale, G. K. *A New Testament Biblical Theology: The Unfolding of the Old Testament in the New*. Grand Rapids: Baker Academic, 2011. [INTERMEDIATE]

Bruce, F. F. *New Testament History*. Doubleday-Galilee ed. New York: Doubleday, 1980. [INTERMEDIATE]

Carson, D. A., and G. K. Beale, eds. *Commentary on the New Testament Use of the Old Testament*. Grand Rapids: Baker Academic, 2007. [ADVANCED]

Carson, D. A., and Douglas J. Moo. *An Introduction to the New Testament*. Grand Rapids: HarperCollins, 2009. [ADVANCED]

Elwell, Walter A., and Robert W. Yarbrough. *Encountering the New Testament: A Historical and Theological Survey*. 3rd ed. Grand Rapids: Baker Academic, 2013. [BEGINNER]

Green, Joel B., and Lee Martin McDonald, eds. *The World of the New Testament: Cultural, Social, and Historical Contexts*. Grand Rapids: Baker Academic, 2013. [ADVANCED]

Gutierrez, Ben, and Elmer Towns. *The Essence of the New Testament: A Survey*. Rev. ed. Nashville: B&H Academic, 2016. [BEGINNER]

Hoehner, Harold W. *Chronological Aspects of the Life of Christ*. Grand Rapids: Zondervan, 1977. [INTERMEDIATE]

Marshall, I. Howard. *New Testament Theology: Many Witnesses, One Gospel*. Downers Grove: InterVarsity, 2014. [INTERMEDIATE]

Schreiner, Thomas R. *New Testament Theology: Magnifying God in Christ*. Grand Rapids: Baker Academic, 2008. [INTERMEDIATE]

Schreiner, Thomas R. *Magnifying God in Christ: A Summary of New Testament Theology*. Grand Rapids: Baker Academic, 2010. [BEGINNER]

Zuck, Roy B., ed. *A Biblical Theology of the New Testament*. Chicago: Moody, 1994. [BEGINNER]

Intertestamental/Second-Temple Literature

Barnett, Paul. *Jesus and the Rise of Early Christianity: A History of New Testament Times*. Downers Grove: InterVarsity, 2002. [INTERMEDIATE]

Blackwell, Ben C., John K. Goodrich, and Jason Maston, eds. *Reading Romans in Context: Paul and Second Temple Judaism*. Grand Rapids: Zondervan, 2015. [ADVANCED]

Carter, Warren. *Seven Events That Shaped the New Testament World*. Grand Rapids: Baker Academic, 2013. [BEGINNER]

Evans, Craig A. *Jesus and His World: The Archeological Evidence*. Louisville: Westminster John Knox, 2012. [INTERMEDIATE]

Helyer, Larry R. *Exploring Jewish Literature of the Second Temple Period: A Guide for New Testament Students*. Downers Grover: InterVarsity, 2002. [INTERMEDIATE]

Bible Backgrounds/Culture

Arnold, Bill T., and Brent A. Strawn, eds. *The World Around the Old Testament: The People and Places of the Ancient Near East*. Grand Rapids: Baker Academic, 2016. [INTERMEDIATE]

Arnold, Clinton E., ed. *Zondervan Illustrated Bible Backgrounds: New Testament*. 5 vols. Grand Rapids: Zondervan, 2019. [BEGINNER]

Bock, Darrell L. *Studying the Historical Jesus: A Guide to Sources and Methods*. Grand Rapids: Baker Academic, 2012. [INTERMEDIATE]

Burge, Gary M., and Gene L. Green. *The New Testament in Antiquity: A Survey of the New Testament within Its Cultural Contexts*. 2nd ed. Grand Rapids: Zondervan, 2020. [ADVANCED]

deSilva, David A. *Honor, Patronage, Kinship & Purity: Unlocking New Testament Culture*. Downers Grove, IL: InterVarsity, 2000. [ADVANCED]

Keener, Craig S., and John H. Walton. *NIV Cultural Backgrounds Study Bible: Bringing to Life the Ancient World of Scripture*. Grand Rapids: Zondervan, 2016. [BEGINNER]

Keener, Craig S. *The IVP Bible Background Commentary: New Testament*. Downers Grove: InterVarsity, 2014. [BEGINNER]

King, Philip J., and Lawrence E. Stager. *Life in Biblical Israel*. Louisville: Westminster John Knox, 2001. [ADVANCED]

McClendon, Adam, and John Cartwright, eds. *Approaching the New Testament: A Guide for Students*. Nashville: B&H Academic, 2020. [INTERMEDIATE]

Walton, John H., ed. *Zondervan Illustrated Bible Backgrounds Commentary: Old Testament.* 5 vols. Grand Rapids: Zondervan, 2009. [BEGINNER]

Walton, John H. *Ancient Near Eastern Thought and the Old Testament: Introducing the Conceptual World of the Hebrew Bible.* 2nd ed. Grand Rapids: Baker Academic, 2018. [ADVANCED]

Walton, John H., Victor H. Matthews, Mark Chavalas. *The IVP Bible Background Commentary: Old Testament.* Downers Grove: InterVarsity, 2000. [BEGINNER]

Bible Maps/Geography/Archaeology

Aharoni, Yohanan, Michael Avi-Yonah, Ze'ev Safrai, Anson F. Rainey, and R. Steven Notley. *The Carta Bible Atlas.* 5th ed. Jerusalem: The Israel Map and Publishing Company, Ltd., 2011. [BEGINNER]

Kennedy, Titus. *Unearthing the Bible: 101 Archaeological Discoveries that Bring the Bible to Life.* Eugene, OR: Harvest House, 2020. [BEGINNER]

Price, Randall, and H. Wayne House. *Zondervan Handbook of Biblical Archaeology: A Book by Book Guide to Archaeological Discoveries Related to the Bible.* Grand Rapids: Zondervan, 2017. [BEGINNER]

Rasmussen, Carl G. *The Zondervan Atlas of the Bible.* Rev. ed. Grand Rapids: Zondervan Academic, 2011. [BEGINNER]

Stiles, Wayne. *Going Places with God: A Devotional Journey through the Lands of the Bible.* Ventura, CA: Regal, 2006. [BEGINNER]

Books Defending Scripture/Bible Problems

Bargerhuff, Eric J. *The Most Misused Verses in the Bible: Surprising Ways God's Word Is Misunderstood.* Bloomington, MN: Bethany House, 2012. [BEGINNER]

Butler, Joshua Ryan. *The Skeletons in God's Closet: The Mercy of Hell, the Surprise of Judgment, the Hope of Holy War.* Nashville: Thomas Nelson, 2014. [INTERMEDIATE]

Copan, Paul, and Matthew Flannagan. *Did God Really Command Genocide? Coming to Terms with the Justice of God.* Grand Rapids: Baker, 2014. [INTERMEDIATE]

Copan, Paul. *Is God a Moral Monster? Making Sense of the Old Testament God.* Grand Rapids: Baker, 2011. [INTERMEDIATE]

Croteau, David A., and Gary E. Yates. *Urban Legends of the Old Testament: 40 Common Misconceptions.* Nashville: B&H Academic, 2019. [BEGINNER]

Croteau, David A. *Urban Legends of the New Testament: 40 Common Misconceptions.* Nashville: B&H Academic, 2015. [BEGINNER]

Geisler, Norman L., and Thomas Howe. *The Big Book of Bible Difficulties: Clear and Concise Answers from Genesis to Revelation.* Grand Rapids: Baker Books, 2008. [BEGINNER]

Gundry, Stanley N., ed. *Show Them No Mercy: Four Views on God and Canaanite Genocide.* Counterpoints. Grand Rapids: Zondervan, 2003. [INTERMEDIATE]

Jones, Timothy Paul. *Why Should I Trust the Bible?* Fearn, UK: Christian Focus, 2020.

Kaiser, Walter C. Jr., Peter H. Davids, F. F. Bruce, and Manfred T. Brauch. *Hard Sayings of the Bible.* Reprint ed. Downers Grove: InterVarsity Academic, 2010. [BEGINNER]

Keller, Timothy. *The Reason for God: Belief in an Age of Skepticism.* New York: Penguin, 2008. [BEGINNER]

Kimball, Dan. *How (Not) to Read the Bible: Making Sense of the Anti-women, Anti-science, Pro-violence, Pro-slavery and Other Crazy-Sounding Parts of Scripture.* Grand Rapids: Zondervan, 2020. [INTERMEDIATE]

Longman, Tremper III. *Confronting Old Testament Controversies: Pressing Questions about Evolution, Sexuality, History, and Violence.* Grand Rapids: Baker Books, 2019. [INTERMEDIATE]

Orr-Ewing, Amy. *Why Trust the Bible?: Answers to Ten Tough Questions.* London: InterVarsity, 2005. [BEGINNER]

Oswalt, John N. *The Bible among the Myths: Unique Revelation or Just Ancient Literature?* Grand Rapids: Zondervan, 2009. [INTERMEDIATE]

Richards, E. Randolph, and Brandon J. O'Brien. *Misreading Scripture with Western Eyes: Removing Cultural Blinders to Better Understand the Bible*. Downers Grove: InterVarsity, 2012. [ADVANCED]

Richards, E. Randolph, and Richard James. *Misreading Scripture with Individualist Eyes: Patronage, Honor, and Shame in the Biblical World*. Downers Grove: InterVarsity, 2020. [ADVANCED]

Trimm, Charlie. *The Destruction of the Canaanites: God, Genocide, and Biblical Interpretation*. Grand Rapids: Eerdmans, 2022. [INTERMEDIATE]

Webb, William J., and Gordon K. Oeste. *Bloody, Brutal, and Barbaric?: Wrestling with Troubling War Texts*. Downers Grove: Intervarsity, 2019. [ADVANCED]

Webb, William J. *Slaves, Women, and Homosexuals: Exploring the Hermeneutics of Cultural Analysis*. Downers Grove: InterVarsity, 2001. [ADVANCED]

Reading and Interpreting the Bible

Duvall, J. Scott, and J. Daniel Hays. *Grasping God's Word: A Hands-On Approach to Reading, Interpreting, and Applying the Bible*. 4th ed. Grand Rapids: Zondervan Academic, 2020. [BEGINNER]

Fee, Gordon D., and Douglas Stuart. *How to Read the Bible for All It's Worth*. 4th ed. Grand Rapids: Zondervan Academic, 2014. [BEGINNER]

Hendricks, Howard G., and William D. Hendricks. *Living by the Book: The Art and Science of Reading the Bible*. Rev. ed. Chicago: Moody, 2007. [BEGINNER]

Osborne, Grant R. *The Hermeneutical Spiral: A Comprehensive Introduction to Biblical Interpretation*. Rev. and exp. ed. Downers Grove: IVP Academic, 2006. [INTERMEDIATE]

Yarbrough, Mark M. *How to Read the Bible Like a Seminary Professor: A Practical and Entertaining Exploration of the World's Most Famous Book*. New York: FaithWords, 2015. [BEGINNER]

Zuck, Roy B. *Basic Bible Interpretation: A Practical Guide to Discovering Biblical Truth*. Colorado Springs: David C. Cook, 1991. [INTERMEDIATE]

NAME AND SUBJECT INDEX

SCRIPTURE INDEX

22:3–5 *142*
22:9–10 *142*
22:12–13 *143*
22:16 *143*
22:22 *143*
22:23 *143*
22:24 *143*
22:25 *143*
22:26–29 *143*
22:27 *143*
22:30–31 *143*
22–31 *143*
23 *30*
24 *138*
25 *138*
27:14 *60*
31:5 *140*
33:20 *60*
37:7 *60*
37:34 *60*
38:15 *60*
42–72 *138*
51 *138*
66 *138*
73–89 *138*
78 *138, 332*
81–83 *138*
86 *138*
86:15 *203*
89 *138*
90 *137*
90–106 *138*
93:1 *363*
103 *30*
103:19 *135*
105 *138*
107–50 *138*
109:8 *31*
119:18 *223*
119:105 *362*
119:166 *60*
130:5 *60*
139 *138*

Proverbs

1:1–7 *145*
1:1–22:16 *145*
1:2 *146*
1:3 *146*
1:4 *146*
1:5 *146*
1:6 *146*
1:8–7:27 *146*
1:8–9:13 *145*
8:1–9:18 *147*
10:1–22:16 *145*
10:1–31:31 *147*
16:18 *196*
16:33 *123*
22:17–24:34 *145*
25–29 *145*
30 *145–46*
31 *145*
31:1–9 *146*
31:10–31 *146*

Ecclesiastes

1:1–11 *149*
1:2 *150*
1:3–11 *150*
1:12–2:26 *149*
1:16 *150*
2:3–9 *150*
2:11 *150*
2:13 *150*
2:15 *150*
2:24 *150*
3 *151*
3:1 *151*
3:1–15 *149*
3:14 *151*
3:15 *151*
3:16–4:16 *149*
3:16–22 *150*
5:1–6:12 *149*
5:8–20 *150*
7:1–8:17 *149*
9:1–18 *149*
10:1–20 *150*

11:1–12:7 *150*
12:8 *150–51*
12:8–14 *150*
12:11 *151*
12:13 *151*

Song of Songs

1:1–2:7 *153, 155*
1:2–2:17 *154*
1:2–4 *156*
1:7–8 *156*
1:8–10 *156*
1:12–14 *156*
1:15 *156*
1:16–17 *156*
2:1–3 *156*
2:2 *156*
2:3 *156*
2:7 *156*
2:8–17 *153, 155*
2:10–14 *156*
3:1–4 *156*
3:1–5 *153–55*
3:5 *156*
3:6–5:1 *154*
3:6–11 *154–55*
4:1–5:1 *154–56*
4:1–15 *156*
5:2–6:3 *154*
5:2–7 *156*
5:2–8 *153, 155*
5:2b *156*
5:9–6:3 *153, 155*
6:4–8:4 *154*
6:4–9 *154–56*
6:10–12 *154–55*
6:13–7:10 *153, 155*
7:1–8 *156*
7:11–13 *153*
7:11–14 *155*
8:1–2 *156*
8:1–14 *153, 155*
8:4 *156*
8:5–14 *154*